Web Graphics For Dummies®

COMPUTER
BOOK SERIES
FROM IDG

Anatomy of the Browser Window

Some elements may look different on different platforms and in different browsers, but most browsers and platforms incorporate these elements.

Navigation buttons

Document title   Document address

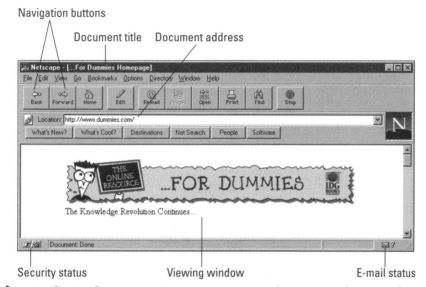

Security status   Viewing window   E-mail status

Web Graphic Formats

Abbreviation	Name	Description
GIF	Graphic Interchange Format	A popular proprietary format of graphics compression to transfer images over the Internet. Pronounced *Jiff* or *Giff* (like *Jerry* or *Gary*).
GIF89a	Graphic Interchange Format, 1989	The flavor of GIF used for animation. Capable of delivering multiple frames in a single file.
JPEG	Joint Photographic Experts Group	Frequently used for photographic-quality images on the Web. JPEGs are best for making small files from big photos. Pronounced *Jay-peg*.
PNG	Portable Network Graphics	A non-proprietary, GIF-like format for transmitting Internet graphics. PNG does not support multiple frames for animation. Pronounced *Ping*.

IDG
BOOKS
WORLDWIDE

Copyright © 1997 IDG Books Worldwide, Inc.
All rights reserved.

Cheat Sheet $2.95 value. Item 0211-5.

For more information about IDG Books,
call 1-800-762-2974.

...For Dummies: #1 Computer Book Series for Beginners

Web Graphics For Dummies®

Cheat Sheet

Graphics System Checklist

Component	Key specification
PC system	Pentium 100 CPU, Windows 95 operating system
Macintosh system	PowerMac CPU, System 7.x operating system
RAM	16MB — minimum
Hard drive	500MB — minimum
CD-ROM	A low-performance drive is adequate for installing software and clip art
Image editor	GIF and JPEG file output
Text HTML editor	Straightforward, direct access to code
WYSIWYG HTML editor	Intuitive operation without inserting nonstandard tags in HTML output

Basic HTML color codes

Name	Hex code
aqua	00FFFF
black	000000
blue	0000FF
fuchsia	FF00FF
gray	808080
green	008000
lime	00FF00
maroon	800000
navy	000080
olive	808000
purple	800080
red	FF0000
silver	C0C0C0
teal	008080
white	FFFFFF
yellow	FFFF00

Web Graphics Software

Program	Function	Platforms	Web address
BBEdit	Text editor	Macintosh	www.barebones.com/
ClarisDraw	Image editing	Windows, Macintosh	www.claris.com
CMed	Text editor	PC	www.iap.net.au/~cmathes/
CorelDraw 7	Image editing, conversion	Windows	www.corel.com
DeBabelizer Pro	Image conversion	Windows	www.equilibrium.coam
DeBabelizer Toolbox	Image conversion	Macintosh	www.equilibrium.coam
Claris Home Page	WYSIWYG editor	Windows, Macintosh	www.claris.com
HotMetal Pro	WYSIWYG editor	Windows, Macintosh	www.softquad.com
Adobe Illustrator	Image editing	Windows, Macintosh	www.adobe.com
Image Alchemy	Image conversion	Macintosh, DOS, UNIX, OS/2	www.handmadesw.com
Adobe PageMill	WYSIWYG editor	Windows, Macintosh	www.adobe.com
PaintShop Pro	Image editing, conversion	Windows	www.jasc.com
Adobe Photoshop	Image editing, conversion	Windows, Macintosh	www.adobe.com
Corel WebMaster	Site manager, WYSIWYG editor	Windows	www.corel.com

®

References for the Rest of Us! ®

COMPUTER BOOK SERIES FROM IDG

Are you intimidated and confused by computers? Do you find that traditional manuals are overloaded with technical details you'll never use? Do your friends and family always call you to fix simple problems on their PCs? Then the *...For Dummies*® computer book series from IDG Books Worldwide is for you.

...For Dummies books are written for those frustrated computer users who know they aren't really dumb but find that PC hardware, software, and indeed the unique vocabulary of computing make them feel helpless. *...For Dummies* books use a lighthearted approach, a down-to-earth style, and even cartoons and humorous icons to diffuse computer novices' fears and build their confidence. Lighthearted but not lightweight, these books are a perfect survival guide for anyone forced to use a computer.

> *"I like my copy so much I told friends; now they bought copies."*
>
> **Irene C., Orwell, Ohio**

> *"Quick, concise, nontechnical, and humorous."*
>
> **Jay A., Elburn, Illinois**

> *"Thanks, I needed this book. Now I can sleep at night."*
>
> **Robin F., British Columbia, Canada**

Already, millions of satisfied readers agree. They have made *...For Dummies* books the #1 introductory level computer book series and have written asking for more. So, if you're looking for the most fun and easy way to learn about computers, look to *...For Dummies* books to give you a helping hand.

™

IDG BOOKS WORLDWIDE

5/97

WEB GRAPHICS FOR DUMMIES®

WEB GRAPHICS FOR DUMMIES®

by Linda Richards

IDG Books Worldwide, Inc.
An International Data Group Company

Foster City, CA ♦ Chicago, IL ♦ Indianapolis, IN ♦ Southlake, TX

Web Graphics For Dummies®

Published by
IDG Books Worldwide, Inc.
An International Data Group Company
919 E. Hillsdale Blvd.
Suite 400
Foster City, CA 94404
www.idgbooks.com (IDG Books Worldwide Web site)
www.dummies.com (Dummies Press Web site)

Library of Congress Catalog Card No.: 97-80119

ISBN: 0-7645-0211-5

Printed in the United States of America

10 9 8 7 6 5 4 3 2 1

1O/QY/QY/ZX/IN

Distributed in the United States by IDG Books Worldwide, Inc.

Distributed by Macmillan Canada for Canada; by Transworld Publishers Limited in the United Kingdom; by IDG Norge Books for Norway; by IDG Sweden Books for Sweden; by Woodslane Pty. Ltd. for Australia; by Woodslane Enterprises Ltd. for New Zealand; by Longman Singapore Publishers Ltd. for Singapore, Malaysia, Thailand, and Indonesia; by Simron Pty. Ltd. for South Africa; by Toppan Company Ltd. for Japan; by Distribuidora Cuspide for Argentina; by Livraria Cultura for Brazil; by Ediciencia S.A. for Ecuador; by Addison-Wesley Publishing Company for Korea; by Ediciones ZETA S.C.R. Ltda. for Peru; by WS Computer Publishing Corporation, Inc., for the Philippines; by Unalis Corporation for Taiwan; by Contemporanea de Ediciones for Venezuela; by Computer Book & Magazine Store for Puerto Rico; by Express Computer Distributors for the Caribbean and West Indies. Authorized Sales Agent: Anthony Rudkin Associates for the Middle East and North Africa.

For general information on IDG Books Worldwide's books in the U.S., please call our Consumer Customer Service department at 800-762-2974. For reseller information, including discounts and premium sales, please call our Reseller Customer Service department at 800-434-3422.

For information on where to purchase IDG Books Worldwide's books outside the U.S., please contact our International Sales department at 415-655-3200 or fax 415-655-3295.

For information on foreign language translations, please contact our Foreign & Subsidiary Rights department at 415-655-3021 or fax 415-655-3281.

For sales inquiries and special prices for bulk quantities, please contact our Sales department at 415-655-3200 or write to the address above.

For information on using IDG Books Worldwide's books in the classroom or for ordering examination copies, please contact our Educational Sales department at 800-434-2086 or fax 817-251-8174.

For press review copies, author interviews, or other publicity information, please contact our Public Relations department at 415-655-3000 or fax 415-655-3299.

For authorization to photocopy items for corporate, personal, or educational use, please contact Copyright Clearance Center, 222 Rosewood Drive, Danvers, MA 01923, or fax 508-750-4470.

is a trademark under exclusive license to IDG Books Worldwide, Inc., from International Data Group, Inc.

About the Author

Linda Richards was born in a log cabin in Nebraska in 1860. . . .

(Editor's Note: Sorry. Wrong author.)

Linda Richards has been doing computer-type stuff for a long time. She's also been doing graphics stuff for a long time, though for years the two things were seen as mutually exclusive. Computers for writing and for fun. Graphics without computers and for food.

In 1986, Linda could no longer keep her head buried from the computer design revolution. Her brother foisted a Mac computer onto her, insisting — over her protestations — that this was the way that the future designed. After playing for a while, Linda sadly agreed. The world was moving on. It seemed like a good idea to move with it.

Those early design computers enforced two realities to the working journalist and graphic artist:

- ✔ She would never again have to retype something she'd written on another computer.
- ✔ She would, after a while, miss the feel of wax under her nails from paste-up. But only a bit.

It wasn't long — in elephant years or football minutes — before telecommunications gave way to the Internet. And not long behind *that* came the World Wide Web. This time, Richards was ready, writing about online connectivity and Internet development early enough that people often looked at her askance and wondered if she was talking sci-fi.

At the time of writing *Web Graphics For Dummies*, Richards has owned over 20 different computer systems (though not all at the same time). From her first home hacker system in 1981, she's followed the twists and turns of the development of the micro computer with alternating joy and despair, depending on which computer company is being silly at the time.

Richards' traditional graphic design background and passion for electronic beasties came together with the development of the Web. Here, finally, is a medium where she indulges in computers and design at the same time — the geek and artist portions of her personality finally at peace together.

Today, Richards writes for many publications and designs professionally for the Web and other mediums. You probably have seen her work in a wide variety of publications — over a thousand of her non-fiction articles have been published on topics as wide and varied as high fashion, the arts, business, and — of course — technology.

Richards lives in the Cold Blue North (read that Vancouver, British Columbia) with the people and pets she holds dearest in the world. Richards rides her bike almost everywhere, but eschews cel phones, "If God," says Richards, "had intended us to use mobile phones, He would have given us antennae."

ABOUT IDG BOOKS WORLDWIDE

Welcome to the world of IDG Books Worldwide.

IDG Books Worldwide, Inc., is a subsidiary of International Data Group, the world's largest publisher of computer-related information and the leading global provider of information services on information technology. IDG was founded more than 25 years ago and now employs more than 8,500 people worldwide. IDG publishes more than 275 computer publications in over 75 countries (see listing below). More than 60 million people read one or more IDG publications each month.

Launched in 1990, IDG Books Worldwide is today the #1 publisher of best-selling computer books in the United States. We are proud to have received eight awards from the Computer Press Association in recognition of editorial excellence and three from *Computer Currents'* First Annual Readers' Choice Awards. Our best-selling *...For Dummies*® series has more than 30 million copies in print with translations in 30 languages. IDG Books Worldwide, through a joint venture with IDG's Hi-Tech Beijing, became the first U.S. publisher to publish a computer book in the People's Republic of China. In record time, IDG Books Worldwide has become the first choice for millions of readers around the world who want to learn how to better manage their businesses.

Our mission is simple: Every one of our books is designed to bring extra value and skill-building instructions to the reader. Our books are written by experts who understand and care about our readers. The knowledge base of our editorial staff comes from years of experience in publishing, education, and journalism — experience we use to produce books for the '90s. In short, we care about books, so we attract the best people. We devote special attention to details such as audience, interior design, use of icons, and illustrations. And because we use an efficient process of authoring, editing, and desktop publishing our books electronically, we can spend more time ensuring superior content and spend less time on the technicalities of making books.

You can count on our commitment to deliver high-quality books at competitive prices on topics you want to read about. At IDG Books Worldwide, we continue in the IDG tradition of delivering quality for more than 25 years. You'll find no better book on a subject than one from IDG Books Worldwide.

John Kilcullen
CEO
IDG Books Worldwide, Inc.

Steven Berkowitz
President and Publisher
IDG Books Worldwide, Inc.

Eighth Annual Computer Press Awards ≥1992

Ninth Annual Computer Press Awards ≥1993

Tenth Annual Computer Press Awards ≥1994

Eleventh Annual Computer Press Awards ≥1995

IDG Books Worldwide, Inc., is a subsidiary of International Data Group, the world's largest publisher of computer-related information and the leading global provider of information services on information technology. International Data Group publishes over 275 computer publications in over 75 countries. Sixty million people read one or more International Data Group publications each month. International Data Group's publications include: **ARGENTINA:** Buyer's Guide, Computerworld Argentina, PC World Argentina; **AUSTRALIA:** Australian Macworld, Australian PC World, Australian Reseller News, Computerworld, IT Casebook, Network World, Publish, Webmaster; **AUSTRIA:** Computerwelt Osterreich, Networks Austria, PC Tip Austria; **BANGLADESH:** PC World Bangladesh; **BELARUS:** PC World Belarus; **BELGIUM:** Data News; **BRAZIL:** Annuário de Informática, Computerworld, Connections, Macworld, PC Player, PC World, Publish, Reseller News, Supergamepower; **BULGARIA:** Computerworld Bulgaria, Network World Bulgaria, PC & MacWorld Bulgaria; **CANADA:** CIO Canada, Client/Server World, ComputerWorld Canada, InfoWorld Canada, NetworkWorld Canada, WebWorld; **CHILE:** Computerworld Chile, PC World Chile; **COLOMBIA:** Computerworld Colombia, PC World Colombia; **COSTA RICA:** PC World Centro America; **THE CZECH AND SLOVAK REPUBLICS:** Computerworld Czechoslovakia, Macworld Czech Republic, PC World Czechoslovakia; **DENMARK:** Communications World Danmark, Computerworld Danmark, Macworld Danmark, PC World Danmark, Techworld Denmark; **DOMINICAN REPUBLIC:** PC World Republica Dominicana; **ECUADOR:** PC World Ecuador; **EGYPT:** Computerworld Middle East, PC World Middle East; **EL SALVADOR:** PC World Centro America; **FINLAND:** MikroPC, Tietoverkko, Tietoviikko; **FRANCE:** Distributique, Hebdo, Info PC, Le Monde Informatique, Macworld, Reseaux & Telecoms, WebMaster France; **GERMANY:** Computer Partner, Computerwoche, Computerwoche Extra, Computerwoche FOCUS, Global Online, Macwelt, PC Welt; **GREECE:** Amiga Computing, GamePro Greece, Multimedia World; **GUATEMALA:** PC World Centro America; **HONDURAS:** PC World Centro America; **HONG KONG:** Computerworld Hong Kong, PC World Hong Kong, Publish in Asia; **HUNGARY:** ABCD CD-ROM, Computerworld Szamitastechnika, Internetto online Magazine, PC World Hungary, PC-X Magazin Hungary; **ICELAND:** Tolvuheimur PC World Island; **INDIA:** Information Communications World, Information Systems Computerworld, PC World India, Publish in Asia; **INDONESIA:** InfoKomputer PC World, Komputek Computerworld, Publish in Asia; **IRELAND:** ComputerScope, PC Live!; **ISRAEL:** Macworld Israel, People & Computers/Computerworld; **ITALY:** Computerworld Italia, Macworld Italia, Networking Italia, PC World Italia; **JAPAN:** DTP World, Macworld Japan, Nikkei Personal Computing, OS/2 World Japan, SunWorld Japan, Windows NT World, Windows World Japan; **KENYA:** PC World East African; **KOREA:** Hi-Tech Information, Macworld Korea, PC World Korea; **MACEDONIA:** PC World Macedonia; **MALAYSIA:** Computerworld Malaysia, PC World Malaysia, Publish in Asia; **MALTA:** PC World Malta; **MEXICO:** Computerworld Mexico, PC World Mexico; **MYANMAR:** PC World Myanmar; **NETHERLANDS:** Computer! Totaal, LAN Internetworking Magazine, LAN World Buyers Guide, Macworld Netherlands, Net, WebWereld; **NEW ZEALAND:** Absolute Beginners Guide and Plain & Simple Series, Computer Buyer, Computer Industry Directory, Computerworld New Zealand, MTB, Network World, PC World New Zealand; **NICARAGUA:** PC World Centro America; **NORWAY:** Computerworld Norge, CW Rapport, Datamagasinet, Financial Rapport, Kursguide Norge, Macworld Norge, Multimediaworld Norge, PC World Ekspress Norge, PC World Nettverk, PC World Norge, PC World ProduktGuide Norge; **PAKISTAN:** Computerworld Pakistan; **PANAMA:** PC World Panama; **PEOPLE'S REPUBLIC OF CHINA:** China Computer Users, China Computerworld, China InfoWorld, China Telecom World Weekly, Computer & Communication, Electronic Design China, Electronics Today, Electronics Weekly, Game Software, PC World China, Popular Computer Week, Software Weekly, Software World, Telecom World; **PERU:** Computerworld Peru, PC World Profesional Peru, PC World SoHo Peru; **PHILIPPINES:** Click!, Computerworld Philippines, PC World Philippines, Publish in Asia; **POLAND:** Computerworld Poland, Computerworld Special Report Poland, Cyber, Macworld Poland, Networld Poland, PC World Komputer; **PORTUGAL:** Cerebro/PC World, Computerworld/Correio Informático, Dealer World Portugal, Mac*In/PC*In Portugal, Multimedia World; **PUERTO RICO:** PC World Puerto Rico; **ROMANIA:** Computerworld Romania, PC World Romania, Telecom Romania; **RUSSIA:** Computerworld Russia, Mir PK, Publish, Seti; **SINGAPORE:** Computerworld Singapore, PC World Singapore, Publish in Asia; **SLOVENIA:** Monitor; **SOUTH AFRICA:** Computing SA, Network World SA, Software World SA; **SPAIN:** Communicaciones World España, Computerworld España, Dealer World España, Macworld España, PC World España; **SRI LANKA:** Infolink PC World; **SWEDEN:** CAP&Design, Computer Sweden, Corporate Computing Sweden, Internetworld Sweden, it.branschen, Macworld Sweden, MaxiData Sweden, MikroDatorn, Nätverk & Kommunikation, PC World Sweden, PCaktiv, Windows World Sweden; **SWITZERLAND:** Computerworld Schweiz, Macworld Schweiz, PCtip; **TAIWAN:** Computerworld Taiwan, Macworld Taiwan, NEW ViSiON/Publish, PC World Taiwan, Windows World Taiwan; **THAILAND:** Publish in Asia, Thai Computerworld; **TURKEY:** Computerworld Turkiye, Macworld Turkiye, Network World Turkiye, PC World Turkiye; **UKRAINE:** Computerworld Kiev, Multimedia World Ukraine, PC World Ukraine; **UNITED KINGDOM:** Acorn User UK, Amiga Action UK, Amiga Computing UK, Apple Talk UK, Computing, Macworld, Parents and Computers UK, PC Advisor, PC Home, PSX Pro, The WEB; **UNITED STATES:** Cable in the Classroom, CIO Magazine, Computerworld, DOS World, Federal Computer Week, GamePro Magazine, InfoWorld, I-Way, Macworld, Network World, PC Games, PC World, Publish, Video Event, THE WEB Magazine, and WebMaster; online webzines: JavaWorld, NetscapeWorld, and SunWorld Online; **URUGUAY:** InfoWorld Uruguay; **VENEZUELA:** Computerworld Venezuela, PC World Venezuela; and **VIETNAM:** PC World Vietnam.
3/24/97

Acknowledgments

Books are made by taking a lot of pieces and then melding them into a cohesive whole. The success of that whole depends a great deal on the people who do the melding. I'm awfully lucky to have a pile of good melders in my life.

Thanks to Pat O'Brien, my editor at IDG Books Worldwide, for . . . well . . . everything. His knowledgeable hand guides his projects with special care and his steel nerves make everything go a lot lighter. His ultra-dry sense of humor doesn't hurt anything either. Nor does the fact that he gets my jokes.

Thanks also to Jill Pisoni at IDG, for her important role in the birth of this project, to Regina Snyder and her production team, for juggling all of the pieces that went into the finished book, and to Joyce Pepple and the media development team for assembling the CD-ROM. Jill, Pat, Gina, Joyce, and all of the other Dummies Press experts work very hard to make their projects look really easy. That's part of the reason for the special light that sets *...For Dummies* books apart.

Thanks always to Brian Gill, my agent at Studio B. Brian does so much to ensure that all of the cool projects he gets me go off really well. Because he's also very funny and understands the importance of laughing at my jokes, he is a consequential agent, indeed.

Thanks to my mom, Lea Huber, for being my mom and because I had the amazing arrogance not to mention her in any of my previous books. Hi, mom.

Thanks to my good friends Thea Partridge and Caroline Broadway. Both are Web professionals who, in their own ways, contributed much to the substance and tone of this work.

Special thanks to my son Michael Richards and my life partner David Middleton for knowing how to put up with me when I'm in the middle of a book and sometimes ever-so-slightly grumpy. They don't walk on tippy-toes around me, but know me well enough not to wonder when I bark at them for asking what time it is. I guess I'm usually so sunny that these temporary slips of temper are entirely acceptable.

David also must be thanked for prising me away from my computer, taking me for walks, and putting food in me when I would otherwise have just propped a piece of toast on the keyboard and kept going. These flashes of light and air describe our relationship very well. He always brings the sun to me — seemingly without effort.

Publisher's Acknowledgments

We're proud of this book; please send us your comments about it by using the IDG Books Worldwide Registration Card at the back of the book or by e-mailing us at feedback/dummies@idgbooks.com. Some of the people who helped bring this book to market include the following:

Acquisitions, Development, and Editorial

Project Editor: Pat O'Brien

Senior Acquisitions Editor: Jill Pisoni

Media Development Manager: Joyce Pepple

Associate Permissions Editor:
Heather H. Dismore

Copy Editor: Felicity O'Meara

Technical Editors: Paul Benson, Paul Osze

Editorial Manager: Mary C. Corder

Production

Project Coordinator: Regina Snyder

Layout and Graphics: Lou Boudreau, J. Tyler Conner, Todd Klemme, Tom Missler, Heather Pearson, Kate Snell

Proofreaders: Betty Kish, Laura L. Bowman, Joel K. Draper, Robert Springer, Karen York

Indexer: Richard T. Evans

General and Administrative

IDG Books Worldwide, Inc.: John Kilcullen, CEO; Steven Berkowitz, President and Publisher

IDG Books Technology Publishing: Brenda McLaughlin, Senior Vice President and Group Publisher

Dummies Technology Press and Dummies Editorial: Diane Graves Steele, Vice President and Associate Publisher; Judith A. Taylor, Product Marketing Manager; Kristin A. Cocks, Editorial Director

Dummies Trade Press: Kathleen A. Welton, Vice President and Publisher

IDG Books Production for Dummies Press: Beth Jenkins, Production Director; Cindy L. Phipps, Supervisor of Project Coordination, Production Proofreading, and Indexing; Kathie S. Schutte, Supervisor of Page Layout; Shelley Lea, Supervisor of Graphics and Design; Debbie J. Gates, Production Systems Specialist; Tony Augsburger, Supervisor of Reprints and Bluelines; Leslie Popplewell, Media Archive Coordinator

Dummies Packaging and Book Design: Patti Sandez, Packaging Specialist; Lance Kayser, Packaging Assistant; Kavish + Kavish, Cover Design

◆

The publisher would like to give special thanks to Patrick J. McGovern,
without whom this book would not have been possible.

◆

Contents at a Glance

Cartoons at a Glance

By Rich Tennant

page 189

page 281

page 125

page 211

page 7

page 69

Fax: 508-546-7747 • E-mail: the5wave@tiac.net

Table of Contents

Introduction

· ·

*U*p late and Web surfing, you make a fast left-click. Slammo! It's a graphic so cool, your head spins. Your purpose on the planet is revealed. You want to create a graphic so earth-shatteringly cool that people stop at *your* Web site to bask in your wonderfulness.

This freedom to create is the very essence of the Web. Sure, there are gobs of information on the Web, but letters and numbers move in many ways. What sets the Web apart are visual feasts for the whole world, with every artist equally accessible. Not only can megaconglomerate companies share expensive graphics with a waiting public, but you can, too.

There are hardware minimums and some software optimums — we'll look at both in this book — but many effective programs for Web graphics are shareware or freeware, and the list grows almost daily. Really lovely commercial software packages are available, too. We'll look closely at both software genres in some of the following pages.

It's heady stuff. With a middle-of-the-road computer system — probably the same computer you're using as a Web surfboard — you have the tools for graphics as wonderful, elegant, and generally nifty as the largest multinational corporation on the planet. The new order never looked so good.

Doing It for Dummies

It should be noted — at least, I want to note — that you, gentle reader, are a smart person. In computer terms, *dummies* aren't dumb. The smartest people I know have *...For Dummies* books in their libraries.

Computers, however, can suck the smarts out of anyone. A computer's implacable, insistent *rightness* unnerves the most confident. Especially when the computer smugly does nothing — despite your well-meant help.

At these times, you *know* it's your fault. Worse, the guy down the street did this same thing on his computer and the computer worked just fine. Who wouldn't feel helpless under those circumstances?

Web graphics are more intimidating than almost any computer topic. Turn away for five minutes and something new has happened. That's a scary environment. You can feel like a dummy for even *trying* to understand it. But stay with it if you can.

I think of Web graphics technology as a river rushing past. The stream always rushes and neither you nor I can stop it. What we can do is find our place in the stream, a place where we fit. Let this book be your map to finding that place.

I'm in this business to put technology to work. Whether working in oils, acrylics, or pixels, designers merge their skills to the tasks and technologies at hand. Beautiful, exciting graphics make the process worthwhile. In *Web Graphics For Dummies,* the technology goes to work.

You, wonderful you

I assume you are an intelligent person with at least a rudimentary knowledge of computers. If you're brand new to computers, this is the right book to learn about Web graphics, but you may need some other help to start your computer or insert a diskette.

Your computer system is less important than your state of mind about Web graphics. Most readers (and Web users) have Macintosh or Windows-equipped computers, so *Web Graphics For Dummies* focuses on Mac and Windows topics. Readers with Unix boxes and other beasts will find much of interest, too.

How this book works

You don't really need instructions for *Web Graphics For Dummies.* This book is simple enough to follow in the order you prefer.

Your habits determine whether you read from front cover to back cover, jump around at spare moments, or read topics as you need them. That's okay. Every part of *Web Graphics For Dummies* is complete unto itself. If you read the whole book, you'll know more, but knowing all isn't always the goal. When you just need to make a particular project work, *Web Graphics For Dummies* is ready to help.

A couple of more technical points about reading this book:

If you're expected to type something in, it appears in the text like this:

Type what you see here

Programming code lines, such as HTML codes, look like this:

```
<HTML>Code Line<\HTML>
```

What's between the covers

Web Graphics For Dummies features good, simple, accurate information on the following topics (and much more):

- ✔ The nature of Web graphics
- ✔ Choosing the best graphics format for the job
- ✔ Creating a Web graphic from scratch
- ✔ Selecting software and hardware
- ✔ Designing for WebTV
- ✔ Adding pictures and sound to Web pages
- ✔ Creating image maps
- ✔ Designing for different platforms
- ✔ Finding answers to questions you haven't asked — yet

The stuff you can skip

Here and there, *Web Graphics For Dummies* has background information and a bit of extra technical detail. (Forgive me, please. I'm a geek. It's my nature.) You can identify these frills because they're printed in special gray boxes called *sidebars*. Sidebars will not endanger your health in any way. Feel free to pole vault right over these gems if you want to.

How This Book Is Set Up

Web Graphics For Dummies lets you read from start to finish or anywhere in between. How you read it is up to you.

- ✔ The *Index* at the back of the book can guide you to a subject. If you want to know what Amaya is, check the index for *Amaya* and go directly to the page referenced in the index.
- ✔ The *Table of Contents* at the front of the book is a map of the whole book. For example, you may be especially interested in linking audio clips to your Web images. The Table of Contents guides you straight to the chapter with the lowdown on graphics and sounds.

✔ Six *parts* consist of several chapters that relate — more or less — to the title of the part.

In the big picture, the parts are a thumbnail sketch of the book. Let's take a look.

Part I: For the Web Newbie

Web Graphics For Dummies starts with a quick tour to lay a good foundation. You'll find Internet basics and the World Wide Web's place in the system. You don't really have to read all of this stuff. Every bit of what's salient to Web graphics covered in this part gets its very own section later in the book.

Part II: Formats for Everyone

GIFs, JPEGs, PNG . . . all these standards seem to have been created with the express purpose of confusing you. But each has a place and a purpose. And graphic format standard are important to the Web. They let other people see your graphics.

This part also peeks at other not-so-basic stuff that it's still really good to know about — if only to show off the next time you're at a dinner party.

Part III: The Sky Is the Limit

Don't think rinky-dink for your Web site. Think "how high is the sky?" There's no reason that the site you build and the graphics that compliment them can't be as tough and elegant as any you've seen out there.

In this chapter we look at some basic basics as well as some swell tricks and tips to get your graphics and Web sites to polished perfection.

Part IV: Things That Make You Say "Hmmmmm"

Lots of Web stuff is visual, and in the dinosaur days, that was good enough. Today's Web, however, is in constant multimedia motion, so it's good to know about these aspects.

There's no rule that says you *have* to have audio on your Web site. Or that you *need* to design for Web TV. However, it's certainly good to know where to start if you want to, or have to. Start here to put the Web in motion.

Part V: The Part of Tens

The traditional *For Dummies* lists of stuff that go together. I spill my guts about the tools you need to make web graphics, top online resources, solutions to common problems, and more — all neatly decimalized into tens.

Part VI: Appendix

Don't dismiss this part because of the uncool name. Unlike nasty school textbooks, there's a lot of cool stuff in the Appendix. The glossary, for instance, gets you up to speed on the lingo fast. And the chapter on what's cooking with the CD-ROM is an important one if you want to take advantage of some of the cool stuff we've included on there. It lets you know just what's there and what to do with it.

Icons

You'll find icons in this book for paragraphs that focus on specific aspects of the technology.

Technical information follows. Read it if you want, or skip it as quickly as possible. Your call.

Hints and shortcuts are flagged with the tip icon.

Elephants might never forget, but we do. This icon helps you remember stuff that'll make your task easier.

There's really not much you can break in a computer system, but sometimes it's just better to *not* do something. This icon will help you stop before you start doing something silly.

Where to Go from Here

You have now been completely prepared to use this book you're ready to get to work. Check out the Index, study the Table of Contents, or just turn the page and begin at the beginning. And then — like the wag said — just do it. I hope all you need for great Web graphics is *Web Graphics For Dummies* and some time alone with your computer.

Part I
For the Web
Newbie

The 5th Wave   By Rich Tennant

"Before I go on to explain more advanced procedures like the 'Zap-Rowdy-Students-who-Don't-Pay-Attention' function, we'll begin with some basics."

In this part . . .

You don't build a solid house without laying a good foundation. You don't drive in the rain without good tires. And though those two are hardly the same, there's a parallel in there somewhere and I'll bet you get it. Web graphics begin at the beginning, even if we spend a lot of the rest of the time going to the place where we most need to be.

This part of the book takes you on a quick tour of the things you need to know to lay a good foundation: Internet basics, and the World Wide Web's place in on the 'Net.

And here's the good part. You don't really have to read all of this stuff at all. Every bit of the stuff that's salient to Web graphics that we cover in this next few pages gets its very own section later in the book. So graze thoroughly or browse happily, depending on your own personal learning curve. Our mandate — yours and mine — is to get to the stuff that interests us quickly because the World Wide Web is expanding by the minute and graphics are waiting to be created.

Let's get busy!

Chapter 1

The Anatomy of a Web Graphic

• •

• •

*N*ot sure exactly how to define a Web graphic? Relax. No one else is, either. Or, if they're sure, they're sure by themselves and no one precisely agrees with them.

Fact is, all of this technology is still so startlingly new. Ten years ago, no one even imagined the Web or coined the phrase "information highway," let alone the graphics that would adorn the sides of the road.

This chapter goes down that road a bit, so feel free to detour to later sections if you prefer. It's possible to put a roof on a house without knowing a whole lot about how shingles are made.

If you prefer to stick around and bandy semantics while getting some background, come on. There's still lots of stuff to understand.

Web Graphics Defined

So on the heels of saying that it's sort of indefinable, I go ahead and try to define it. I like to bandy semantics. Anyway, it's my job.

A Web graphic is any piece of (relatively) static art that is created or reinterpreted to be included on a Web page or other HTML (Hypertext Markup Language) computer document and intended for viewing by a wide variety of people on different platforms.

I say *(relatively) static* because simple GIF animations are Web graphics. They are, after all, viewed by the same software. An extra bonus is that they're incredibly easy for the designer (that's you!) to produce.

What's a Web graphic?

Because of the nature of the World Wide Web and HTML, only certain types of files can be viewed on a Web page. Theoretically, any type of graphic file format can be used, but there has to be enough people prepared to meet that format. For instance, and again theoretically, a standard TIFF (Tagged-Image File Format) file — popular with many digital designers — can be used. But there are a couple of reasons why they're not. In the first place, TIFF files tend towards the huge. They're big and cumbersome and would be time-consuming to download on conventional analog modems.

Size aside, if you stick a TIFF file on your Web page, most people can't see it. Most browsers display only certain kinds of files, and TIFF isn't one of them.

So Web graphics must use one of several popular formats for other people to see them!

Popular formats

If we boil things down very tightly, essentially three types of file formats can be used in a Web page.

JPEG (Joint Photographic Experts Group)

JPEG is one of the two most popular formats for display on a Web page. JPEG files are usually the smallest files. Unfortunately, at least part of this is because JPEG is a "lossy" method of compression. Basically, that means that when saving a file as a JPEG squeezes important bits out in the compression process, you experience some "loss" of information. In certain situations, that's okay. For instance, losing less than critical bits of information that doesn't actually effect the quality of the image a great deal. On the other hand, with some images, you really see the difference. Figure 1-1 is an original TIFF file.

Figure 1-2 is a JPEG file, saved at medium quality for a real reduction in file size. Figure 1-2 is only 11K, but you can see where some of the information has been lost, particularly when you look closely around the cow's head and neck area.

GIF (Graphics Interchange Format)

Sometimes you hear GIF files referred to as CompuServe GIF files, and herein lies the biggest problem with this format. Depending on whom and when you ask, GIF *may* be owned by the good folks at CompuServe. Or maybe not (again, depending upon when and whom you ask). The complications are

Figure 1-1:
This cow is
shown here
as a .tif file,
at 121K. A
lovely
animal,
but too
cumbersome
a file for a
Web page.

Photographed by David Middleton

Figure 1-2:
Same cow,
JPEG
perspective.

obvious. Who wants to save files in a format that may actually have an owner? The future ramifications are potentially frightening. Especially because GIF remains one of the more popular file formats for Web graphics.

Figure 1-3 illustrates our friend from the preceding figures as a GIF. And — like the JPEG — she's come in at 11K. This time, some of the loss has occurred in her flank.

PNG (Portable Network Graphics)

PNG is the Web-developed non-proprietary answer to GIF. No one owns it. And because — unlike JPEG and GIF — it was developed for the Web for use on Web pages, it is a superior Web format in many ways. PNG retains all of the information in the original file (it's not at all lossy!), which makes it a "non-destructive" format. Some bad news: PNG files generally are at least slightly larger than JPEGs or GIFs. Another negative: As of yet, many browsers don't support the PNG file format, so using the format on your Web pages may not be a good idea . . . yet.

 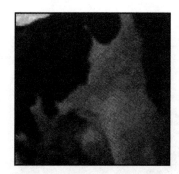

Figure 1-3:
Again the cow, but now she's a GIF.

Bossy is back and better than ever as a PNG file in Figure 1-4. The particular save configuration I chose came up with a whopping 33K for this image. Twice as big as the other two, but still considerably smaller than the original TIFF file. But notice the smooth grayscale tones. There appears to have been no loss of information.

Figure 1-4:
Our cow is now a PNG.

More, of course, on all of this later. But this gives you the beginnings of a working knowledge on the three contending file types. I talk about them a lot.

It's about limitations

And, really, it's about overcoming those limitations in a way that satisfies your creative sense. At first glance, designing for the Web is very confining. International struggles about both standardization and market share leave the user feeling somewhat confused and certainly constrained.

In the first place, the Web surfers who view your graphic are most likely using one of two browsers: Netscape or Microsoft Explorer. Unless they aren't. Either way, viewers on different browsers experience your Web site in an entirely different way, even apart from the differences they bring as individuals. They actually *see* different things. Which brings us to the second place.

Different platforms

If it isn't already bad enough that different browsers make things look entirely different, those same browsers look different again on different platforms. The Macophile using Netscape sees something different than the Windoze user running the same program.

Bandwidth considerations

Part of the experience is how quickly it all comes down. One of my Web designer pals just showed me his prize creation, the jewel in his Web designing crown. It's really lovely, but the graphics are *huge*. "No problem," he said. "It's aimed at business users. Business users all have really fast connections." Which is wrong. Even though an increasing number of people in some areas have T1s and so on at their place of work, lots of business people like to do their surfing at home. And lots of *those* kinds of users still struggle along at 14,400 and 28,800 bps.

So, even the size of your graphics affects your view. Sure, a 300K JPEG of one of your creative creations looks super cool, but who's going to know that when your viewers click off somewhere else before they even get a chance to see it?

When limitations turn into challenges

So you're looking at several limitations:

- The format you choose to display your graphics affects both how the graphic looks as well as the site viewer's ability to see it.
- A visitor's platform greatly affects how Web images look.
- The speed of a viewer's modem connection, the speed of your server's connection, and the way those things coincide directly affects the viewer's experience of your images.

These variables alone may be quite daunting in a less dynamic medium. Because it's the Web, things change quite quickly. What looks problematic today is likely being scrutinized by industry experts who see the problem as well.

Meanwhile, stay flexible. Don't get married too closely to a single idea or way of doing things.

To really check how others — at least some of them — see your graphics, you need at least two browsers on your computer. Keep tabs on what's popular. As I write this, the dynamic duo are Internet Explorer and Netscape Navigator. Fully, 85 percent of surfers use one of these two.

Your Web Graphics Can Look As Good As Anyone's

In the long ago (that really wasn't!), a $100 million a year company out-promoted you. They threw a lot of money at designers and printers and reps. The big kids looked more professional because of high-dollar technology that was inaccessible to little guys.

Enter the Internet, where all graphics are created equally. By assembling some basics, you have the same tools available to you as the highest priced designers at the most famous agencies. A successful Web site isn't made by simply burning money. It's created by careful applications of a series of tools.

The really good news? You can do that, too!

Chapter 2

Getting Right to Work

● ●

In This Chapter

▶ Preparing a graphic for the Web

▶ HTML quick and dirty

▶ Using images with HTML

● ●

Creating a graphic for the Web is an easy operation if you have a few tools. Here and now, let's make a very simple GIF file.

Preparing Graphics for the Web

To create a Web graphic, you need only a few simple tools and skills. The good news is, you probably already have most of these right now!

✔ A computer! Preferably one purchased in this decade.

✔ An image editing or converting program. You can start with an expensive, multifunctional image editor like Adobe Photoshop or a simple shareware converter, such as GIFConverter.

✔ An image. For this exercise, use one of your own or — to follow along with the exercise — open FLYGUY.TIF from the *Web Graphics For Dummies* CD-ROM.

Let's make a GIF file. For demonstration purposes, I used the popular image converter DeBabelizer. Any image editor or converter works as well and in a similar manner.

1. **In your image editor or converter, open FLYGUY.TIF from the *Web Graphics For Dummies* CD-ROM.**

   If you are working with one of your own files, make sure that it's cleaned up and ready for conversion. The sample graphic is shown in Figure 2-1.

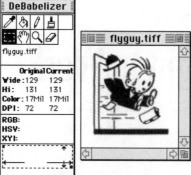

Figure 2-1:
Getting
ready to
convert a
TIFF file into
a format
suitable for
the Web.

2. **Select Save As from the file menu.**

3. **A dialog box offers you several save schemes and naming options, as shown in Figure 2-2. Choose GIF from the many file types offered.**

   Many programs will automatically append the .GIF suffix to whatever name the file already had. Check to make sure that this has happened; if it *hasn't,* do it yourself. For simplicity, leave the color setting at the default, 256. This creates a compact, usable GIF file.

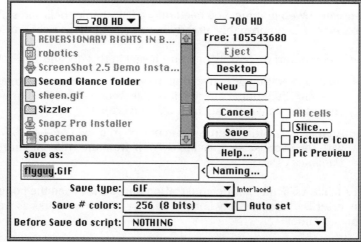

Figure 2-2:
When you
select Save
As in
almost any
graphics
program,
you get a
list of
possible file
types.

When you work with Web graphics, you also work with several different file types. Make sure that you append the file type to the file when you name it. For example, you can make a Photoshop TIFF file into both a GIF and a JPEG. Imagine the eye-crossing confusion if you *didn't* tell the files what they were and then tried to figure it out on your own.

Another key detail. Most modern programs can tell what type of file something is just by looking at it. But some can't. In this case, you must append the file type so that the dumb ol' computer knows what to do with it.

4. **Choose Save from the dialog box and — whammo-presto! — you are the proud owner of a graphic suitable for Web publication.**

You can make many possible refinements to the Web graphic you just created. You can affect transparency and choose whether to dither. You can control colors and how they're represented. All of that is covered in other chapters of the book. However totally technical or confusingly complicated graphics seem, remember this lesson. All those refinements help you make better Web graphics. Or, at least, different ones. But the very simple image in the preceding example works. And — depending on the starting image — it'll probably even work well. The confusion comes with the technical refinements.

The really salient thing here? Even simple graphics work. When surfers get to your Web site, they see your images. Everything beyond that is icing!

A Quick Take On HTML

When we really get cooking, we can boil HTML down to three key issues:

- ✓ Creating the graphic to be made into one that is Web-appropriate (that is, one that people can see when they visit a Web site).
- ✓ Converting the graphic into a popular Web format, such as JPEG, GIF, or PNG.
- ✓ Incorporating the graphic into a Web page in a way that is efficient and gorgeous.

What is HTML?

HTML is sometimes called a programming language which — in the strictest sense — it absolutely is not.

The "hyper" in Hypertext is the key to understanding the function of HTML. "Hyper" describes how a Web page connects from place to place on a page, its host site, or another site anywhere in the world. They're *hyper* because they're jumping.

Early in my design career (now I'm gonna show my rings), I trained for a CompuGraphic typesetting machine. Later, I first saw HTML. I said, "Wow! This looks like typesetting code." Other former typesetters say the same, no matter what type of machine they were trained on. Typesetters train to make code that translates into beautiful designs. Building Web pages isn't much different.

Being a really whizz-bang creator of Web pages and worker of HTML requires both sides of your brain. The best Web page designers consider the technical issues of Web site design, how the page looks, and how users move around the site. The best Web designers are in touch with both their inner artist and their inner geek. Both are equally necessary for excellence.

What's it made outta?

HTML can seem unwieldy and unforgiving. That's because — mostly — HTML is unwieldy and unforgiving. The Web and HTML were developed by high-energy physics geeks to show off their cool physics-geek documents. HTML and the Web weren't intended for fancy-shmansy designers.

If designing for the Web seems like a designer's nightmare, that's why. The rocket scientists who invented the Web didn't invent it for you or me. For their own super-geek purposes, it was perfect.

Why not use a WYSIWYG editor?

All of this HTML stuff is enough to make your eyes cross. After all, there are programs out there that do all this stuff without ever looking at the code.

The problem really takes us right back to that greatest of all challenges when designing for this medium. Everything looks different when you're standing somewhere else.

A bit of a for-instance: When I design a page in Quark or PageMaker — for the world, not the Web — there are incredible levels of interfaces between me and my code. I mean, it looks like I'm dropping a photo on the type and all the type is obediently running around it, just as I specified. But, in reality, there is a drop-dead WYSIWYG editor doing all that interpreting for me. If I dug down far enough, I'd find code because computers use codes and numbers to do everything: even if it looks like they don't.

The reason why I don't (thank goodness!) need to dig down to code level in Quark is because I have specified in my work *exactly* what the finished product should look like. I told the program I want my margins here and a release there and throw exactly *that* typeface here where I told it to go. And if I send it to my laser printer, it'll print in exactly that way. That's the nature of the program and the work it's meant to do: Programs like Quark and PageMaker were designed to let you easily specify things with a great deal of precision right to the point where you output the file.

And then there's the Web.

Because everyone uses different viewers and monitors and computers to view your work, you have a great deal many more variables than you do for work that is intended to be somehow hard copied. And while a WYSIWYG HTML editor can be helpful — and in truth they're getting better all the time — I don't foresee a time in the professional Web designer's future when it will entirely replace at least some hand coding.

Even if you find a really good HTML editor — say one that hasn't been invented as I write this — to do large quantities of your dirty work, it's still a good thing to have at least a knowledge of the code. And failing the knowledge, then the reference. I guess that's what I'm doing here!

HTML Crunched Down

This is not an HTML book. It doesn't even play one on TV. Lots of books are dedicated to that topic. However, I go over some of the high notes here, especially as they relate to executing your Web graphics in real time.

- ✔ When you parse the code of a Web page, you quickly get a feel for what you're looking at. Some of the writing is set apart in <SYMBOLS>, like that. And, when you look again, the stuff set apart doesn't appear when the page is "published" in a Web browser.

- ✔ Things that appear in lesser than and greater than symbols (<>) are the business end of HTML. They contain the secret codes that make everything happen.

To look at it up close and personal, lets look at a for-real Web page, and what the code does within the file.

```
<HTML>
<HEAD>
<TITLE>HTML at a Glance</TITLE>
</HEAD>
<BODY BGCOLOR="#ffffff">
```

(continued)

(continued)

```
<PRE><CENTER><TT><FONT SIZE=+4>What the HTML!?!</FONT></
        TT></PRE>

<P><CENTER> If you want to build Web pages, you have to at
        least know what HTML looks like. And what it
        looks like is this. Looking at the code might
        initially make your eyes want to cross, but it's
        really pretty simple once you:</CENTER></P>

<UL>
 <UL>
   <LI>1. Get the hang of it, and
     <LI>2. Take the time to look carefully at it and break
        down all the parts
   </UL>
</UL>

<P><CENTER><IMG SRC="horse1.gif" WIDTH="155"
        HEIGHT="131"></CENTER></P>

<P><CENTER> And  —  just in case you're wondering  —  this
        horse serves no particular purpose here. I just
        thought he was cute and that it would be a good
        place for you to see an image tag.</CENTER>
</BODY>
</HTML>
```

In a World Wide Web browser, the preceding code translates to Figure 2-3.

A closer look

Let's take another look at the same code from a closer angle.

1. First, open the HTML file and specify a head, title, and body color.

```
<HTML>
<HEAD>
<TITLE>HTML at a Glance</TITLE>
</HEAD>
<BODY BGCOLOR="#ffffff">
```

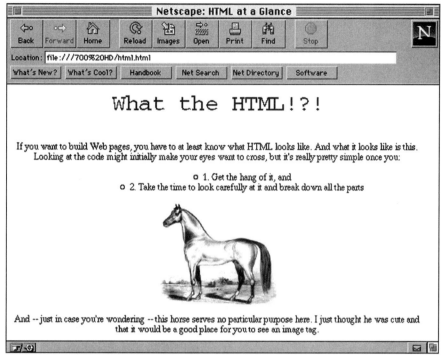

Figure 2-3:
All of that
code adds
up to a
pretty
simple file.

2. **Then specify a little centered type.**

   I dislike the standard Web font for headlines, so here I specified teletype <TT> for the font of the first block of type. To my eye, it gives it a smoother look, but that's a very personal thing.

   In the same block, specify a font size, then add the type, and then close off all that early stuff.

   ```
   <PRE><CENTER><TT><FONT SIZE=+4>What the HTML!?!</FONT>
   </TT></PRE>
   ```

3. **Now some basic body copy. Centered, but only because I like to see it that way sometimes.**

   See, it's really pretty simple when you break it down. Here, the results of the coding are fairly obvious.

   ```
   <P><CENTER>If you want to build Web pages, you have to
              at least know what HTML looks like. And what it
              looks like is this. Looking at the code might
              initially make your eyes want to cross, but it's
              really pretty simple once you:</CENTER></P>
   ```

4. Now some tricky stuff that isn't, really. A (short) centered list is also indented a couple of times. It jumps out from the rest of the stuff a bit without overpowering the whole page.

```
<UL>
  <UL>
    <LI>1. Get the hang of it, and
    <LI>2. Take the time to look carefully at it and
        break down all the parts
  </UL>
</UL>
```

5. Now the image, just for good measure. I centered this one again, in addition to sizing it on the Web page. (Width and height specifications are in quotes in the following code.)

```
<P><CENTER><IMG SRC="horse1.gif" WIDTH="155"
        HEIGHT="131"></CENTER></P>
```

6. A bit more text that tells you what's going on.

```
<P><CENTER>And — just in case you're wondering —
        this horse serves no particular purpose here. I
        just thought he was cute and that it would be a
        good place for you to see an image tag.</CENTER>
```

7. Finish with the traditional HTML signoff, just so the server never hangs while looking for the end of our Web page.

```
</BODY>
</HTML>
```

Lots of bits and pieces, but pretty simple overall.

Of course, there are lots more commands, and much more to learn. But what I'd like to see with this is at least a slight comfort with HTML. As well as recognition that it's possible to get your hands dirty in the code without ever blowing your cool.

If you want to get your hands *super* dirty with code and just learn everything there is to know about HTML, you can check out the World Wide Web Consortium's Web site at http://www.w3.org where you find not only the complete standards for HTML 3.2, but also any changes that are being considered.

Weaving images into HTML

In this book, the thing that is most interesting about HTML is how it's used to weave Web graphics into a Web page. This is salient even if you have people around who do the actual coding for you. Knowing how your image will be applied in actual usage helps you design it in the most effective way.

Tools you'll need

Using some of the skills looked at in this chapter, let's build a simple Web page around that first graphic. Here's what you need.

✔ Some sort of HTML editor. Ideally, there'll be some way for you to peek at code as you work. Check out CMed for Windows and BBEdit for Macintosh. There are others — many of them good — but these two are longtime favorites with a lot of the Internet community.

✔ A GIF file. You can use FLYGUY.GIF that you made in the exercise earlier in this chapter.

Let's get started!

1. Open your HTML editor and start a conventional file:

```
<HTML>
<HEAD>
```

This part of the code is to establish that — yes — this is an HTML file and that a head will follow.

2. Think of a title for your Web page. As you can see, mine wasn't terribly original.

```
<TITLE>Adding a Graphic to an HTML File</TITLE>
</HEAD>
```

A salient title is an important part of a Web page. Search engines often reference things by title. Also, if someone likes your page well enough to bookmark it, a good title will help them remember just why they wanted to keep it!

3. And then the body of the HTML document.

```
<BODY>

<P><CENTER><FONT SIZE=+4>HTML Exercise #2</FONT>
      </CENTER></P>
```

(continued)

(continued)

```
<P><FONT SIZE=+2>It's a simple matter to add
one of your Web graphics to an HTML file. And
this is how we do it...<FONT></P>
```

This is where you get down to business. As you can see, in the body of this document, a headline and some copy is included.

4. **And now the moment we've all be waiting for: adding the image. As you can see, the image is centered in this example.**

```
<P><CENTER><IMG SRC="flyguy.GIF"></CENTER>
```

As you can see, adding the image is the easiest part of the page in this instance.

5. **Finally, the page is properly closed off:**

```
</BODY>
</HTML>
```

The resulting page looks like Figure 2-4.

Figure 2-4:
The teeny little page resulting from all of that code. Note that adding the image was the very easiest part.

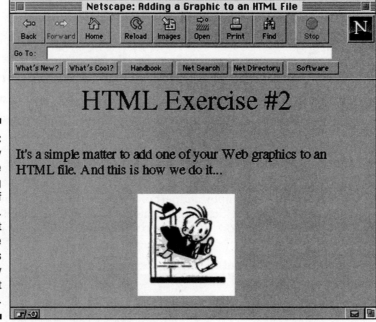

Chapter 3

When Your Web Graphics Become Image Maps

· ·

In This Chapter

▶ What's an image map?

▶ Client-side and server-side image maps

▶ Creating clickable graphics

· ·

*I*mage maps — and their cousins, clickable graphics — are one of the reasons the Web is such a delight to navigate and negotiate. What could be simpler than arriving at a site and discovering that all you have to do to find your way around is click on the pretty picture?

At some point you'll find yourself wanting to add some of this clicking ease to your own Web work. While the technique for creating this type of graphic is precisely the same as for other types of Web graphics, what you actually *do* with that graphic once you've made it is quite different.

The Image Map Demystified

When you're surfing, image maps look horribly complex to create. How could they not be? What you see as a surfer is a single, elegant graphic that somehow links you through to a number of areas in a site. How could something that makes things that easy for you as a Web surfer *not* be difficult to create? The old axiom holds true here, though: Everything is easy when you know how. And while this may not hold up for astrophysics, it's pretty much true for image maps.

What's an image map good for?

There are several things that an image map is useful for. The most simple type of image map is one that takes you from one location — in this case, a Web graphic — to another location on a Web site. In this instance, it's not so much an image map as a clickable Web graphic.

The image map that links to a single location can be helpful in just moving things along effortlessly on a Web site. A single button on a Web site moves surfers from one place to the next, as shown in Figure 3-1. The one illustrated is, of course, from the first page of my own Web site. Clicking on it bypasses a whole bunch of business stuff and takes visitors straight to my own area on the site.

Figure 3-1:
A simple
clickable
graphic.

However, when someone says "image map" we most often think of a larger graphic that directs a Web site's traffic to several different locations, either on or off the site. The classic example would, of course, be an actual area map where the site visitor can click on an area of interest and get zoomed there easily, without having to read text that says, "For Southern California, click here" and so on.

Another useful example would be of a floor plan, or locations in a mall — either a virtual mall, or a real one. An image map where the surfer can easily click through to the desired location makes things easier for a Web visitor to negotiate.

Lots of people surf the Web without graphics enabled in order to speed things up. And many people use browsers — like Lynx, for example — that don't have the capacity to view graphics. For both groups it's important to:

✔ Make sure the graphics in your image map are small, so that people who make a choice about what graphics they view will want to view yours.

✔ Use ALT (alternate) tags to give a type label for every graphic you use. This should be true not only of your image maps, but of all the graphics you embed into HTML.

A common use for image maps is routing traffic easily to other areas. For instance, in the example shown in Figure 3-2, visitors to my Web site can click on pictures of some of my friends to find out more about them. The Web graphic was created in Photoshop using several different images and backgrounds and then saved as a single file. The resulting file channels visitors to pages that talk about these friends and to their own Web sites. All in all, it's a very fun use of a whole lot of technology.

Figure 3-2:
My Friends
Page is
actually a
single
image,
compiled of
several
images in
an image
editor.

How to make an image map

There are two ways to make all this happen.

 ✔ You can hand-code the image map's instructions in the editor you commonly use for HTML coding.
 ✔ You can use an image mapping program.

While the second way is the easiest if you use one of the powerful mapping programs out there, it's good to know how to do it the old-fashioned way — that is, by hand — so you know what it is you're actually doing.

Having said that, there are some really powerful image mapping aids out there — some of which are included on the Web Graphics For Dummies CD-ROM that comes with this book — that take all the tedium out of calculating image maps. There's no real reason not to use one of them. Mapedit for Windows and WebMap for Macintosh (both included on the CD-ROM) are good examples of shareware image-map editors designed by others to make your life easier. There doesn't seem to be a good reason to wander around in the forest when other people have already made a path.

In addition, an increasing number of WYSIWYG HTML editors include some type of image mapping facility. Adobe PageMill, for example, includes a good one.

I discuss both options later in the chapter.

Client-side and server-side image maps

At the technical end of things, image maps can be specified in one of two ways: as *server-side* or *client-side*. The server-side image map is the only type that was available in the bad ol' days, before image map–supporting browsers added extra fun.

All the current and recent releases of the more popular browsers (Netscape Navigator, Internet Explorer, Cyberdog, Spyglass Mosaic, and others) support client-side image maps.

Specifically, in a server-side image map, instructions for the locations of the *hot spots,* or links, on your graphics are stored on the remote server, in a file separate from the HTML or graphics files the map relates to.

Client-side image maps look exactly the same to the innocent surfer, but they are created quite differently. On a client-side image map, the instructions for the hot spots on the graphics are contained within the HTML coding.

While both methods have something to recommend them in certain situations, client-side image maps are the most popular at present, for a couple of reasons:

  ✔ Server-side image maps demand more of the server's time and attention because the person viewing your file pulls down not only your graphic and HTML files, but the additional CGI (Common Gateway Interface) file as well. That means additional trips to the server and more demand on the bandwidth.

  ✔ Client-side image maps are easier for the Web designer to control and edit. This is because the coding for the map resides inside the page's regular HTML coding. No special thought needs to go into storage and maintenance for the map to work.

Because coding in CGI and all things to do with it are outside the scope of this book, I leave discussions of server-side image maps right there. The balance of image mapping discussions is around client-side maps.

The Old-Fashioned Way: Creating a Simple Clickable Graphic

While not, strictly speaking, an image map, this seems like a logical place to talk about straight-up clickable graphics. While the techniques behind creating the single graphic that is clickable and creating an image map are completely different, the results look very similar to the Web surfer.

What you need

For this exercise, you need:

- ✔ An HTML editor. One that lets you get in there and muck with the code yourself.
- ✔ A graphic to make clickable. If you don't have one handy that you'd like to use, open SINGLEHOTSPOT.GIF from the CD-ROM that's included with this book.

Making that clickable graphic

1. **Open your text editor.**

   For this example, I used BBEdit for Macintosh, which is a very simple, shareware Macintosh HTML editor. You can use anything that will let you get in and mess with the text. An example of what *not* to use would be Adobe PageMill 1.0 because it doesn't allow the user to actually see the resulting code (Version 2.0 of PageMill corrects this oversight).

2. **You need to create a working file so that you can view the results when you're done, so mark it up the way you would any new HTML file: with open HTML tags, a title, and so on, like this:**

   ```
   <HTML>
   <TITLE>Clickable Graphic Exercise</TITLE>
   <BODY>
   <P ALIGN=CENTER><FONT SIZE=+4>Clickable Graphic
          Exercise<BR><BR></FONT></P>
   ```

So you're creating a file — I saved mine as CLICK.HTML, to demonstrate a clickable graphic. If you're following along so far, you have something that looks like Figure 3-3 if viewed in an Internet browser.

3. **Now the graphical stuff. The coding is not a lot different from the coding for any graphic, with the big difference being that you're giving a "target" URL — where you want the click to be. Like so:**

```
<P ALIGN=CENTER><FONT SIZE=+4>Clickable Graphic
        Exercise<BR><BR>
</FONT><A HREF="clickthru.html">
```

CLICKTHRU.HTML is what I named the target file for this exercise, and the ones that are to come. But notice, I specified a font size for my little headline and then gave the HREF as the name of the target file.

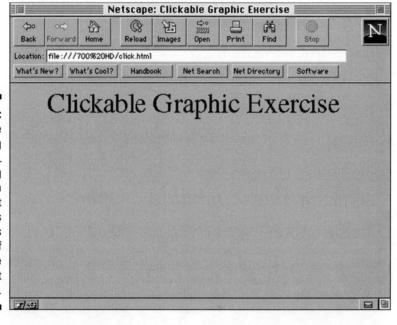

Figure 3-3: The preceding HTML coding gives you a file that looks like this example. Of course, the best is yet to come.

On the same line — though I broke it up here just to tell you about it — are the specifications for the image on *this* page: your clickable graphic. SINGLEHOTSPOT.GIF (what a mouthful) is the graphic you're making clickable. Note the material that's behind the ALT command. This stuff is important. Like it says in the tag, it lets people without graphics capabilities, or those who surf with graphics turned off, know what is *supposed* to be in this spot. In some cases, you want to use ALT to tell people what to do if they don't see any graphics.

Another possibility: Should your graphic be broken, for some reason, surfers will still see something useful besides an empty old box.

```
<IMG SRC="singlehotspot.gif" ALIGN="BOTTOM"
NATURALSIZEFLAG="3" ALT="It's important to indicate what
          the function of this graphic is, in writing.
          That way, someone without a graphics-enabled
          browser will still be able to negotiate your
          site."
BORDER="0"></A> <BR>
</P>
<P ALIGN=CENTER><TT><FONT SIZE=+1>This is a single
          clickable graphic. Accomplished, you will have
          noticed, very simply.</FONT></TT>
</BODY>
</HTML>
```

And that's it — a clickable graphic that looks just like Figure 3-4 when downloaded by an Internet browser.

Figure 3-4:
The completed single clickable graphic exercise. If you click on the graphic, it takes you directly to the specified page: CLICKTHRU HTML.

Note the BORDER="0" portion of the coding above. If you choose *not to* leave it at 0 — say if you choose "1" instead — you get a visible border around the graphic, in the color chosen for links.

Now that you've made a clickable graphic, jump straight into the image map.

The Old-Fashioned Way II: Making an Image Map

All preamble aside, get your hands right into a for-real, client-side image map.

What you need

For this exercise, you need:

✔ An HTML editor. With the same specifications as the last exercise: one that lets you get right into the code yourself.

✔ An image mapping utility. Several are included on the CD-ROM that comes with this book. For this exercise I used the shareware program WebMap for the Macintosh. You'll find that all image mapping utilities work very similarly and on the same principle.

✔ A graphic to turn into an image map. If you don't have one of your own that you'd like to use, open HOTSPOT.GIF from the Web Graphics For Dummies CD-ROM.

Making that image map

1. **In your HTML editor, create four target files that you'll be linking your image map to.**

   These files need only be very simple files, but name them carefully so you can remember which is which. In this example, they're TARGET1.HTML, TARGET2. HTML and so on:

   ```
   <HTML>
   <HEAD>
   <TITLE>The target of all our exercises!</TITLE>
   </HEAD>
   <BODY BGCOLOR="#ffffff">
   <H1><CENTER><TT>This is Target One </TT></CENTER></H1>
   ```

```
<H1><CENTER><IMG SRC="target.gif" WIDTH="212"
        HEIGHT="260"
        ALIGN="BOTTOM"
NATURALSIZEFLAG="3"></CENTER></H1>
</BODY>
</HTML>
```

2. **Open HOTSPOT.GIF in your image mapping package, as shown in Figure 3-5.**

   What you'll be doing in the image mapping utility is specifying areas to be defined as coordinates for a Web surfer to click to when on a Web site. So remember the names of the four target HTML files you create.

Figure 3-5:
HOTSPOT.GIF ready to be image mapped. The interface shown is WebMap for Macintosh. Most image mapping utilities work in a very similar way. Note the *x* and *y* coordinates in the lower left corner. The utility finds these easily for you, so that you don't have to calculate them.

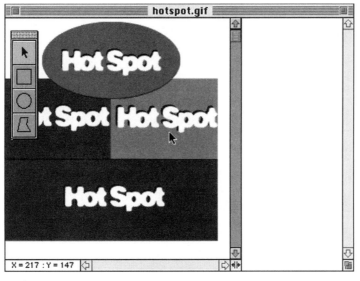

3. **With the circle tool selected, define a circle in the *Hot Spot* circle icon on the graphic as shown in Figure 3-6.**

   Don't worry if you don't get the circle in exactly the right place right away. When you stop drawing the circle you'll notice a little handle on the bottom right of the shape that you can grab to reshape the circle.

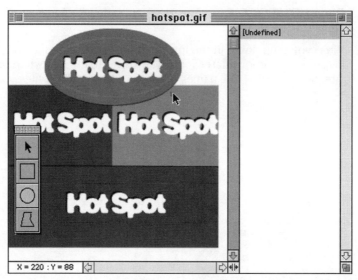

Figure 3-6:
If you miss on your first try, don't worry. It's very easy to move and reshape these areas in MapEdit.

4. **After you've drawn the circle, notice the word *[undefined]* pop up in gray in the right portion of the screen. This is the place where you input your target HTML file. Simply move your mouse to the grayed-out word and double-click.**

   A dialog box like the one shown in Figure 3-7 appears, prompting you for the name of your target file.

5. **The oddly shaped boxes created by the overlapping circle could be handled in a couple of ways. You could use the polygon tool, seen in Figure 3-8, to define the area accurately. Or you could use the rectangle tool shown in Figure 3-9 to define the area roughly.**

Figure 3-7:
When you double-click on the highlighted word that is associated with the shape you've just drawn, you're greeted with a dialog box that prompts you for the name of the HTML file to be targeted by that area.

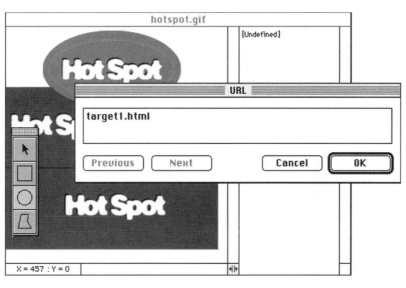

Figure 3-8:
Use the polygon tool in the image map program to precisely define an uneven area.

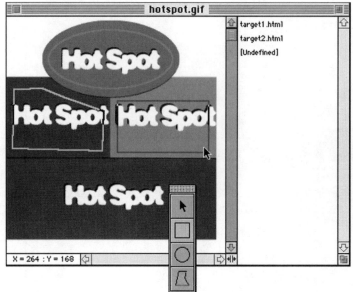

Figure 3-9:
Sometimes close is good enough. At those times, you can use a rectangle tool to define the hot area within a rough-edged shape.

6. **Select the rectangle tool to define the space within the largest box at the bottom. Click on the fourth highlighted area to define the space within this rectangle as TARGET4.HTML.**

   That's pretty much it for the mapping part of image mapping — easy enough to make early trepidation seem silly. Just two steps remain. You have to perform *both* a Save As and an Export As Text command for the image mapping to work once you actually have it in an HTML file, so . . .

7. **Choose Save As from the file menu. You can safely save over the original version.**

8. **Then choose Export As Text from the file menu. You get a dialog box like the one shown in Figure 3-10, asking you for the name. Take out the extra dot (.) that the program sticks in until you have a name that's acceptable in HTML, as shown in Figure 3-11.**

Figure 3-10:
A dialog box prompts you for a name and supplies one. Remove the extra dot (.) for something that looks more like Figure 3-11.

Figure 3-11:
The dot from Figure 3-10 has been deleted.

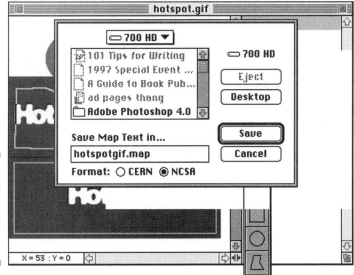

Working with the mapped image

Now that you have your image mapped, it's time to do something with it.

Your image mapping utility — WebMap or Mapedit — will have saved a map file that includes all the calculations it saved you from doing. In the case of my hot spot file, it saved it to my HTML editor — BBEdit — by creating a text file that really could be opened in any text editor, such as a word processor or any type of text handling program. The resulting file looks like this:

```
#
# Created by WebMap 1.0.1
# Wednesday, April 30, 1997 at 7:36 PM
# Format: NCSA
#

default hotspot.html
circ target1.html 56,16 223,93
poly target2.html 9,92 7,170 130,173 132,120 83,104 50,91
         9,92
rect target3.html 148,107 271,175
rect target4.html 6,187 275,280
rect hotspot.html 0,0 0,0
```

Of course, the first part is pretty much just the job output — WebMap's way of telling me what it is, when it was done, and by what. Details like this are ultimately important to geeks. You don't need it at all.

The second — and last — chunk is the business end of the whole production. These are the precise mathematical locations of the maps you specified. Aren't you glad you didn't have to figure that out yourself? Now that you've got them, you can plug them into an HTML file.

1. **In your HTML program, start a normal file. Open HTML and specify a head and title:**

```
<HTML>
<HEAD>
<TITLE>Image Mapping Exercise</TITLE>
</HEAD>
```

2. **In my example I specified a white background because I like the way the colors I chose look on that color:**

```
<BODY BGCOLOR="#ffffff">
```

3. **Tell the file what the GIF is that is to be mapped:**

```
<P><CENTER><AREA><MAP NAME="hotspotgif.map">
```

4. **Here's where you get to the business part of the image map. Plug in the coordinates established for you in WebMap or Mapedit (or whatever utility you used) so that the file knows which click produces what result.**

Don't let the algebraic look of the coding give you heartburn. It looks a lot ickier than it is. And broken down, it's really pretty simple. Here's the first one broken down to look at its components:

```
<AREA SHAPE="rect" COORDS="56,16 223,93"
HREF="target4.html">
```

- The AREA SHAPE defines the shape chosen. In this case, it's a rectangle.

- The COORDS and then the appropriate numbers specify exactly where the image is clickable. Where, in other words, the live areas are to be found.

- The HREF specifies what a click in the live area will produce — where on the map a click will take you. In this case, it's a file named "target4.html."

5. **Then you deal individually with the balance of the shapes in the map:**

```
<AREA SHAPE="polygon" COORDS="9,92 7,170 130,173
        132,120 83,104 50,91 9,92 "
HREF="target3.html">
  <AREA SHAPE="polygon" COORDS="148,107 271,175"
HREF="target2.html">
  <AREA SHAPE="circle" COORDS="6,187 275,280"
        HREF="target1.html">
```

6. **Establish that you've dealt with all aspects of the map </MAP> and that there will be no visible border around the whole map itself or any of its components. USEMAP tells the file that the map information is here (remember, you just did that) and not on a remote server in a CGI file:**

```
</MAP><IMG SRC="hotspot.gif" BORDER="0"
        USEMAP="hotspotgif.map"
```

7. **As with almost any image-wielding HTML file, specify the size of the total map.**

This saves some time in the download process because the size information is in the code, so the downloading browser doesn't have to wait to see the file to size it. There are fewer surprises.

The ISMAP command tells the browser that it has an active image coming its way and to look out for it. A simple command, but if you forget it, the whole shebang won't work.

```
WIDTH="280"
HEIGHT="363" NATURALSIZEFLAG="3" ALIGN="BOTTOM" ISMAP>
<ISMAP="#imagemap"></CENTER></P><P><AREA>
```

8. **Then, as always, you end the HTML nicely, by coding in a finale. In this way, you prevent the browser from cliff-hanging by looking to see just what the heck happened to the end of the file:**

```
</BODY>
</HTML>
```

All that coding produces a pretty simple file, as can be seen in Figure 3-12, but one that will elegantly take surfers deeper into your Web page. And in an entirely graphical way.

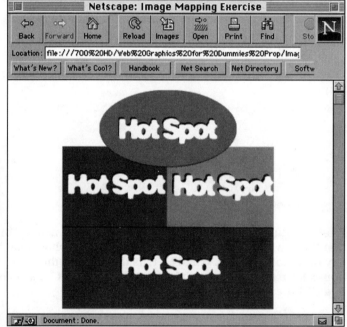

Figure 3-12:
The completed image map shown within an HTML file on a Web browser.

Image Mapping with a New-Fangled Web-Weaving Tool

If an image mapping utility makes image mapping easy, doing the same chore with one of the latest generation of WYSIWYG Web design tools practically does the job all by itself.

PageMill 2.0 from Adobe and Microsoft FrontPage are just two of the Web-weaving programs that make image mapping a breeze.

If you are thinking about using a WYSIWYG Web design tool, make sure that it lets you view the HTML code easily. Some of them don't. I find that sometimes it's a lot simpler to be able to get into the code and throw in a good ol' <CENTER> command instead of fighting your way through to finding why it's not doing it. Also, future edits to the file are sometimes easier when you can get straight to the code.

The very newest generations of Web-weaving tools all seem to offer easy access to the HTML source code as an option, while some of the earlier versions of the same software did not. Insist on having this capability. That way, it's always there when you need it.

1. **Create a multishape or multicolor document in any image editor that supports one of the Web formats. Or open MAP.GIF from the CD-ROM that comes with this book.**

   For this exercise, I created a graphic intended to be clickable in Microsoft Image Composer 1.0, as shown in Figure 3-13. It's a down and dirty graphic: I did it quickly, having fun with shapes and playing with opacity and colors. It was intended only for this exercise. You can do the same:

Figure 3-13:
The graphic was created quite quickly in Microsoft Image Composer, then saved as a .GIF file. It's a teeny file that was designed with this exercise in mind.

2. **Select New page from the File menu in FrontPage, and from there select the Normal Page template or wizard, and do a little preliminary housekeeping.**

I gave the file a name and a headline — a couple of things I always like to do — as shown in Figure 3-14. If you're not using FrontPage, you'll find that most WYSIWYG HTML creation tools work in a similar way. Of course, Microsoft has brought along those pesky wizards, but they're really just templates with irritating names. Anyway, all WYSIWYG editors on most platforms will easily let you set up a file and start to work.

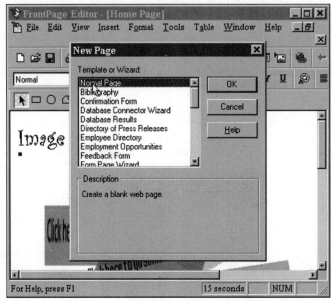

Figure 3-14: You're looking for a nice surface where you can start laying down your image map.

3. **Import the graphics file you've prepared (or opened from the CD-ROM).**

   Most of the WYSIWYG editors let you do this very simply, usually with some type of graphic image that you click to go get your file, as shown in Figure 3-15.

4. **To activate your graphic and prepare it for image mapping in FrontPage, simply double-click on the image itself.**

   The tools you need spring into action as shown in Figure 3-16.

Figure 3-15:
Introducing a graphic into your WYSIWYG file is usually quite easy. You just point to an image of a graphic on the toolbar; in FrontPage it's the little image of a landscape, third icon from the right on the toolbar.

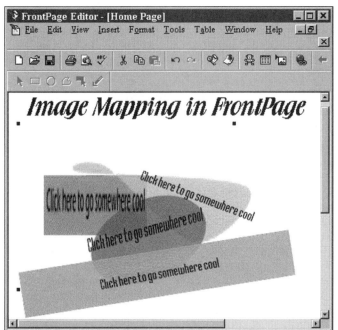

Figure 3-16:
In FrontPage, simply double-clicking on the imported image brings to life the tools you need to do the image map.

5. **Select the tool most appropriate to the first portion of your image map. If you used the image from the CD-ROM, you'll be using the polygon tool (the oddly shaped box, fourth from the left) a *lot* because even the rectangles are at funny angles. Use the tool to describe the shape, just as you did in the previous exercise.**

You'll notice that as soon as you complete the description, a dialog box like the one in Figure 3-17 appears, prompting you for a target URL. Once again, I prepared a simple HTML file for this purpose. This one is called *target.htm* and I have all roads end there.

6. **Type the name of the target HTML file in the space asking for it in the dialog box. I created just one target file for this exercise.**

You now have a completed image map file ready for testing and uploading. Too easy? I know — makes you wish you'd done it sooner. If you like, ask FrontPage (or whatever editor you're using) to show you the HTML code. You'll see that the thing you created looks very much like the code in the previous exercise, only it *was* slightly less labor intensive. Is that a good thing? Sometimes. As good as WYSIWYG editors are, there are certain times where I wouldn't like to be without my hands-on-and-get-your-hands-dirty HTML editor. In the case of image maps, however, the code — and the result — look just as pretty. Take a look at Figure 3-18.

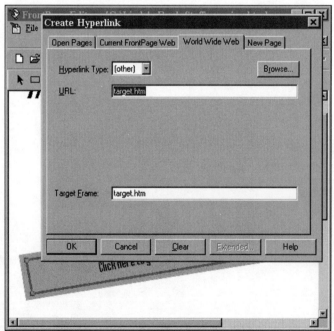

Figure 3-17:
Enter the name of the target HTML file.

Figure 3-18:
Ta da! And voilà! The finished image map — and you hardly had to get your hands dirty to do it. Sometimes I hate it when technology makes very complicated things very, very easy. This time, I'm happy.

Chapter 4

Platforms

*A*fter decades of worrying about computer platforms and incompatibilities, we're just starting into a time where this is increasingly not a consideration. The advent of the Internet as a major means of computer communication has hastened the process of helping computers talk to each other sensibly.

Setting Formats

Web formats like JPEG and PNG can be read by all types of computers. This cross-platform compatibility has set up an industry-wide demand for files and programs to be readable on an ever-wider range of computers. Now, many programs ship both Macintosh and Windows versions of software on a single CD-ROM. Users, software vendors, manufacturers — even book publishers — have fewer headaches by shipping for multi-platform machines. One disc fits all!

The other side of the compatibility issue is that not all machines are created equally. Although a graphics file may be readable on two completely different machines, the parameters of those computers often make the file in question appear quite different. Commonly, a Web image that reads perfectly on a Macintosh computer appears quite dark on a PC. Conversely, the perfectly balanced PC image appears slightly washed out on the average Macintosh. Figure 4-1 is a hand-tinted photograph from the 1930s that shows the tonal difference on the Macintosh and PC computers. If converted to a Web format and uploaded as it is, the image on the left would appear dark to a unacceptable percentage of viewers.

Figure 4-1:
This hand-tinted photograph from the 1930s shows the tonal difference on the Macintosh and PC computers.

What is Gamma?

A difference in apparent tonality is due to the different ways various computers look at light and compensate for it. That's gamma.

Gamma is the difference between the voltage applied to your monitor, and the resulting light or brightness of the image. In essence, then, gamma is the way brightness on your monitor is gauged.

Gamma on the Web

While gamma has always influenced how you see things on your computer, it wasn't until we started designing images for viewing on *other* computers that gamma played such a significant role. As long as the printer delivered what we wanted, ignorance was bliss. However, gamma on other monitors is one more decision we can't control. And if we want others to appreciate our images, gamma becomes an issue.

Gamma begins at home

Gamma on your own computer is, of course, something you can control. How bright an image looks on your monitor is determined by several factors:

✔ Monitor gamma setting (most often software accessible)

✔ Ambient light in your work area

✔ Brightness setting of the monitor

The Macintosh computer does gamma correction somewhat automatically. Most PCs don't. The upshot of this is that if something looks good on a Macintosh display, it's too dark on a PC.

Majority Rules

The safest course is to correct for the PC. There are a couple of reasons for this:

✔ More Web surfers are riding PC-powered surfboards, so it makes sense to make sure your images look best on the platform with the most viewers.

✔ PC-corrected images are acceptable on a Mac. Images that are corrected for Macs are darker on a PC, so they're hard to see on a PC.

Correcting gamma

In a perfect world, you have the facilities to load and view all of your images on both a Macintosh and a PC. The fact is, however, that even if you have both platforms Web-ready in your studio, viewing all Web graphics in this way may be time prohibitive.

If you accept that files prepared on a PC are normal, PC Web designers can skip ahead to the next part. Mac designers, however, still have some work ahead of them.

Shooting the gamma gap

The simplest gamma-correction option is a monitor brightness setting that is right between the Macintosh and the PC. In doing this, images seem just a little too bright on the Macintosh and a little bit too dark on the PC. While this is a viable alternative that many designers are opting for, it also means that no one sees the images in the way they were originally intended. Sort of a compromise where no one is entirely happy, like politics.

On the other hand, it's easier, so you may find it a viable alternative. (Is that why politicians compromise so frequently?)

The most common gamma setting on a PC is 2.5. On the Macintosh it's 1.8. Splitting the difference places your gamma setting smack-dab in the middle, around 2.2.

How you set your gamma depends on your hardware and software configuration. Some image editors, such as Photoshop, ship with a gamma control. With a control of this nature, setting gamma is a simple matter of activating this control, as shown in Figure 4-2.

Figure 4-2:
The Gamma
control
panel that
ships with
Photoshop
makes it
very simple
to adjust
gamma
on the
Macintosh.

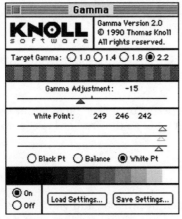

Consult your hardware manuals for specifics on setting gamma on your particular machine.

The fast track

Adjusting your gamma for ultimate exposure is somewhat complicated, but there are acceptable shortcuts.

PC tricks

Forget the median. Because the largest percentage of users are on your platform — and Mac users viewing your images see them slightly lighter than intended and therefore acceptable — your gamma concerns are minimal.

Macintosh tricks

If you don't feel like going through the gamma hassle, at the very least give your images an overall lightening, as shown in Figure 4-3. An easy way to do this is with the brightness/contrast command under Image: Adjust in Photoshop. Other image editors have similar commands.

Figure 4-3: Brightening the image with a brightness command can correct the gamma sufficiently to make the image readable to most Web users.

In some ways, this slap-dash method is like halftoning a photograph for newsprint reproduction. And — like that operation — it works simply, but well. On your Macintosh, make the image slightly lighter than ideal. PC surfers should read it perfectly.

Browsers

A lot of things happen on the Web that a designer should never have to deal with. Traditionally, graphic designers precisely control exactly how all aspects of their work are viewed. Computers were just a tool to create beautiful files that were then reproduced by traditional methods and then shared with the world. The Web makes a mockery of this control. Not only do we have to worry about the gamma on various platforms, our concerns are even more basic than that.

The most popular Web browsers at press time are Netscape Navigator and Microsoft's Internet Explorer. Netscape and Microsoft browsers show our work in entirely different ways, so a Web page designed for one looks entirely different in another.

From a designer's standpoint, it gets worse. Even within the *same* browser, users have a fair amount of control over their viewing environment. For example, your carefully planned HTML type has different line breaks in small monitors and big monitors (as shown in Figure 4-4 and Figure 4-5). Worse, users can change type styles for certain functions, override link colors, even — gasp! — opt to ignore graphics altogether. All of this adds up to nightmares for designers who are used to absolute control of their work.

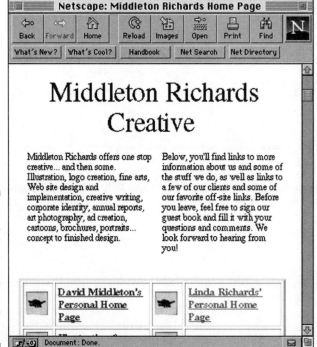

Figure 4-4: HTML pages change, depending on how the Web window is set.

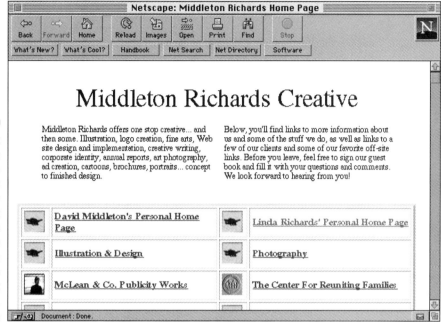

Figure 4-5:
The same
Web page
viewed at a
radically
different
width. Note
the havoc
this wreaks
on the
HTML-set
type.

An Acrobatic attempt

There is no absolute way to control exactly what the viewer of your images sees when visiting a Web page. Adobe Acrobat allows for PDF files which force the viewer to download the entire page exactly as designed. While this does give the designer absolute control over how the design is viewed, it *takes* all of the control from the Web surfer, who is used to it. Worse, PDFs are mostly fairly large files that force the surfer to download 100K+ files to their own computer, and then not really be able to interact with the file in the same way that they can with an HTML-prepared Web file.

At present, I feel that PDF files have their place. Within organizations, for example, where it might be desired for the page of a manual to be represented in a very precise way. But PDF is a long way from solving the problems designers face in this new and interactive medium.

Meanwhile, though, if you *do* encounter a PDF file on the Web, I've included the Adobe Acrobat reader on the *Web Graphics For Dummies* CD-ROM.

There's no solution!

That's the hard fact that classically and traditionally trained graphic designers have to get used to. There is no way to make all things precise and consistent from platform to platform and from machine to machine. The very things that make the Web the exciting, powerful tool that it is just won't allow it. There are, however, ways to ensure — at least, *attempt* to ensure — that your viewing audience sees something good, even if it isn't exactly what you want them to see.

Setting the boundaries

Some designers — some of them quite notable — actually make an image file of a width indicator for their Web pages and instruct visitors to these sites to, "Set your screen width from here to there," as shown in Figure 4-6.

Figure 4-6:
Some designers make an image file of a screen width indicator to tell Web surfers how wide their screen should be set for optimum viewing of their pages.

While this does tell Web visitors the optimum viewing width, it always strikes me as at least a little bit bossy. Also, for my part, when I look at Web pages, I'm *surfing* and just can't be bothered with re-adjusting my screen and slowing things down still further.

However, if you're very concerned that your Web pages are seen at a certain width, this is one way to go.

All things to all people

Because of the wide range of platforms and browsers you will be designing for, it's best to have access to as many browsers and computers as possible with which to check your pages.

At the very least, having both Internet Explorer and Netscape Navigator installed on your machine will let you check the way things look on both of these popular browsers.

Chapter 5

Frames and Tables

. . . .

In This Chapter

▶ What's a frame?

▶ When can you have too many frames?

▶ Enter frames with caution

▶ What's a table?

▶ What you need to build a table

▶ How to check your work

▶ Constructing a table on a background

▶ Specifying percentages of screen size within tables

. . . .

Strictly speaking, frames and tables don't have a whole lot to do with Web graphics, except when they do. It is possible to do either of these things in a quick and dirty way, without any thought to the finesse of the thing.

On the other hand, incorporating either or both of them gently and properly into a Web page, with the graphics they are displayed with ultimately in mind, can make all the difference. They can, in fact, make a site more successful. Keep these graphical aspects of frames and tables in mind while approaching this topic.

As a general rule, then, use both frames and tables in a gentle way and use them like salt: sparingly and only when necessary. Overuse may be detrimental to your health!

Just What Am I Talking About?

Before I get too far ahead of myself, let's see just what I'm talking about. Why wouldn't everyone want to look through a frame? And just what the heck *is* a table, other than a place to eat your dinner and balance your books?

The frame boiled down

In Web parlance, a frame is actually a set of HTML coded pages nested within one another in order to make navigation easier for a visitor in a Web site, as shown in Figure 5-1. A link from within a frame to another page actually forces the viewer to see the site from within the parameters of the frame.

I've seen frames used to advantage on online magazine sites, where narrow strips form tables of contents and mastheads. On retail sites, strips list products for sale so that they stay in the viewer's face at all times. However, I've seen more bad uses of frames than good ones — sites where frames seem good for little besides showing that the Web designer can do them, and not necessarily well.

Because frames — very generally speaking — are really pages within pages within pages and maybe more, top notch organization of your material is absolutely imperative. Bad organization at the design level not only looks cheesy, but confusing as well.

Figure 5-1:
A simple frameset looks something like this. Narrow strips top and left assist the site's overall navigation, while the big frame front and center is where the action is.

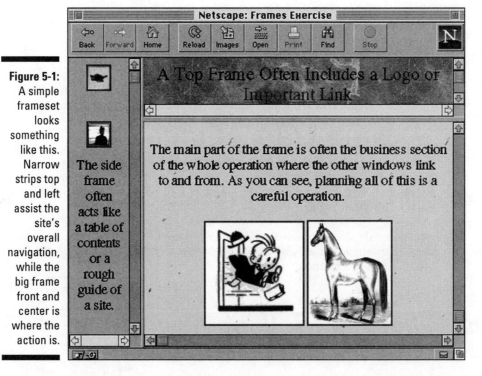

How many is too many?

While there is no top end to the number of frames you can have in a frameset, I've seldom seen a useful site with more than three in the window at one time. More than this can be not only confusing, they can be down-right taxing to the surfer with a slower modem.

Frames Help No One When Everyone Can't See Them

Even when you bust your buns making a gorgeous frame-driven site, there's a good chance that a whole whack of people won't be able to see them anyway. Frames are one of the newer features supported by HTML, so the first generation of most of the popular browsers aren't able to read them. And stats show that lots of people still use those older browsers.

Partly because of this, most successful sites currently using frames also offer a "non-frame" version for surfers who either have browsers that don't support frames, or for those who just don't want to see them.

So when you really feel that the site you're designing requires frames, do design an alternate route for those who can't or don't want to partake of your frames.

The table boiled down

Like the frame, the table can be a useful device for organizing information on a Web site, though an entirely different method of organization. You can see, as shown in Figure 5-2, that a table — properly used — can help people negotiate your site more easily.

Though the source code for an HTML file that incorporates tables can be scary, tables are actually pretty simple to build. Really, only three HTML tags make the whole thing happen:

- ✔ <TABLE> which is the main tag and tells the browser that a table is incoming.
- ✔ <TR> which stands for Table Row and defines the horizontal row of table cells.
- ✔ <TD> which stands for Table Data and defines the cells within a table row.

Figure 5-2:
A simple table. It's really about organizing information in a way that makes it easier to negotiate a site.

As an illustration of this, let's look at the same page with the all that pesky table information turned off, as shown in Figure 5-3. You can see that, in this instance, the table really does help organize the information in a palatable way. And you don't need any carpentry tools!

Let's jump right in and build one together. You just need a few tools to get started:

- ✔ A get-the-hands-dirty HTML editor that lets you create the code.
- ✔ An image editor.
- ✔ A GIF file to include within one of your tables.
- ✔ A browser to view your handiwork.

Building a graphical table

Tables are sometimes referred to as "easy" or more or less "difficult," but — really — they're all just zebras with differently angled stripes. The table you're going to build would be considered a more advanced table in some schools of thought, but — realistically — it's just a table with more stuff in it.

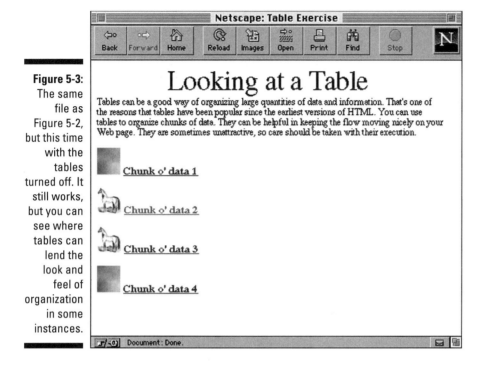

Figure 5-3:
The same
file as
Figure 5-2,
but this time
with the
tables
turned off. It
still works,
but you can
see where
tables can
lend the
look and
feel of
organization
in some
instances.

I've chosen this particular table because it's an especially useful one for our purposes. It allows you to take a simple and teeny background file and use the table tags to create an HTML file that many designers would find a place for on their sites.

A table is a table is a . . .

Remember that tables can be easily sliced down to digestible portions. As you move through this code, think about how it all breaks down and think of how it all fits together.

Checking your work

When you work in a pure code HTML editor, it's a good idea to have one of your browsers open at the same time so you can watch your work progress.

It's easy on most platforms to "flip" back and forth between your editor and your browser to check and make sure that the stuff you're coding is really what you want.

WYSIWYG editors aren't infallible, either. This is pretty new technology. Some of the things — especially more advanced things — you ask it to do can produce some wonky and unacceptable results. Periodically looking at your work in a browser helps spot this stuff early.

Remember, the changes won't be reflected in your browser until you've saved your working file. Then it's a simple matter to ask the browser to *reload* or *refresh* your working file for your inspection.

Building the Background for the Table

In the chapter on backgrounds, I go in deep on backgrounds and the facts and philosophy behind them. I'm not going to double up on all that here. But I want you to build a cool table that rests and works over a sharp background, so begin at the beginning and do this whole deal in a couple of stages.

If any part of the background aspects of this description confuses you, jump ahead to the background chapter where all is made clear.

1. **Open a new file in your image editor. Make it 900 x 50 pixels on a white background, as shown in Figure 5-4.**

   You end with a long, skinny file intended to give you a small file that's as wide as most browser's windows, and then some.

2. **Using the rectangular marquee or draw tool (depending on what program you're working in), draw a rectangle the height of the larger rectangle, about 100 pixels wide.**

   You can use the image editor's ruler tool to help you with this. Color the rectangle you draw a nice, rich color that isn't so dark that text doesn't show up on it. You should end up with something that looks very much like Figure 5-5.

3. **Save two versions of the file.**

   First save it in the format you're working in. For example, if you're working in Photoshop, save the file in Photoshop format. This is in case you're unhappy with the final result and want to go back and change something — you don't have to start over!

4. **Next, save the file in GIF format, or move to a program like DeBabelizer where you can convert it. When you're working in Photoshop, choose Export from the file menu and save as GIF89A.**

Now you're ready to move on to the for-real table stuff.

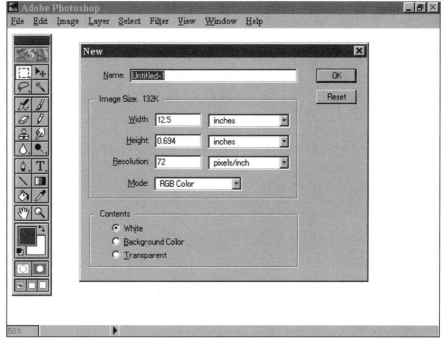

Figure 5-4:
Open a file
in your
image
editor that
is 900 x 50
pixels, as
shown
in the
illustration.

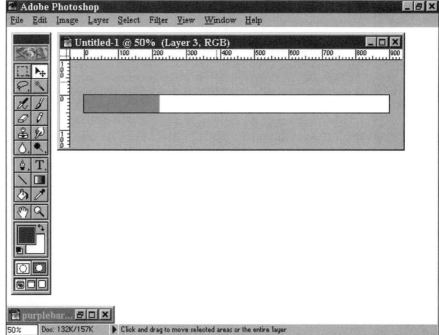

Figure 5-5:
You're
going to end
up with a
long, skinny
file that
makes up a
background
to artfully
lay your
tables on.

Building the Table for the Background

Now, the table-y stuff. You've built a background that is designed for text that is positioned by tables. The finished effect you want is something like a nicely laid out magazine page: different elements, lined up where they're supposed to be.

1. **Open a new file in your HTML editor using all the standard stuff, like this:**

```
<HTML>
<HEAD>
```

2. **Give the beast a title. Something that you'd like to show up on the title bar in a browser.**

```
<TITLE>A Cool Way to Use a Table</TITLE>
</HEAD>
```

3. **Here's where you get to the part where you use your nifty and newly created background graphic. At the same time — and in the same line — specify a background color. I specified white.**

```
<BODY BACKGROUND="PURPLEBAR.GIF" BGCOLOR="#ffffff">
```

4. **You're going to be laying in some type, so you specify the size you want now. You can come back and change the file size later if you don't like it.**

```
<FONT SIZE=5>
```

5. **Now the part you've been waiting for. The table itself. Remember earlier I talked about the parts of the boiled down table? Here's where they come in. You're going to specify that your table width is 100 percent of the screen, regardless of screen size. You may also, if you want to, enter a specific size; it will give you a slightly different effect. For now, percentages are a little easier to comprehend than hard numbers.**

```
<TABLE WIDTH="100%" BORDER="0" CELLSPACING="1"
        CELLPADDING="0">
```

This tag specifies that the width of the table is 100 percent of the screen size; no border around the cells to indicate where they are; CELLSPACING specifies how much space to put between the cells; and CELLPADDING specifies how much to put inside the cell.

6. **Now you need to define your table row. First, let it know that it's going to happen:**

```
<TR>
```

7. Now specify your first Table Data cell and the information in it.

```
<TD WIDTH="30%"><BASEFONT SIZE=5>
<TT>A table can be an ultra-cool way of using some of
      that neat-o background stuff. What could be
      easier and look better and neater than using
      atable to contain various thoughts and pieces of
      information. Life is good.</TT></TD>
```

Lots of types of things work well in this format. I just stuck in a block of text, but you may have active links, staff names with e-mail flags, you name it.

8. Now you set a command to make a single skinny cell that is just to hold the place between the two working cells. It looks like this:

```
<TD WIDTH="10%"></TD>
```

9. Now make your third and final cell. This is the big one: As you can see, I gave it a whopping 60 percent of the screen size. As well, I stuck some text in it. Here again, you may use this space for myriad things and can include links out — or anything — if you want.

```
<TD WIDTH="60%">
<P><CENTER><FONT SIZE=+2>Then you can use this chunk for
      other stuff. Or even some pictures.</FONT>
      </CENTER></P>
```

10. Being a smartypants, I want you to stick a graphic in here, just so you can see how easily it's done. Note that you're still working within that third cell as you specify the location and size of the graphic.

```
<P><CENTER><IMG SRC="cow.GIF"
WIDTH="293" HEIGHT="162" ALIGN="BOTTOM">
```

11. It's important to end things properly. In this step, you sign out of everything: the center tag, then the various table tags, and finally the document itself.

```
</CENTER></TD></TR>
</TABLE>
</BODY>
</HTML>
```

Don't forget to save before you truck off to look at your document in a browser — a document that should look very much like Figure 5-6.

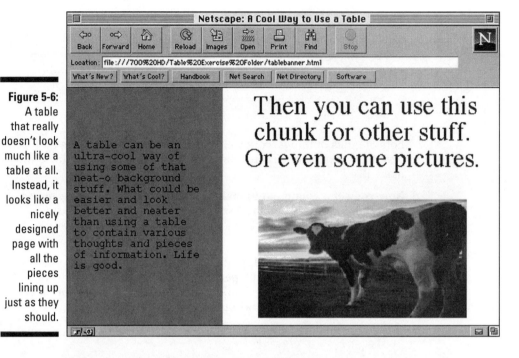

Figure 5-6:
A table
that really
doesn't look
much like a
table at all.
Instead, it
looks like a
nicely
designed
page with
all the
pieces
lining up
just as they
should.

A table can be an ultra-cool way of using some of that neat-o background stuff. What could be easier and look better and neater than using a table to contain various thoughts and pieces of information. Life is good.

Then you can use this chunk for other stuff. Or even some pictures.

Why use percentages?

Take a peek at why you used percentages for the Table Data cells in the example, rather than using fixed widths.

Sometimes, fixed widths really work best, like when you're using the table for data, for instance, and not as part of a design. But when the table is a design element, percentages are frequently superior.

You've seen sites with fixed tables, especially when you have a monitor that's under 15 inches. Lots of designers use bigger ones and forget about the poor mortals that don't have their computing power. By assigning percentages, you know that your tables aren't going to get cut off. This is because the browser has been told how wide the table is: as wide as the open browser window.

Using your example, someone surfing by with a really teeny monitor would see something like Figure 5-7. None of the type has been cut off. The width of the background banner of color hasn't changed, because that's fixed (we had to fix it when we created it — it can't be a variable). However, all of your type is still nicely tabled. It flows differently, but when you work with that design it still looks good.

Actually, this smaller version even looks sort of cool. A much larger version would look different again. It's best to be able to view the results on different monitors or with different browser window sizes to be sure that your table parses the way it's supposed to.

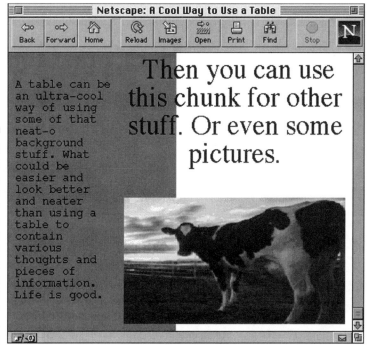

Figure 5-7: Using percentages, surfers with a smaller window still see all your tabled information on the width of their screen.

Part II
Formats for Everyone

The 5th Wave   By Rich Tennant

"Hold your horses. It takes time to build a home page for someone your size."

In this part . . .

Graphic formats are important to the Web. They're what makes it possible for you to see pictures on the Web. More importantly, they're what let's other people see *your* graphics. That being the case, it isn't really possible to know too much about the formats those graphics will be viewed in.

We also peek at other not-so-basic stuff that it's still really good to know about. If for no other reason than to show off the next time you're at a dinner party.

Chapter 6

Giffing It Up

*T*he GIF (Graphics Interchange Format) is the most controversial of the common Web graphics formats. And the controversy starts with the name. It's known that the originator of the GIF format pronounced it with a hard "G". But a lot of people pronounce it with a soft "G", like a brand of peanut butter.

Regardless of how it's pronounced, GIF is also one of the most widely used of the Web formats, and all browsers read it as a matter of course. That means that using it ensures that your graphics are viewable by the largest number of people.

Where the bigger part of the controversy comes in is that GIF is a commercial format, and it's a proprietary specification of CompuServe. Several years ago, Unisys announced that they would sue all developers of GIF software for patent fees. This possibility put wings on the feet (and the developing hands) of a large number of proponents of nonproprietary graphics enthusiasts. The resulting formats, such as PNG, are beginning to make their presence felt.

It should be noted that the controversy over the legal status of GIF affects you, the user, not at all. No one talks about filing suits against people who actually *use* the GIF format to save files, but rather against those who created the software to prepare those end-user GIFs.

Meanwhile, despite whatever legal wrangling takes place, GIF continues to rule the Web as a format for graphics display. This is for a couple of reasons:

✔ It's fast. GIF files can be made to squeeze a lot of information into a pretty teeny package. This is great for those of us (most of us!) with limited bandwidth.

✔ It's efficient. GIF files offer a number of options that let the user have a great deal of control over how the graphic displays on the Web. For instance, an *interlaced* GIF comes up a bit at a time while downloading (see Figure 6-1). Figure 6-2 shows the complete download.

✔ Everyone can see it. Because all browsers ship with the ability to view GIF files, all potential viewers can see your graphics. This can be a big plus — you actually want people to be able to see the stuff you've created.

Figure 6-1:
An interlaced GIF file shows up a bit at a time while downloading. This can be a good option because it doesn't leave your potential viewers staring at an empty hole on the page while it loads.

Making a GIF File

To make a GIF file, you need an image editor or image converter that supports GIF. Because most do, this isn't a problem at all.

When you don't have an image editor that supports GIF, don't despair. Several shareware converters help you with the final stage.

Figure 6-2:
The fully
downloaded
GIF.

Creating a GIF file with an image editor

Creating a GIF file is very easy, it's really just an extension of any type of image creation you've ever done.

For example, if you've ever created a Photoshop or CorelDraw file and saved it as another format, you have all of the skills you need to create a GIF formatted file.

For demonstration purposes, I chose the popular image editor, Photoshop. And though mileage varies from software package to software package, the basics are similar.

1. **Begin with an image that you've somehow gotten into your computer (something you've scanned, manipulated, or even created right here in your image editor).**

2. **Without altering the currently saved format, do whatever finishing and clean-up that needs to be done to the image, as shown in Figure 6-3. Resize as necessary before conversion, and add any color or image changes to the file.**

As a general rule, it's a good idea to do as much clean-up of an image as possible before you convert to a Web format. Ideally, prior to conversion, your image should be resized, cleaned up, and ready for viewing by a Web audience near you!

horse1 @ 100% (Layer 1, RGB)

100%   Doc: 432K/499K

3. **In Photoshop, choose Export from the file menu. Choose GIF89a Export from the fly-out menu, as shown in Figure 6-4.**

   Many programs let you save to GIF by using the Save As command. If you can't find it under Export, try Save As.

4. **After you've chosen to export the file, the GIF89a Export dialog box appears (see Figure 6-5), offering you a few fairly simple options. Choose the Adaptive rather than the Display palette.**

   This is because Display, in this instance, refers to your own system. Choosing Adaptive means it adapts for the Web's color palette. Choose Interlace if you want the graphic to display as it downloads. The Colors you choose to render your graphic are determined by the type of document you display. The lower the number, the smaller the resulting GIF file.

5. **In Photoshop, exporting to GIF automatically results in the .GIF suffix being attached to your file, as shown in Figure 6-6. This helps you distinguish it from other versions of the same file. Also, because converting the image type flattens out any Photoshop layers or other cool stuff, you need your original work file in case you want to make changes.**

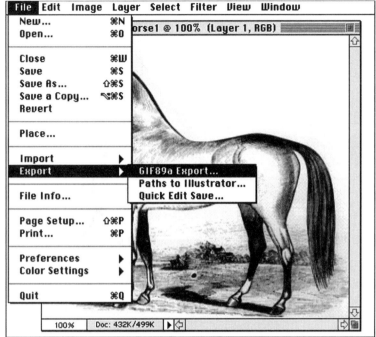

Figure 6-4:
Saving a file
as a GIF is
actually an
export
function in
Photoshop.

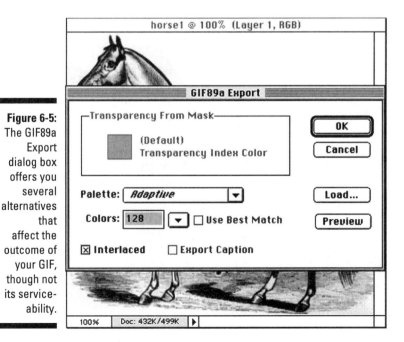

Figure 6-5:
The GIF89a
Export
dialog box
offers you
several
alternatives
that
affect the
outcome of
your GIF,
though not
its service-
ability.

700 HD
Sterling Quote
System Stuff
TE080596.DOC
This day first...
To Do
700 HD
Eject
Desktop
New
Cancel
Export to GIF File:
horse1.gif
Save

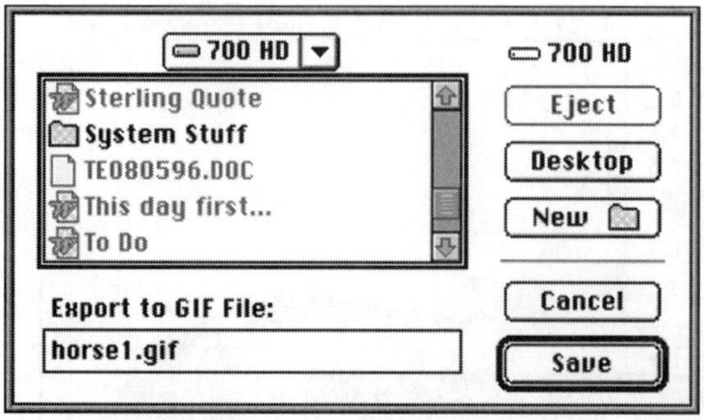

Figure 6-6: Make sure that you append the suffix .GIF to the file when you change the format. It saves some confusion later.

6. Your GIF file is now ready for uploading (see Figure 6-7).

Again, your mileage will vary, but this particular file started out as a 649K Photoshop file (read that: over half a meg!) and is just 55K after a first run at exporting it to GIF. Still too big to be really happy about, but already a huge improvement.

horse1.gif @ 100%
100%
Doc: 144K/144K

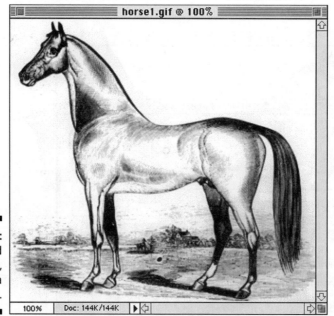

Figure 6-7: The finished GIF file, ready for a Web page.

GIF and GIF89a

You see references to GIF files, as well as references to GIF89a. This seems a good place to talk about the difference; those differences are subtle, but important.

In the first place, we should all agree that GIF89a is a stupid name. If we followed the naming pattern, then GIF would actually be GIF87A, because the standards that specify what a GIF file is were established in 1987.

With that hint firmly in place, can you guess when the standards for GIF89a came to be? I knew you could!!

So the specifications for the GIF format were released in 1987, and the specifications accommodated these things:

✔ Interlacing

✔ LZW compressed images

✔ Multiple images encoded within a single file

GIF89a is an extension of the original GIF specification, and was released (you guessed it) in 1989. The newer specifications added

✔ Transparency options

✔ Unprintable comments

✔ Display lines of text

✔ Application-specific extensions within the file

This all means a couple of really important things:

✔ GIF89a supports more sophisticated animation (more on this later) than the earlier specifications.

✔ You can tell GIF89a what level of transparency you want and — in fact — whether you want transparency at all.

Transparent GIFs

Transparency in GIFs is yet another feature that didn't get fully appreciated until the advent — in a big way — of the Web. And transparency is frequently an important aspect of a Web design, so make sure that the version of GIF you're using supports it.

When the name isn't on the label

If your image editor or converter specifies *GIF89a* as a file type, transparency is supported.

If it says *GIF87a,* it doesn't. And — most often — when it simply says *GIF,* it actually *means* GIF87a and doesn't support transparency.

Again, don't despair. Several shareware and online transparency applications make GIF87a easy.

Image Converters

Regardless of what software you ultimately choose to prepare your graphics for the Web, you'll probably find that you seldom create one in the format in which it is be displayed.

Because all Web formats include some type of compression, it's usually faster and easier to work in the format most native to the software (for example, Photoshop format in Photoshop) and then convert the image before uploading to a Web site.

Dithering is a good and important thing

Whenever you hear "dither" in relation to computer graphics, you can be sure that it's not about someone getting all worked up about something. In fact, it's so far from that I wonder how it got this name at all!

Instead, when you choose the dither option when converting within a program, you actually tell the program to substitute colors or shades that are unavailable with ones that are.

While graphic dithering in one form or another has been around for a long time, it's especially useful in making Web graphics. In color files for the Web, you only have a maximum of 256 colors at your disposal. And less is better, because the fewer you use, the smaller your file. In grayscale images, dithering is helpful as well because the less shades of gray you use, the less information has to be stored and — again! — the smaller your file.

Finding just the *right* dither for the particular file you're working on is part science, part experience, and part just fooling around. After doing it for a while, you get a feel for where to start without going through all the permutations. In the next exercise, you do a lot of dithering to help you get the hang of it.

Converting an image

You can use any Image Conversion software package to convert an image from another format to GIF or to make a file already saved as a GIF smaller, as shown in the following example.

For demonstration purposes, I used the popular graphics production toolbox DeBabelizer. A demo version of this software is included on the *Web Graphics For Dummies* CD-ROM, which comes with this book.

Many Image Conversion programs do things in a very similar way.

1. **Open the GIF file you just created in Photoshop, as shown in Figure 6-8, or some other image editor.**

   I'm going to assume that all of your editing has already been done in the previous step. Although some very basic editing is possible in most image conversion programs, this is not really what they're intended for. In most cases, it's best to bring in a file that is ready for conversion.

Figure 6-8:
The PNG file you created in Photoshop is edited and ready for conversion. If you didn't do the Photoshop exercise, open the file called HORSE1.GIF from the *Web Graphics For Dummies* CD-ROM.

2. Choose convert to B&W/Grayscale from the Palette menu, as shown in Figure 6-9.

In DeBabelizer — as in several other image conversion programs — you have the opportunity to reduce the file size without greatly altering the appearance of the file. Because this is a non-color image, you can do several things.

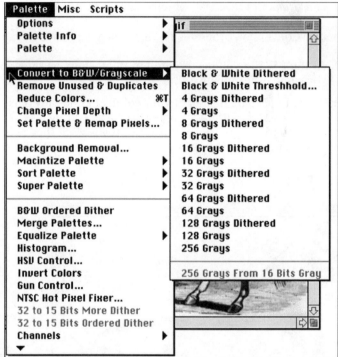

Figure 6-9: Choosing Convert to B&W/ Grayscale from the Palette menu gives you several options from a fly-out menu.

3. To get a feel for what this means, choose Black & White Dithered, as shown in Figure 6-10.

Options on the fly-out menu let you convert your image to anything from a black & white dithered image all the way to 256 grays. In this case, it's a pretty interesting effect, and can be acceptable for some uses. The real bonus is the reduction of the file size. If you save it (don't do it!), you have a pretty teeny file (around 11K), even though it takes up a fair amount of area. Choose Undo from the Edit menu.

Figure 6-10:
Choosing
Black &
White
Dithered
in this
instance
produces a
pleasing
pointillist
effect. It
also makes
for a really
small file.
But it looks
totally
different
than the
original, so
it may
not be
acceptable.

4. **This time, choose Convert to B&W/Grayscale from the Palette menu and choose 256 Grays.**

   With your horse restored to his multi-grayed glory, you can experiment a bit more. Notice that the image doesn't appear to change at all; you can't add pixels that are no longer there. The original file is 128 Grays, so no enhancements can be made at this stage. So, by extension, when you now choose 128 Grays Dithered, no visible change occurs. For this reason, it is not necessary to undo either of these steps.

5. **Next choose 64 Grays from the same menu.**

   A lot of the background "noise" we had happening before disappears as though by magic (see Figure 6-11). It isn't. Magic, that is. But it is useful. And it also illustrates why absolute formulas are so difficult in creating Web graphics. Almost everything that follows the basic rules works. However, some work better than others in terms of giving you the small size you need and the quality you like.

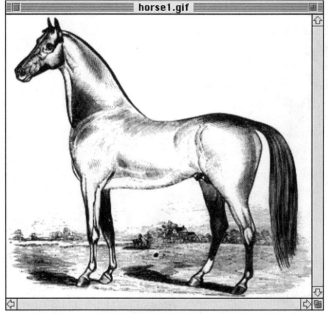

Figure 6-11: Choosing 64 Grays from the Convert to B&W/ Grayscale has produced a cleansing affect in this instance.

6. Next choose 8 Grays Dithered from the Convert to B&W/Grayscale menu (see Figure 6-12).

Notice that, because you've reduced the tonality to just eight scales of gray, you do lose some of the richness in the horse's coat. But, for this particular image, these results would be quite acceptable for most uses. Not bad, as well, considering that your file is now down to about 22K with very little effort.

You now have a finished GIF, ready for uploading to a Web site.

While these instructions are specific to DeBabelizer, most converters offer you some type of control over the level of dithering when you specify your GIF file. Quite often, it pops up in a dialog box after you choose Save As. Remember, feel free to play with the various dithering possibilities. None of the selections are absolutely wrong (so don't worry about screwing anything up!), but a few are better than the others. Look for this golden mean.

Figure 6-12:
With 8
Grays
Dithered,
some of the
detail is
lost, but the
horse's coat
still has a
sheen and
the detail of
the drawing
is apparent.

Chapter 7
Animated GIF Files

• •

• •

I've had a love-hate relationship with Web animation since the first time I saw it. On one hand, a really good GIF Web animation makes surfers really sit up and take notice. On the other hand, GIF animation is something of an artform in itself.

The Low Down Dirty on Animation

For every single really excellent GIF animation, we are subjected to twenty that are marginal, or worse. What is the point of twinkling bullets? Or wriggling icons? They're cute the first time. After that, just what *is* the point?

Here's what I hate most: a useless animation spinning on a Web site. Because of the animation, I can't tell when the page is finished downloading. Worse, the animation can be looped in such a way that it's almost impossible to escape. Every time any link on the page is clicked, the animation reloads.

What's the point?

Animation has a place on the Web. But it's a small place, much smaller than the one it currently occupies. If you're thinking about adding an animation to your Web site, ask why.

✔ Does animation make your Web site better?

✔ Is animation the best tool?

✔ Are you just showing off?

I never have favorable answers for these questions. My Web page is devoid of animations and will stay that way in the forseeable future.

It's fun!

If you gather that I don't actually like Web animations, you're half right. I don't like the way animations impact on my surfing time. However, Web animation is fun! I keep making cool Web animations when no one is looking. Considering the coolness factor, they're amazingly easy.

What's Animation?

Animation is simply individual "cels" (pictures) shown one after another so you perceive a continuous action. Remember playing with flip books when you were a kid? Animation works like a flip book — the pictures change so fast that you think there's a moving image.

On the Web, the most expeditious way of implying that movement is a GIF89a file that's been specially prepared for that purpose. GIF89a files store more than one image in the same file, so they're ideal for animation.

A GIF animation is completely downloaded to the viewer's browser on their machine, then plays from start to finish. Such a download assures a smooth-appearing animation, because a playing GIF animation doesn't depend on images that haven't yet been downloaded.

Not all browsers display animated GIFs, although all of the newest ones do. The good news is that browsers that don't support GIF animations don't show a big hole where your animation is supposed to be. If ill-equipped surfers hit a animated GIF, they see either the first or last frame. That means the first and last frames in any animation should be useful on their own.

Adding animation to your Web site

The business end of GIF animations is part of what explains their popularity. Adding a GIF animation to your code is as easy as adding a static image — the familiar IMAGE tag is used for both animated and non-animated GIF files.

To add an animation to a Web page (such as the GIF animations on the *Web Graphics For Dummies* CD-ROM), the basic coding looks like this:

```
<IMG SRC="animation.gif">
```

Though actually creating an animation from scratch is a little more difficult, it's a lot easier than the finished work suggests. Animated GIFs require a few elements — you probably already have most of what you need.

✔ Special software to animate your GIF sequences. Some of these are available online. Some can be purchased, and demo versions of some are included on the CD-ROM that came with this book. The most popular shareware GIF animators are GifBuilder for Macintosh (http://iawww.epfl.ch/Staff/Yves.Piguet/clip2gif-home/GifBuilder.html) and GIF Construction Set for Windows (http://www.mindworkshop.com/alchemy/alchemy.html). A recent non-shareware GIF animator is offered by Totally Hip Software http://totallyhip.com.

✔ An image editor to tweak graphics.

✔ An HTML editor to add the animation to a Web page.

✔ An idea!

Making a simple animation

There are a few minimum steps to make an animation. In the following example, I'm animating a word.

1. **Open your image editor.**

   I've used Adobe Photoshop for this exercise, but just about anything that allows you to work with some colors and some text in an RGB file works for this.

2. **In the image editor, select your type tool, select a color, and type a word.**

   I've used the word "Animation" but any old word will do for this simple exercise, as shown in Figure 7-1.

Figure 7-1:
Animating
"Animation"
seemed like
a fun thing
to do. So I
started
there.

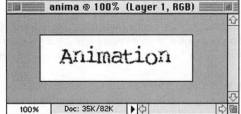

3. **If you're working in Photoshop, you can create the second frame in your animation by adding another layer. If you're not in Photoshop, you can save this image as ANIMA1 and then alter it, saving the result as ANIMA2, and so on.**

   In this example, using the layering in Photoshop, I'm again using the type tool to set exactly the same word, but in a different color, and with a slightly different alignment.

4. **We can stop here, but a three-cel animation is more fun than two. I set the same word again, but this time make it bold and change the color again, as shown in Figure 7-2.**

Figure 7-2:
Another
layer in
Photoshop.
This time
the type is
bold with a
slightly
different
alignment.

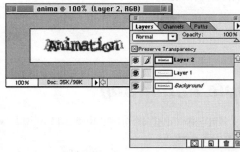

5. **I add a fourth layer (new color, no bold), then save the file in Photoshop format and close it. Easy.**

6. **In either GifBuilder or GIF Construction Set (depending on your platform), open the file you just created, make sure the Preview window is selected, and choose Run or Start to see your animation, as shown in Figure 7-3.**

It's not award-winning, but it works.

Figure 7-3:
Photoshop's
layers
function is
super-cool
for doing
animations
because it
is very
polite about
dumping all
of those
layers into
separate
frames.

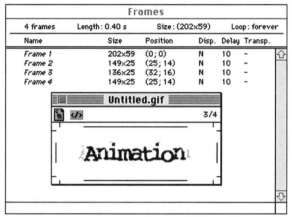

If you don't use an editor that supports layers, getting your animation running will take a little longer. Choose Open A New File in the animating software, and then add each of the files you made as a New Frame. Then select Start or Run and watch the magic.

Making an animation with your eyes closed

Not really, but almost. If you're running under Windows 95, try this ultra-fast and easy way of making an animation.

You'll only need a few things for this simple animation:

✔ A computer running Windows 95

✔ An image editor. (An editor that exports to GIF89a makes the work easier.)

✔ The shareware program *GIF Construction Set*.

This is about the easiest way on the planet to make a GIF animation. In fact, it practically does it all by itself.

1. **Create a few frames for animation. Even unrelated GIFs can produce a cool slide show. For this demonstration, I used PaintShop Pro 4.0 because it's easy to create a little work area and save it out as a GIF, as I've done in Figure 7-4. For this exercise, I've gone for the classic ball example.**

   Classic, because just about every animation program going includes some type of ball example with their software.

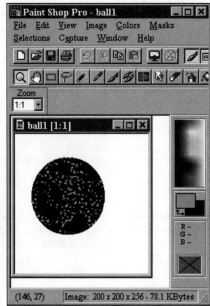

Figure 7-4: An image editor like PaintShop Pro makes it easy to create simple images and then save them as GIF files.

2. **In total, I did five different frames. For each frame, I moved the ball, slightly changed the color, and then saved it as a GIF file. Saving them as BALL1.GIF, BALL2.GIF, and so on (as shown in Figure 7-5) makes the order easy to remember. Each was constructed on a work area of just 200 x 200 pixels.**

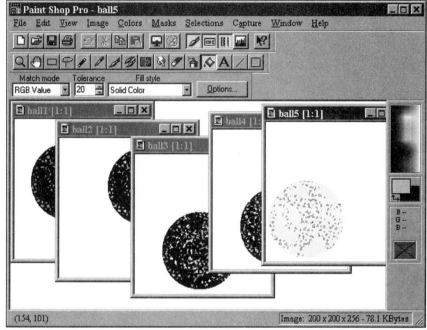

3. Now, the super-easy animating part. Open the Animation Wizard from the File menu in GIF Construction Set.

The screen looks like Figure 7-6.

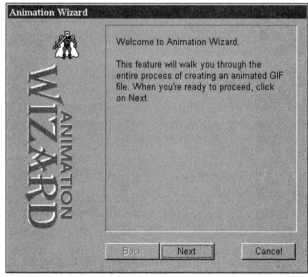

4. **The Animation Wizard asks a series of painless questions. It's like any good Windows 95 Wizard. Just select the functions you want and then click Next to move on. When the Wizard asks you to select the source files for your animation, choose Select and then navigate to the place where you saved your GIFs, just as you would for any image-related material.**

   After you've selected all of the images, you'll have a list that looks like Figure 7-7. Choose Next after the images have been selected.

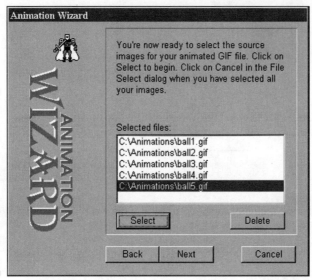

Figure 7-7:
When prompted to select the source files for your animation, just browse to where your GIFs are saved.

5. **After you've selected the source files, you're set. GIF Construction Set maps the files for you and presents the finished animation on a page that looks like Figure 7-8.**

   It's the boring-but-necessary part of the animation. The good news is that you didn't have to do any of the boring part! It's easy to make changes at this stage. You can choose to insert or delete frames at will.

6. **To see the animation, choose View from the toolbar and watch it fly, as in Figure 7-9.**

   The illustration, of course, doesn't do it justice: We couldn't figure out how to make it move right here on the page!

7. **To use your animation on a Web page, choose Save As from the File menu in GIF Construction Set. Save it with some name you haven't used yet, and you're away.**

   You've just made the world's easiest animation!

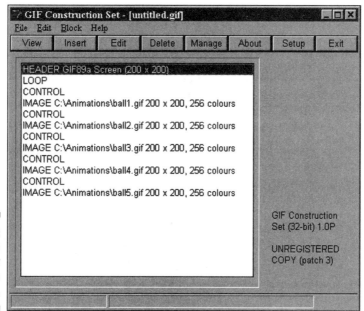

Figure 7-8:
The summary page for the animation.

Figure 7-9:
The finished animation is shown running when you choose View from the toolbar.

While we used an ultra-simple subject for this demonstration, the same technique would work for virtually any subject.

Don't get antsy about making animations. It really is this easy. If your animation doesn't come out the way you want, no worries. You can either tweak it or toss the whole thing out and start again. There's so little time in the animating process that it doesn't feel too bad if you have to do this.

Beyond Simple Animations

Many shareware programs animate frames that you've made in other image editing programs. Usually, this is enough. But a new generation of programs combines the two processes, and adds more. One of these software packages is WebPainter from Totally Hip Software.

WebPainter takes animation beyond simple support for GIF89a multiple frames. Unlike some of its brethren, WebPainter presents a toolbar in its main window, complete with a full selection of drawing and painting tools, as shown in Figure 7-10. Not only can you animate, but you can draw and paint and otherwise manipulate your animation cels.

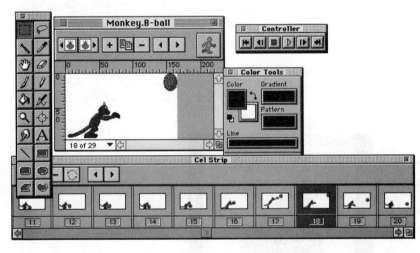

Figure 7-10:
The
WebPainter
window
reveals
powerful
controls.

WebPainter imports finished images to be animated and also offers tools to create images. Your choice depends on whether you work fastest and most comfortably by using another program.

A simple WebPainter animation

And now it's time for that classic bouncing ball. Hurray! You knew it was coming sooner or later, didn't you? Here's what you'll need:

  ✔ WebPainter 1.0 or 2.0

Hey, that was a short list! Let's get going.

1. **Create a new document in WebPainter. When you see the Create New Document dialog box, as shown in Figure 7-11, choose 8-bit depth for the color, Windows Netscape for the Color Table, and make the Cel Size 200 x 200. Leave the other input items at their defaults.**

Figure 7-11:
The Create New Document dialog box gives you the opportunity to input various pieces of information to customize your document.

2. **The work area will, at first, be unadorned. Customize it by getting the toolbars you need from the Windows menu. For this exercise, you'll need the Color Tools, Controller, and Paint Tools palettes, all accessible from the Windows menu. Choose them now, and arrange them however feels most comfortable. You'll end up with a work area that looks like Figure 7-12.**

3. **To help position your animation, select the registration tool, as shown in Figure 7-13. Point it at the middle of your document and click once to make it stick.**

You don't *have* to use the registration point, but it helps when you line things up later.

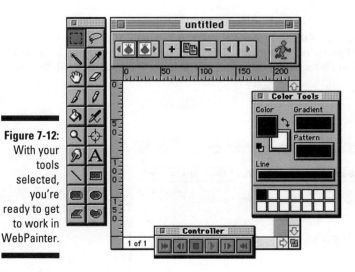

Figure 7-12:
With your
tools
selected,
you're
ready to get
to work in
WebPainter.

Figure 7-13:
The
registration
tool is
located on
the Paint
tools
palette.

4. **Select a nice color for your ball, something ball-like. I chose red. Then using the oval tool, draw a circle in the upper-left hand portion of the cel, as shown in Figure 7-14.**

5. **Now choose the Duplicate Cel icon as shown in Figure 7-15, to create a new cel that looks like the old one.**

6. **The Duplicate Cel icon gives you a cel that looks just like the one before, only this one will be numbered 2/2. In order to see what went before, select the Onion Skin Previous icon as shown in Figure 7-16.**

   That way, when you start to move things around, you'll have a ghosted image of what came before.

Figure 7-14:
After selecting a color, use the oval tool to define a small ball in your work area. Behold, the beginning of your bouncing ball!

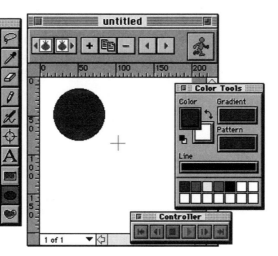

Figure 7-15:
The Duplicate Cel icon.

Figure 7-16:
The Onion Skin Previous icon is on the left. Onion Skin Next is on the right. The little onions make them pretty hard to miss.

7. Use the magic wand tool to select the ball in the second cel.

As soon as it's selected, you'll see that your pointer turns into an arrow. You can use this arrow to slide the second cel's ball into position, which is slightly below the first ball, as shown in Figure 7-17.

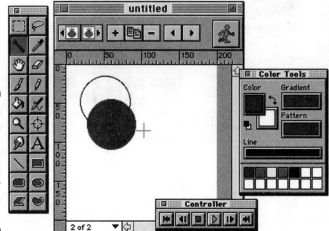

Figure 7-17:
Position the
second ball
on the
second cel
slightly
below the
first.

8. Repeat the previous steps a couple more times. With the size ball I defined and the course I took, I did the fall in five frames. You can use however many (or few!) you'd like. With your ball just prior to contact with the bottom of the frame, choose to add a new cel by selecting the big plus sign icon to the left of the Duplicate Page icon. This will give you a shiny new cel to work in. With your original color still selected, once again use the Oval tool to define a squished ball near the bottom of the frame, as shown in Figure 7-18. This gives the feeling of the ball hitting the ground.

9. Choose Show Cel Strip from the Windows menu. This palette shows you the progression on the cels you've already built, as shown in Figure 7-19.

10. By highlighting each of the cels in the downward progression individually, you can use the duplicate cel icon to duplicate the cel and then drag it into position at the end of the animation.

You have to do this for every cel in the animation in order to get the full up and down feel of the bouncing ball.

Figure 7-18:
An oval slightly wider and not as high as your ball at the bottom of the frame is intended to indicate the ball hitting the ground.

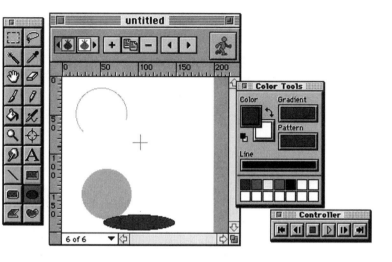

Figure 7-19:
The Cel Strip palette shows a thumbnail version of your animation in storyboard format.

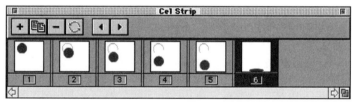

11. **Turn off the onion skins, and run your animation. You do this by selecting the go button on the Controller panel, which will look pretty familiar to you.**

    It looks and acts pretty much like the control panel on your tape deck or VCR. And now, behold the bouncing ball you've created!

12. **To use your new animation on a Web page, choose Export from the file menu as shown in Figure 7-20. Choose Animated Gif File and then follow the bouncing ball to include it in your HTML document.**

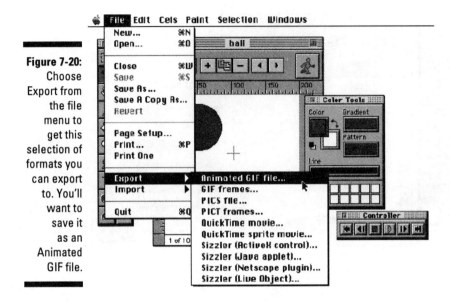

Figure 7-20:
Choose
Export from
the file
menu to
get this
selection of
formats you
can export
to. You'll
want to
save it
as an
Animated
GIF file.

Programmers Need Love Too

Shareware doesn't mean free. Shareware developers work hard to create fun and functional programs. Trying is free, but if you find yourself actually using a piece of shareware, look for the flag that tells you where to send your hard earned bux. Most of the time, shareware fees are very low — $10 or $20. And quite often paying for the right to use it will even get you added stuff, as well — things like upgrades that aren't downloadable or being sent newer versions as they come out.

When you see the prompt or "nagscreen" on a piece of shareware you enjoy, think about the programmer who created the software and what a difference your little contribution can make, both to his pocketbook *and* his self-esteem.

Working demos, like that of WebPainter, aren't shareware at all. They're software that a company has provided you with for the purpose of evaluation. Some of this demo software is crippled. For instance, it won't let you do a save, or some other critical thing. Other packages give you the full version, but only give you 30 days to try it. This is pretty generous, and a wonderful boon for consumers of software. It means that the days when we shelled out a couple hundred bucks for a piece of software that doesn't suit us at all are pretty much gone.

Chapter 8
Making and Using JPEGs

In This Chapter
▶ Decision-making guidelines
▶ JPEG-making tools
▶ File-conversion decision

*J*PEG (Joint Photographic Experts Group) is often considered to be the best method of displaying truecolor photographs on the Web. Pronounced "jay-peg" — maybe like a bird with a wooden leg — the format can often produce really teeny files in places where GIF can't. However, because JPEG is an extremely "lossy" method of compression, detail can be squeezed out of your JPEG files and lost forever.

Going Back and Forth

After you've saved a file as a JPEG, you *can* convert it back into a GIF, a TIFF, or whatever you like. However, any information lost in the conversion process is gone for good. That's not quite as nasty as it sounds. As long as you keep a copy of the original file around, you can just go back to that and start making clean conversions. But when you convert *from* your JPEG file, don't expect quality to get back to original levels, because it can't.

To get the most of your files, you shouldn't make a decision between JPEG and GIF: neither is inherently better. However, you need to spend some time experimenting with both formats to get a feel for which works best for each type of document.

When is JPEG better?

JPEG is better equipped than GIF for several reasons:

✔ When you're starting with a truecolor or grayscale photograph. In general, JPEG gives you a smaller file and better color representation than GIF.

✔ When your largest goal is the smallest file. When you're concerned about quantity (not much!) and not quality, JPEG fits the bill.

✔ Subtly colored artwork and computer drawn images.

When is JPEG wrong?

In a couple of scenarios, JPEG really is too big a loser:

✔ When there are only a few colors, choose GIF first. GIF is lossless, so all of your data is retained. In such cases, GIF is usually smaller anyway.

✔ Sharp edges in images blur in JPEG. Text, bordered icons, and hard-edged borders usually look better as GIF.

✔ Two-level images — pure black-and-white images — never do as well in JPEG as in GIF.

As a general rule of thumb, don't use JPEG compression until you're over 16 levels of gray.

JPEG in action

To demonstrate some of this, let's watch JPEG in action.

1. **In your image editor or conversion program — I used DeBabelizer for this example — open HORSE1.GIF from the *Web Graphics For Dummies* CD-ROM that comes with this book, as shown in Figure 8-1.**

   The file as saved on the CD-ROM weighs in at a fairly hefty 55K.

2. **Choose** Save As **from the** File **menu.**

3. **From the many options given, choose JPEG.**

4. **Most image editors supply a name for your new file at this point. In most cases, it comes up like** HORSE1.JPEG. **If the file type is not appended, add it yourself before hitting** enter **or** return.

   This saves you from trying to figure out which type each file is. Or worse, overwriting your original file when working on your own material.

5. **Some type of JPEG Save Options dialog box appears (like the one in Figure 8-2), no matter which software you're using. For now, choose medium quality. More on quality levels later in the chapter. Press** enter **or** return.

Figure 8-1:
HORSE1.GIF
as saved on
the *Web
Graphics
For
Dummies*
CD-ROM.

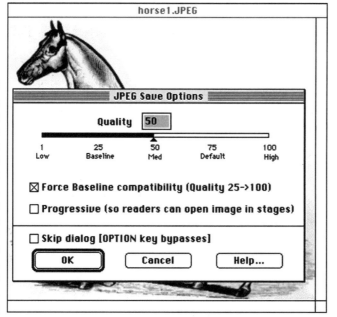

Figure 8-2:
The Save
Options
dialog box
looks
similar to
this one,
regardless
of the
software
you're
using.
Choose
medium.

By doing this very simple operation, you have just created a much smaller file, as shown in Figure 8-3. Just how small depends on the editor you used. Photoshop, for instance, doesn't seem to like to go out of its way to make teeny files in JPEG. The same operation in Photoshop on this image yielded a file of 55K: precisely the same size as the original. In DeBabelizer, however, you're down to 22K with very little effort.

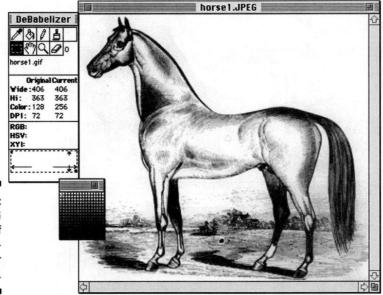

Figure 8-3:
The JPEG version of the now-familiar horse.

Not all image editors and converters are created equally. It can seem a little confusing until you've done a few and can chalk up the experience.

The thing that can keep the slight confusion from turning into frozen inaction is that — in the very end — it really doesn't matter. Though one method may produce a smaller file or a slightly clearer one, any method of saving to JPEG or GIF produces usable Web files. That knowledge is freeing, because you *know* that you can make it happen. And — in a pinch — you can make it happen better next week or next try.

Now that you've looked at JPEG from a couple of angles, go create one from the early stages.

Creating a JPEG File

To make a JPEG file, you need either an image editor or an image converter that supports the format. Because most do, this isn't a problem at all.

Tools you need

When you don't have a program that supports JPEG, all is not lost. There are several shareware converters for several platforms that help you with the final stage.

Creating a JPEG file with an image editor

It's very simple to create a JPEG file. You start with the same skills that you already have to make any type of image file, then add knowledge about what to do with compression and quality controls.

If you've ever created a Photoshop or CorelDraw file and saved it as another format, you have almost all of the skills you need to create a JPEG formatted file.

For the demonstration part of this exercise, I used the popular image editor, Photoshop. If you're not using Photoshop, some of the finer points are slightly different, but the overall commands and results are very similar.

1. **Start with an image that you've somehow gotten into your computer (something you've scanned, manipulated, or even created in your image editor). Remember, JPEG tends to do a superior job on files that are somewhat photographic in nature, so choose this type of file. If you want to follow right along with me, open the file COW.TIF from the *Web Graphics For Dummies* CD-ROM that comes with this book.**

2. **Without changing the currently saved format, do whatever finishing and clean-up that needs to be done to the image, as shown in Figure 8-4. Resize as necessary before conversion, and make any color or image changes to the file.**

Figure 8-4:
The original image — here saved in TIFF format — cleaned up, resized, and ready to become a Web graphic.

As a general rule, it's a good idea to do as much clean-up of an image as possible before you convert to a Web format. Ideally, prior to conversion, your image is resized, cleaned up, and ready for viewing by a Web audience near you!

3. **In Photoshop, choose** Save As **from the file menu. Choose JPEG from the many options available. You are prompted for a file name. To avoid confusion later on, remember to append the suffix** JPEG **to your new file at this point.**

4. **After you chose to save the file, the JPEG Options dialog box, as shown in Figure 8-5, appears, offering you a few simple options. For this first JPEG, choose** Medium **quality. (If you choose a higher quality, you get a larger file.) Lower quality gives you a smaller file — size wise — but may cut the quality back severely, depending on the image. Medium tends to be a good starting point, until you get a complete understanding of your own needs and expectations for your JPEGs. For now, leave the other format options at the default settings (that is, as they come up). They will not unduly affect the results of your file.**

5. **You have now created a JPEG file ready for inclusion on a Web page. This file, which started as a 121K TIFF file, is now a 22K JPEG file.**

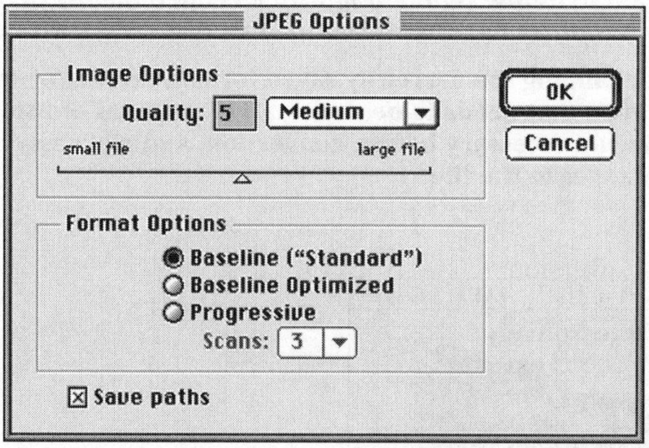

Figure 8-5:
The JPEG Options dialog box in Photoshop is echoed by similar dialog boxes in other programs. Simple commands help control the size and quality of files.

JPEG Options

Image Options
Quality: 5 Medium ▼
small file   large file

OK
Cancel

Format Options
● Baseline ("Standard")
○ Baseline Optimized
○ Progressive
Scans: 3 ▼

☒ Save paths

A Word on Conversions

As with the other file formats, sometimes what's really needed is to take an image that you've polished in some other program, and convert it to a format appropriate to the Web. After all, image editors like Photoshop and CorelDraw allow you to create and manipulate wonderful graphics. When they don't always do the best job possible on conversion to Web formats, you shouldn't be that surprised.

On the other hand, conversion programs like Ghostscript, GIF Construction Set, GIFConverter, Image Alchemy, DeBabelizer, and others are pretty much for just this type of conversion. Some of them with the Web largely in mind.

This being the case, image conversion programs can often be your very best bet in terms of getting the kind of results you need for Web display.

Because all Web formats include some type of compression, it's usually faster and easier to work in the format most native to the software (for example, Photoshop format in Photoshop) and then convert the image before uploading to a Web site.

Converting an image to JPEG

You can use any Image Conversion software package to either convert an image from some other format to JPEG, or to convert a file already saved as a JPEG in order to reduce the size of the file for Web display, as shown in the following image.

For demonstration purposes, I used the shareware program GIFConverter. A demo version of this software is included on the *Web Graphics For Dummies* CD-ROM, which comes with this book.

Many Image Conversion programs work in similar ways.

1. **In an Image Conversion program, open the JPEG file you just created in the previous exercise: COW.JPEG. Or open COW.JPEG from the *Web Graphics For Dummies* CD-ROM that comes with this book.**

   All of your editing should already have been done in the previous exercise. Although most image conversion programs can do some basic image editing, it's usually best to bring in a file that is ready for conversion. Or — as you're doing now — one that has already been converted but needs some fine tuning.

2. **For this demonstration, I used DeBabelizer. There is a demo version of this program on the *Web Graphics For Dummies* CD-ROM that comes with this book. But any Image Conversion program will do these basic things in a very similar way. Choose** Save As **from the file menu. Choose JPEG from the many file types available. If the program doesn't automatically append the file type, do it now. Name the file COW1.JPEG to distinguish it from the JPEG file you previously made of the same image. Press** enter **or** return.

3. **You see some type of JPEG Save Options dialog box, as shown in Figure 8-6, similar to the one you saw in the previous exercise. Again, start at the middle ground by choosing a medium quality file (as shown). Leave the other options at the default settings. Press** enter **or** return.

You now have a finished JPEG, ready for uploading to a Web site. This one is just 11K (half the size of the JPEG you created in Photoshop and a fraction of the size of the original TIFF file).

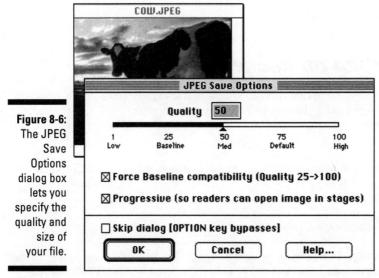

Figure 8-6:
The JPEG
Save
Options
dialog box
lets you
specify the
quality and
size of
your file.

Getting good at creating great JPEG format files is really about mastering the tradeoffs. As operator, you have control over the compression parameters. The larger the size, the better the quality. But when teeny is the order of the hour, you can dump that quality way down to create truly small files. The flip side is: When you create a JPEG you're not happy about, you can make a larger, better file.

Experiment with these compression parameters. You get a feel for exactly what that tradeoff means and how it affects your own files and work.

Chapter 9
Sum-ping for Everyone

In This Chapter

▶ PNG positives and negatives

▶ Image editors that support PNG

▶ Converting to PNG

*I*f you paid attention to every new Internet trend that ran up the pike, you'd never get any sleep. In fact, I often tell people, *"Don't think about all the new stuff that's coming out all the time. It'll just make your ears sweat. It just isn't worth the aggravation, because more than half of that hot new stuff will end up in that great geek junk bin in the sky before the year's out anyway."*

Can You Hear the "But" Coming?

But (there it is!) every now and again some new technology rises to the top of the dreck heap. And it's really hot, really exciting, and we know that it will make a difference to the way we do things.

Portable Network Graphics is one of those things. Shortened to PNG to make it a convenient file extension, it is usually referred to in print with just those three letters. For some silly reason that probably nobody besides the creator (of the format, not the world) knows for sure, PNG is pronounced "ping," so it sounds like "sing," which is, after all, better than pronouncing it "pnnoodg," as the letters may suggest.

The word on the 'Net is that — unofficially — PNG stands for "PNGs Not GIFs." As that implies, PNG was designed to replace the potentially litigious GIF format that may or may not be owned by CompuServe, depending on who you're listening to at the moment.

GIFs, like JPEGs, are designed for a wide variety of uses (none of them actually for the World Wide Web, because both formats pre-date the Web). PNG, however, has Web usage in mind. That being the case, several advantages recommend the format to the Web designer.

First of all, it's easy. And to show you just how easy, go ahead and make a PNG file right now.

Making a PNG File

In order to make a PNG file, you need either an image editor or an image converter that supports PNG.

Tools you need

When you don't have an image editor that supports PNG, don't despair. Several shareware converters can help you with the final stage.

Creating PNG files

Creating a PNG file is relatively simple, and will seem very familiar if you've already made a GIF or two. PNG files have a few extra options. Their purpose is not to confuse you, but to give you full power over the finished file.

The type of options you are offered vary from editor to editor. And many editors mean many options. All of them are based on a combination of offerings of Adam-7 interlacing, compression filters, and palette types. Remember, no matter what you choose, you are creating a usable PNG file.

For demonstration purposes, I chose the popular image editor and manipulation program, Adobe Photoshop.

Adobe Photoshop 4.0's handling of PNG files is flawed, because you are not likely to see great savings in file sizes when using Photoshop. A Photoshop PNG file is about the same size as a Photoshop GIF. Future releases of Photoshop may correct this problem.

1. **Start with an image that you've somehow managed to get into your computer (you've scanned the dog, squeezed the cat, or created something in a draw program or your image editor).**

2. **Without altering the currently saved format, do whatever finishing and clean-up that needs to be done to the image, as shown in Figure 9-1.**

   As a general rule, it's a good idea to do as much of this stuff as possible before you convert to PNG — or any other Web format. So resize as necessary before conversion, and make any color or image changes to the file.

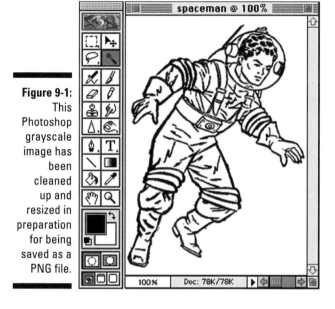

Figure 9-1:
This Photoshop grayscale image has been cleaned up and resized in preparation for being saved as a PNG file.

3. Choose Save As from the file menu.

You get a list of options of file types. Choose PNG, as shown in Figure 9-2.

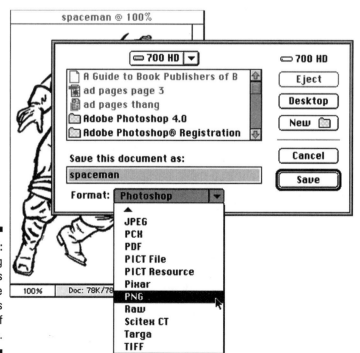

Figure 9-2:
Choosing Save As from the file menu gives you a list of options.

4. **When the dialog box prompting you for a file name appears, give your file the suffix .PNG so that you can easily determine it from other versions of the same file.**

   Also, because converting the image type will flatten out any Photoshop layers or other cool stuff, you want to keep your original work file around in case you want to make changes.

5. **You are now presented with the PNG Options dialog box, as shown in Figure 9-3. For interlace, choose Adam7.**

   This means that, on a fully PNG-enabled browser, your image will display as it loads, giving it that quasi-animated look that many Web users have come to enjoy. Choosing None from the interlace options gives Web users a blank wait while the graphic loads.

   Six filter options relate to how the image data is transformed. In PNG, different types of images respond better to certain types of filtering than others. For now, use the default "Up."

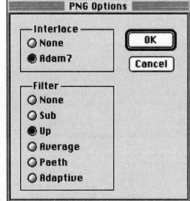

Figure 9-3:
The PNG
Options
dialog box
in Adobe
Photoshop.

You now have a fully functional PNG file ready for Web uploading.

Converting to PNG

Whatever your current Web design software of choice, you will find that you seldom create a graphic for the Web in the format it is displayed in. It's important to keep the final format in mind, of course, and not design beyond the basic limitations of the final file type. However, because all Web formats include some type of compression, it is usually faster and easier to work in the format most native to the software (for example, Photoshop format in Photoshop) and then convert the image before uploading to a Web site.

Converting an image

You can use any image conversion software package to either convert an image from some other format to PNG, or to convert a file that is already saved as a PNG in order to reduce the size of the file for Web display, as shown in the following example.

For demonstration purposes, I used GIFConverter, which is a Macintosh shareware program available for trial by download on the Web at `http://www.kamit.com/gifconverter.html` and is also one of the image conversion packages included on the *Web Graphics For Dummies* CD-ROM.

Many image conversion programs do things in a very similar way.

1. **Open the PNG file you just created in Photoshop, as shown in Figure 9-4.**

   I assume that all of your editing has already been done in the previous exercise. Although it is possible to do some primary editing in many image conversion programs, this is not their strength. It's best to bring in a file that is ready for conversion.

Figure 9-4:
The PNG file you created in Photoshop is edited and ready for conversion. If you didn't do the Photoshop exercise, open the file called SPACE.TIF from the *Web Graphics For Dummies* CD-ROM. For this exercise, this file will work just as well.

2. **Choose Save As from the file menu.**

3. **You are presented with a long list of file types. Choose PNG, as shown in Figure 9-5.**

   Note that, if you're not already working with a file with a PNG suffix, Converter will add it for you. Give the file a name that is slightly different from the Photoshop PNG file you made so that you'll be able to see the converted one at a glance. You can check file sizes later on. Press return.

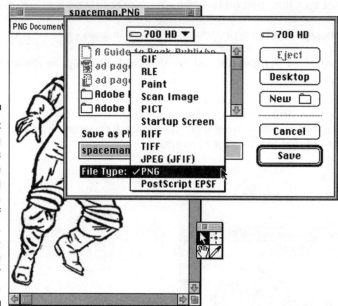

Figure 9-5: Choosing Save As from the file menu brings up a long list of possibilities. Choose PNG to begin your conversion.

4. **You're now given a PNG Option dialog box similar to the one you got in Photoshop, as shown in Figure 9-6. Only now you have more options (still not all of those available to PNG, but this is better).**

   Leave on the Adam7 Interlacing; for depth choose 256 colors, leave Compression level at the default of 6, and choose Up for Filtering method. Press return.

   After the file has completed writing, compare the size of the PNG file you just converted to the one you created in Photoshop. You'll see that it's substantially smaller and now truly ready for uploading.

   When you want to play a bit to see what the different options do, go for it. A PNG file is a PNG file, and one is just as viewable as the next. What is altered by your playing is the level of compression, and this can be radically different in PNG. These vast differences come from PNG's

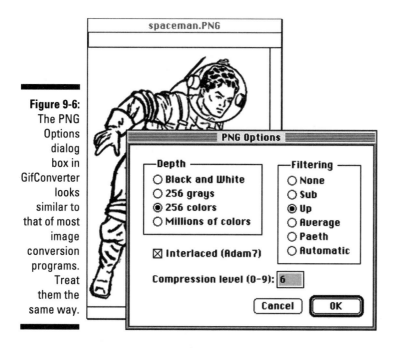

Figure 9-6:
The PNG
Options
dialog
box in
GifConverter
looks
similar to
that of most
image
conversion
programs.
Treat
them the
same way.

ability to mix image types. And that ability is directly related to the software you use to create your PNG file. Remember, all of the options create a PNG that is as equally as viewable as the next. Even PNG developers say that, at present, finding the best algorithms to make the most effective files requires a little "black magic." So be prepared to play to find the magic that works best for you!

Pros and Cons of PNG

Seems like there's always good news and bad news. The good news is that PNG can do a lot of stuff that GIF and JPEG can't. Or certainly, that they don't do as well. For starters, the PNG format produces smaller files. Files saved in the PNG format are usually 10 to 30 percent smaller than GIF files.

Like GIF, PNG supports 1- to 8-bit palettes, as well as 1- to 16-bit grayscale. In addition, it supports full alpha blending and truecolor. If your eyes are starting to glaze at some of the technical description, take a deep breath now. Boiled down, all it really means is that PNG does more cool stuff better than GIF. Best of all, it's non-patented so no one in another five or so years will come and try to claim it. In many ways PNG was created by and for the Web community, and everyone stays happy and royalty free that way.

One of the other main things in PNG's favor is that the format offers practically lossless compression. Translation: More of the pixels you want will get to the people who want to see them. In Web graphics design, very little beyond that matters.

The downside of PNG

You knew that there had to be one, right? At present, probably 75 percent or more of Web users don't have their browsers configured to view PNG files. Which is a bad thing. It means that if you go off tomorrow and build a site entirely around PNG graphics, a lot of viewers will see big holes where your pretty pictures are supposed to be. And that's not good either.

It's all about PNG's relative newness. All of the "right" people in the "correct" places are supporting PNG. Following their lead, developers are adding PNG support to the newest releases of image editing and viewing software and graphical Web browsers. So, software that's really new, as well as the stuff that is yet to be released will — most likely — support PNG.

How animated can PNG get?

The simple answer is, it can't. While PNG was meant to duplicate or outperform the features found in GIF in a non-patented environment, there is one very important GIF feature that PNG has avoided. The developers of PNG opted not to try for the multiple image support that has made GIF so popular for simple Web animations. Word is, there is a PNG-like extension in development called MNG to handle animations under its own file extension.

Theoretically, this sounds good to me. Although the proof is in the pudding (in this case, ming pudding). A file format that tries to be all things to all people is likely to be flawed, as is the case with GIF.

Ready for PNG?

So what does it all mean? A superior file format that offers you . . . what? Better looking graphics that most people can't see. Great. Like the kid who can't get a date for the prom. And his mom tells him he's very handsome and has many sterling qualities. "So I know it, and you know it," he says. "In what way does this help me now?"

Those dateless prom guys are usually worth watching. They quite often go on to have fabulous lives and make up for all that early datelessness. PNG will, I think, be like that. As I said, all the right people are supporting it. Heavy hitters like Adobe and Netscape have paid enough attention that they've added support for the format in their newest releases. Developers of many shareware applications have been quick to see the advantages.

All of this should mean that in a relatively short time, PNG support will be pretty universal. Relatively short? Ten Web years (which in real time means maybe 11 months).

At present, some gung-ho Web producers are putting PNG files on their Web pages, while also offering GIF or JPEG alternatives. When you're really determined to lead the pack, you can do all your files in PNG, but offer links so that users can download plug-ins that will enable them to actually see the files, if they so desire.

However, unless you really have a reason to want to support PNG (such as your sister-in-law was one of the developers) you may be better served by sitting on your haunches for a bit. You have the knowledge. Now watch the Web and watch what your fellow Web designers are up to. When most — if not all — people have the capability of viewing PNG, Web developers will start including PNG files. And you — with all this foreknowledge — can as well.

Chapter 10
Beyond Basics

● ●

In This Chapter

▶ Why should we look further?

▶ VRML

▶ Java

▶ Multimedia

● ●

*O*nce upon a time in this book, we defined Web graphics. Beyond flat art, Web graphics are expanding into motion and 3-D. Such technologies may become essential to designing Web graphics in the not-too-distant future.

Why Do I Wanna Know This Stuff?

This knowledge has purpose:

✔ Mastering the basics now makes it likely that you'll be up to speed when you need to be.

✔ As ideas mature, you'll be expected to weave them into our sites.

✔ It helps you talk to clients.

✔ It impresses people at parties. You can't talk about sports and the weather all the time!

No, Not Vermin!

Virtual Reality Modeling Language is always shortened to VRML and is always pronounced as though it made sense: ver-mil or ver-mle.

VRML is an unbearably cool tool for drawing. (How's that for an incredible oversimplification?) A set of standards for displaying 3-D virtual worlds on the Web, VRML is a 3-D analog of HTML. Where HTML is a language to make flat pages, VRML is a language to work with 3-D objects and graphics.

Still very much an evolving set of standards, some practical applications of grown-up VRML may be an online tour through a condo development, or an up-close and under-the-hood peek at Detroit's latest steel mobile. At present, VRML hasn't evolved much beyond interaction with 3-D boxes and a few online games. Still, it's a technology worth watching, especially if you think your art or your business might benefit from VRML additions to your Web site.

Different flavors of VRML browsers are available. Most are plug-ins for popular Internet browsers, such as Netscape and Internet Explorer. And VRML browsers are available for most platforms.

If you want to check out some of these virtually real worlds for yourself, your best bet is a search of VRML on one of the popular search engines (such as AltaVista at `http://altavista.digital.com`) and seeing what comes up. Last time I did this, I got 9,000 connections.

After you find a VRML to view, chase down the browser you need to see it. All VRML is not created equally, so one VRML browser may not view worlds built with other VRML tools. I have half a dozen VRML browsers on my computers. In general, I find the Mac VRML browsers lame, but I remain hopeful that a good browser will be released.

On the Windows front, VRML browsers are better. My VRML browser of choice is Cosmo Player 2.0 from Silicon Graphics; it's downloadable at `http://vrml.sgi.com`. (You'll find more cool samples and tools to download here, too). Today, building VRML worlds is a pastime I'm reserving for my twilight years. It gives me something to look forward to.

Java Break

Java is important stuff to the designer of Web graphics. Chances are, if you get serious about Web graphics you'll want to know *lots*. At that point, you'll need another book, because Java is a huge topic by itself: more important to the Web technologist than to the designer of Web graphics.

Nevertheless, Java is a good thing to know about, if only to follow conversations on the topic while the technology grows up. Java is cool, it's cutting edge, it's all that and a bag of chips. Despite all that, hardly anyone knows

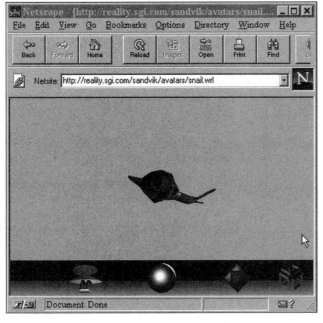

Figure 10-1:
Sample
graphics
from the
Silicon
Graphics
VRML
archives.

what to do with it yet. Java is on lots of Web sites, but mostly they aren't good or unique uses. In fact, many Webmasters use Java for jobs more easily and rapidly accomplished by other methods. But I've jumped way ahead of myself.

What is Java?

If you're in Seattle, you've got your own answer. But the rest of us think differently. I pride myself on knowing how things get their names, but I've never heard an explanation for this one. I have a hunch that someone at Sun just thought it was cute.

Sun Microsystems is where Java started, not that long ago. If you visit the Sun site (http://www.sun.com), you'll see that Java has evolved into a vibrant portion of the company's business. Java is a resource hog, so a Sun workstation to run Java applets isn't such a bad idea.

Java is actually a programming language — developed by Sun — and is a favored niece of the complicated programming language C++. Like CGI programs, Java "applets" cause cool stuff to happen when your Java-enabled browser hits a Java-powered Web page. Your browser actually downloads the Java code and executes the code. In the online game illustrated in Figure 10-2, you can stop your Internet connection and continue to name those animals, because the Java applet is now running on your system.

The pieces of Java

Java technology is broken down into several important parts.

- ✔ HotJava — Sun's original Java browser, which has been superseded by plug-ins for other Web browsers.
- ✔ Applets — Most correctly, these are Java programs or applications. Applets are usually small, as modern applications go.
- ✔ JavaScript — The Java scripting language developed by Sun Microsystems and Netscape.

Brewing Java on your Web pages

Breaking the process down, applets are written in Java and then compiled in a Java compiler. If you don't have a burning desire to program, don't try this at home. It is possible, however, to download public domain and shareware applets for your Web page. If you have a specific need to run Java on your own Web page, you can even hire a programmer to do the nasty bits for you.

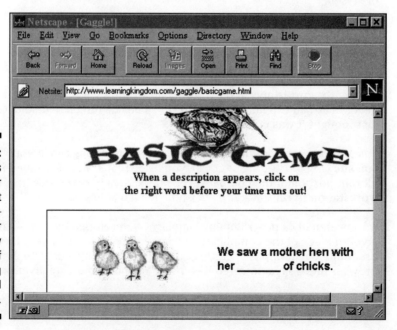

Figure 10-2:
This particular Java applet lets you — or your kids — play a game of identifying animal groups.

After you've begged, borrowed, or bought your Java applet, you embed it into your HTML code with the <APPLET> element of HTML. This is neither the time nor the place for a serious discussion on making that happen, but you now have enough to bluff your way through an office discussion!

Multimedia Web Sites

There's a lot of talk about multimedia Web sites these days. Defining a multimedia Web site is as challenging as defining multimedia. Ask three "experts" and you're likely to hear three different answers. They aren't confused. In this new world of technology, there are fewer rules and more possibilities.

Classically, the term "multimedia" has been given to works of art made of more than one type of material. A painting that is painted with both acrylic and gouache is a multimedia work. Collages made of more than one type of material are also considered multimedia.

If we use the classic definition and apply it to the Web, then any site that uses more than one type of technology is — in the strictest sense — multimedia. Straight HTML combined with a Java animation is multimedia. Add sound or video and you've reached anyone's definition of multimedia.

Looking Sharp with PDF

Portable Description Format is a mouthful, so it's usually named by just three letters: PDF.

PDFs come in a couple of flavors. The most popular is Adobe Acrobat.

Acrobat comes in two parts. The Acrobat Reader is widely available on the Net and other sources (including the *Web Graphics For Dummies* CD-ROM). The Reader gives you the ability to look at files prepared in the creator program, Adobe Acrobat. Acrobat changes almost any document you create by traditional computer methods into a format readable by any computer with a Reader.

PDF gives absolute control of how documents look when downloaded. You prepare the document on any word processor or page layout program just as you would for printing, including color graphics, fonts and — in the latest version — sounds and interactivity. Then, using Acrobat, convert the file to PDF. It's ready to embed into a Web page.

There's good news and bad news

At present, PDF has an equal number of detractors and supporters. It's easy to see why. On one hand, traditional documents are presented exactly as they should be seen. On the other hand, the files to do all of this aren't teeny and visitors must have the Acrobat Reader.

The case for PDF

In certain situations, though, PDF is exactly right. Software manufacturers, especially those who market and distribute entirely on the Web, make excellent use of the technology, as shown in Figure 10-3. Image Alchemy's entire manual is in the PDF format. When new users download a copy of the program of the program's demo from the Web, they get a copy of Alchemy's 228-page manual as well. In the PDF format, the manual is around 500K. This is a hefty file, but it provides a lot of information in an easy format.

Software manuals are a no-brainer for PDF, because you can assume that someone downloading an imaging utility is motivated to use the manual. A retailer of gardening tools, on the other hand, may still prefer printed catalogs. With Adobe pushing for wider use of their Acrobat Reader and add-ins for popular Web browsers PDF technology may get easier for the masses to use.

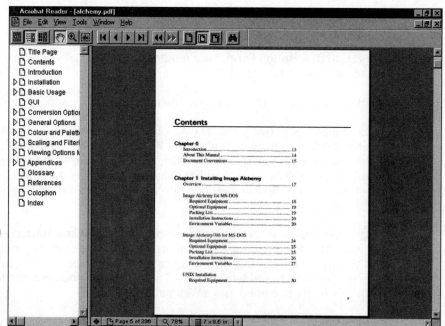

Figure 10-3:
Image
Alchemy's
manual in
PDF format.

Part III
The Sky Is the Limit

The 5th Wave — By Rich Tennant

"ISN'T THAT OUR WEBMASTER? THESE PEOPLE ALWAYS FIND A CREATIVE WAY TO INTERFACE."

In this part . . .

Don't think rinky-dink for your Web site. Think "how high is the sky?" There's no reason that the site you build and the graphics that compliment them can't be as sharp and elegant as any you've seen out there.

Here are some basic basics as well as some swell tricks and tips to create graphics and Web sites with polished perfection.

Chapter 11

Heads Up with the Big Kids

*T*he Internet has often been called the great equalizer. This is because it is simply the only medium where a home-based business has the power to put on as good a show as a multinational corporation. The only venue where there is a very real possibility of your personal gallery getting as much traffic as a Matisse opening. That's pretty heady stuff.

Build It and They Will Come

This is an overstatement and a common misconception for new Webmasters. There *is* more to generating Web traffic than simply putting up a site. Of course, I don't go into that here. That's the topic of a whole other book! The key is going to the edge without going overboard.

Think big

The core of the beast, the essential pull the makes a Web site special, is just as possible for a lone designer as for the large dollar-driven agency. You don't need to spend thousands of dollars creating color printing plates and tens of thousands to distribute copies of your work.

When you think about it, there's really nothing that a high-powered agency can do that you can't do on your own Web site. This very fact has created some stars in the boondocks over the last few years. The tools you need for mind-blowing Web sites are in your hands.

Going overboard

The very best sites don't have too much shiny stuff on them. Their animations are elegant and appropriate, their forms are simple, their use of tables is studied and careful.

In short, the best way to compete most often is by speaking gently. Keep the fireworks to a minimum so your message doesn't get lost in the wash.

Polishing Your Graphics

Certain errors scream "amateur" in any type of graphic production, including graphics for the Web. So give *your* graphics the professional look.

Color

Color within graphics is important to the finished piece. Choose your colors with the final purpose in mind. Remember, you may be playing with "millions of colors" on your computer, but you're limited to 256 *max* on the Web. Make sure that the colors you choose for your graphics translate to Web colors. Also, make sure that the colors you choose fit into your page design.

Size

Large graphics don't make your site look worse, though it may make it invisible. Not only do really huge graphics files on a Web site make you look amateurish, they also scare surfers away. I'm the classic example of this. If I have to wait for a 288K GIF to download, I'm outta there. Tight, small graphics are the answer.

Planning

Think about form and function. Design your graphics with the finished site in mind, even when you're not designing the site yourself.

The Web graphic itself is only part of the whole. Even super-killer-drop-dead graphics lose their impact on an unrelated page. Make sure that you have a good idea of what the finished site will look like so that you can create your graphics to work within that framework.

Gimmicks

Don't overuse them. A single animation that's nicely and thoughtfully executed can give a site a really finished look. More isn't better in this case. Four marginal animations will look like just that. And it doesn't matter whether they're 20-cell animations that took you 16 hours to produce. The understated three-cell animation that really works on your site will look a lot more professional.

Audio can also be a gimmick. An optional link to a rendition of your company song is fun. But RealAudio hitting you in the face at every corner — and when not asked for — can be irritating. Especially when the site depends on it.

White space

Well-trained designers understand the importance of white space, which just means eliminating visual competition. Don't clutter every inch of your site or your graphics with gratuitous *stuff*. Sure, pack the info in. But pack it carefully. Know your message, and then be honest about whether that message pops out.

As a Web designer, you have a powerful asset denied to traditional print artists: flexibility. Web pages can be any size you need, if they work, and you can divide your work into as many pages as you want. So don't lock yourself into packing everything on one page. Leave some space around the items surfers should notice and invite your guests to jump to related pages.

Type

Think carefully about the typefaces you choose and use. What kind of message are they sending, and is it the message you want? Certain fonts are known to be easy to read, some are even designed for easy reading. These are fonts like Helvetica, Garamond, and Palatino; they don't appear to have a whole lot going on, but they're easy on the eyes. Other fonts grab your attention, still others create moods.

Learn as much as you can about typography and then think carefully before plunking type onto your Web pages or in your Web graphics.

Chapter 12

Cleanliness Is Next to Cleanliness

In This Chapter

▶ The importance of graphics to a Web page

▶ The layers of a Web graphic

▶ Using someone else's Web graphics

▶ Before Web graphics: preparing for conversion

Graphics are an important part of Web pages. Some would say *the* most important part. A picture, they've been saying for years and years and years, is worth a thousand words. But a picture on the Web can be worth so much more. That's because a Web graphic can serve many uses:

- ✔ An image map
- ✔ An icon
- ✔ An illustration
- ✔ A company logo or other statement of identity
- ✔ An animation
- ✔ Specially set type, saved in a graphic format

Because Web graphics can be so many different things to so many people, it makes sense that learning to create them effectively is a multi-faceted deal. There are, after all, an increasingly sophisticated set of criteria. Increasing, that is, because as you get more proficient, your demands will go up.

It's sort of like peeling an onion. At the center of the onion is the Web graphic. The layers upon layers surrounding it are increasingly light: increasingly subtle. The onion without the layers is still an onion, but the layers around it make it a better, bigger, more fulfilling onion. As far as onions go.

Don't Sweat It

Creating a Web graphic is not difficult. The crudest, easiest GIF or JPEG that can be made will often suffice, at least as you begin. The subtle layers you add with knowledge and experience — and that's just great. But don't be put off from putting your graphics on your Web site *right* now. You can fine tune them as you go.

The Layers of the Onion

If the making of a Web graphic really is something like the many layers of an onion, let's look at that onion now.

At the heart of the whole thing is the Web graphic itself. This is, of course, the most important thing. But it's also the easiest to create. That is, it's a simple matter to create some kind of Web graphic that will serve on a Web site.

After that simple core, things get progressively more challenging. Not necessarily difficult, mind you. But obviously more finesse is involved with making a really great Web graphic than with making a crude one.

Some of the possible progressions:

1. **A Web graphic is created within a conventional image editing program by Saving As or Exporting to GIF or JPEG formats.**

2. **The same graphic is reopened in DeBabelizer or Image Alchemy or any one of a number of other conversion programs. The colors are adjusted to maximize the palette, a narrower bit-depth is selected to reduce the size, and the file is resaved, now considerably smaller than it was previously.**

3. **Once on the Web, an online image checker like GifWizard at** `http://www.gifwizard.com` **is used for further size reduction and image tightening.**

The result is a graphic that's tight, clean, and ready to be made into a really great pasta sauce.

Don't Want to Make Graphics?

Or do you want someone else to make them for you? Or even, do you want to use other people's graphics to springboard from?

Many sites on the Web offer public domain and royalty free clip art, backgrounds, and buttons that you can download just for that purpose.

http://www.jiffyart.com/

Jiffy Art is a pay as you go site, but there is some free stuff available here as well. The pay stuff seems pretty reasonable, and the shopping cart site is fun to look at. A good place to get ideas.

http://www.ender-design.com/rg/

Realm Graphics is filled with all types of Web-suitable art that is apparently free of copyright. As always with this kind of stuff, do your own homework to make sure that the image you're using doesn't belong to someone else!

http://www.net-user.com/counter/

Net-User is another location filled with downloadable graphics of the help-yourself variety. It asks that you read the terms and conditions before getting download happy. It's a good idea to do so.

http://www.geocities.com/SiliconValley/ 6603/index.html

The Graphic Station has "more free stuff" for people building their Web pages. In fact, according to the Web site, they have "everything you need for your Web site," which makes it a fun site to peek around.

Preparing a Graphic for Conversion

There's more to creating a graphic for the Web than just creating a graphic. That is to say, it doesn't take much at all to make some type of graphic that will display in someone's Web browser. The trick is in making one that looks just the way you want it to; uses hardly any colors, but gives the impression of using many; and — last but not least — takes up so little room that it takes no time at all to download. Even at a modem speed of 14.4 Kbps.

Creating tight, clean graphics

The preceding may well be a statement of goals, because sometimes it seems like the ultimate challenge is just to keep hacking away at a graphic. That is, you create it, you convert it, and then you put it on your Web site, knowing full well you'll come back to it and back again in the effort to one day — finally — save it as the perfect graphic. One that takes up a whole screen, looks full color, and yet takes only 11K. And sometimes you get the feeling that if you play with it long enough — manipulate it, massage it, soothe it, even — it will finally happen.

Before conversion

You can take some steps with your graphic *before* you convert to a Web format.

Let's go step-by-step through preparing a graphic for the Web.

1. **Start with a freshly scanned image.**

    The image in Figure 12-1 is straight-up line art.

Figure 12-1:
The newly
scanned
graphic.

2. **Because it was scanned as line art, the first step is to convert the file into a format that the computer is happy with. In Photoshop, the only possibility from bitmap is grayscale. Do this conversion by selecting Image⇨Mode⇨Grayscale.**

3. **You already know that you're going to be adding color to this image, so at this point go ahead and convert it straight to RGB mode. This is accomplished by selecting Image⇨Mode⇨RGB.**

4. You don't have the image perfectly straight on the scanner bed, so it's a little crooked and needs to be straightened up. In Photoshop, do this using the Free Transform tool.

5. You know that you want to end up with a 72 dpi image, the better to make a teeny Web image later on. So now is the time to make sure that you're at 72 pixels, and convert if necessary. Do this by choosing Image Size from the Image menu, and then making the necessary adjustments in the dialog box.

   This time enter 72 pixels and — because that reduces the size of the image — you enter the physical size you want the image to be. You're finished. (Figure 12-2 illustrates the Photoshop Image Size control panel.)

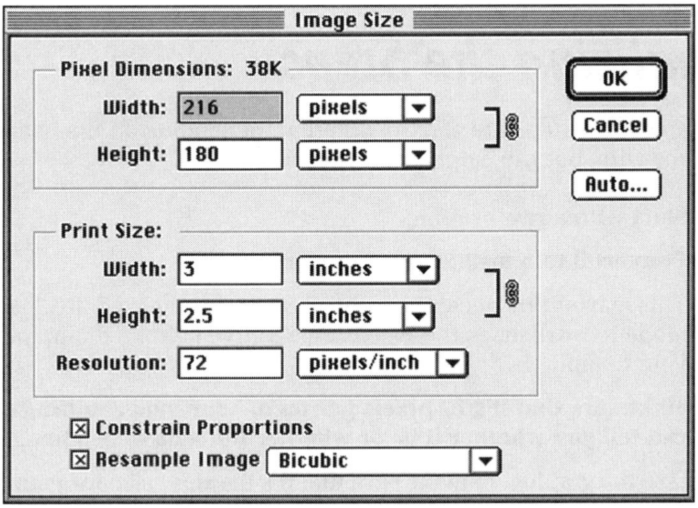

Figure 12-2:
You're
going go to
want to end
up with an
image that's
72 pixels
per inch.

6. You've got enough work in now that you'd be annoyed if the thing crashed, so it's time to save. Do this in the Photoshop format. All options are open to you from the program's own format.

7. With your image looking clean and in the format you currently need it to be, it's time to play a bit. The creative part: Where you do all the things you want to do before you get ready to make it into a for-real Web graphic. Depending on the image, this is where you apply filters, lay in shadows, and so on.

   For this particular one, I just added a bit of color, so I made a red hammock, gave him bright yellow hair, colored his pants and sweater, put a little color in his hands and cheek, and gave that darned bug multi-colored wings. (See Figure 12-3 for the results.)

With your graphic cleaned, sized, creatively manipulated, and freshly saved, you're ready for Web conversion.

Figure 12-3:
Ready
now for
conversion
to a Web
format.

Individualizing the Steps

The preceding steps are slightly different, depending on the image you're working with, but the emphasis is the same.

1. **Start with a raw graphic.**

2. **Convert it to a format you can work with.**

   This may not be necessary, but needs to be checked. RGB is an ideal mode to work in, as the Web is an additive light medium, the same as your computer.

3. **Make sure that it's 72 pixels per inch. Your image editing program can tell you whether it is, or whether it needs to be changed.**

4. **Size the graphic, to make sure that it's the right size for your purposes.**

   If you're not sure, you can always change the size later. But I like to work in the size I'm going to end up with, when possible.

5. **Make sure that the image is straight and clean.**

   Here's where you take out any of the icky bits that got left on in the scanning or creation process.

6. **Add the creative finishing touches. Smooth and streamline a photo, creatively beautify any type of graphic.**

7. **Make sure that your graphic is saved in the format native to the program.**

   You are now ready to convert to Web format. Be sure, however, to leave behind a pre-Web format version. That is, choose Save As, rather than Save when you're making your Web graphics. That way, if you change your mind or want to touch up later, you don't have to go all the way back to the beginning. Having that unconverted backup goes a long way to freeing your mind to experiment with different things in Web formats because you know that it's easy to start over.

Chapter 13

Building Graphics Around Type

In This Chapter

▶ Surfing up examples of type

▶ Creating type as an image

▶ Typography in HTML

Typography is important in almost all disciplines of design. It's well known that type can create mood and feel. That's why multi-national corporations spend the big bucks on designing logos that often consist of nothing more than a couple of stylized letters.

Web Graphics and Type

To fully understand the importance of typography to Web design, do a little surfing on your own. Go to your favorite sites and pay special attention to the way they've used type, and what that usage says to you. Elegant type, carefully used, can go a long way in setting the tone for a site.

Pay close attention to the "feel" of various sites and how its attained. You'll see some commonalities. Notice how the type is used on sites that seem:

✔ Happy and cheerful. What about the type contributes to this?

✔ Elegant and understated. Usually lots of serifs and white space.

✔ Knowledgeable and perhaps scientific. Is the type blocky and strong? With little space given to joviality of anything not related to the topic.

It's interesting how strongly type can convey feeling or mood. It's also interesting how little we pay attention to this; we take it for granted.

Creating Type-Based Graphics for the Web

A lot of the coolest uses we see of type on the Web really don't have much to do with the Web at all. Lots of type is created in other image-editing programs and then saved in a Web graphic format, the way you would any type of graphic.

A lot of the *very* coolest stuff is created in several passes. The initial type may be set in Adobe Illustrator or CorelDraw, for instance, then imported into Adobe Photoshop for a final pass before conversion to one of the Web formats. A long process for one little word, perhaps. But the looks you can get this way are hard to beat.

Let's have a closer look.

Setting type as an image

For demonstration purposes, I'm using Adobe Photoshop. If I'm using kerning, I set the type in a drawing program and then export it to my usual image editor.

1. **In your image editor, open a new file that's 72 dpi and 300 x 300 pixels. Select a red background for the file.**

   Isn't that just awful? So red it hurts your eyes! (Check it out in eye-friendly gray in Figure 13-1.)

2. **Select the type tool and find a font you want.**

   It can be fun to play with your name or that of your business. I set the words "The Image of Type" just because that strikes me as having some fun variables. I decided that bright white type would show up nicely on this dark red. And because I'm a nut for little shadows, I did one here as well. I simply duplicated the layer the type was on, filled it with a very dark green (to really contrast with the red) and then nudged it into a shadow-y sort of position. It wouldn't be hard to duplicate these results in many image editing programs.

3. **Save the file in the image editor's own format.**

4. **Time to lose the red background. In Photoshop, I just dumped the whole layer my background was on right into the trash, as shown in Figure 13-2.**

5. **Now crop in fairly closely to the type. The less you take with you, the smaller your file is.**

6. **Now do what you need to do to create a GIF file. In Photoshop it's an export function. Choose Export GIF89a from the Export menu under the file menu. Give the GIF a name, and you're away. Figure 13-3 shows the results.**

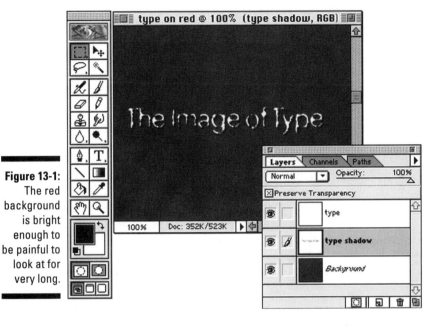

Figure 13-1:
The red
background
is bright
enough to
be painful to
look at for
very long.

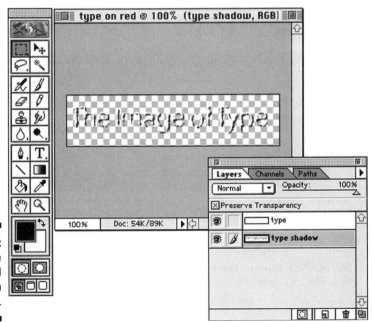

Figure 13-2:
Lose the
background
and crop in
close.

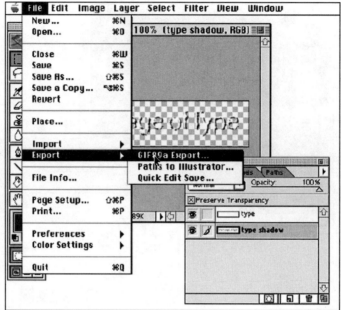

Figure 13-3:
Saving a file
as a GIF in
Photoshop
means
exporting it
using the
Export
GIF89a
function.

Using type in HTML

Now that you've created some type, let's use it in an HTML file just to see
how it all fits together.

1. **Start a file in the usual way, and give it a title.**

```
<HTML>
<HEAD>
<TITLE>Type on the Web</TITLE>
</HEAD>
```

2. **Now assign a nice, deep red background color (Ow!) similar to the
   color that was originally your background color.**

```
<BODY BGCOLOR="#BE1626">
```

3. **Include the type in the HTML, just as you would with any image file
   in HTML. I centered the type, as well, but you don't have to.**

```
<P><CENTER><IMG SRC="type.gif" WIDTH=280 HEIGHT=87>
      </CENTER></P>
```

4. **And then close off the HTML file, just as you would for any complete file.**

```
</BODY>
</HTML>
```

5. **Now preview your file in a browser. Yikes! You find something horrible: antialiasing. Yuck. Check it out in Figure 13-4.**

Figure 13-4:
The
dreaded
antialiasing.
Make it
stop!

What's Antialiasing?

Antialiasing is one of the "nice" things many image editors do for you to make your printable graphics look cooler. It actually smoothes the edges of your graphics by adding intermediate value pixels.

While this is fine, super, and great for a graphic that is intended to end up as a hard copy somewhere, it doesn't do much for images published on the Web.

What to do?

In order to avoid antialiasing, turn antialiasing off whenever possible when working on Web graphics. In some programs, this can be hard to do. Antialiasing is such a *good* thing on traditional publishing that some long-standing programs have it pretty much built-in. Also, the antialiasing controls are all over the place. For instance, in Photoshop, there is an antialiasing check box under preferences. There is also one within the type tool. Make sure that both are *not* checked when working with type for the Web.

Back to the drawing board

Of course, you can go back and rebuild the final part of the graphic with antialiasing turned off. But you get an even cooler, more finished look by incorporating the type onto a background: in this case, a background of solid color. Do that now.

1. **Open the file you saved in Step 3 in the last exercise.**

2. **Using your marquee tool, describe a square of about one inch. Copy it into your clipboard, and — without altering this file — open a new file. Figure 13-5 shows the selected square.**

3. **Paste the chip of red background into the new file. Crop tightly around the red square and export to GIF. I called mine "typeback.gif" for wont of anything more exciting.**

4. **Back in the original file, crop fairly closely around the words, like you did last time. Only this time, don't ditch the red background. Export the file as a GIF.**

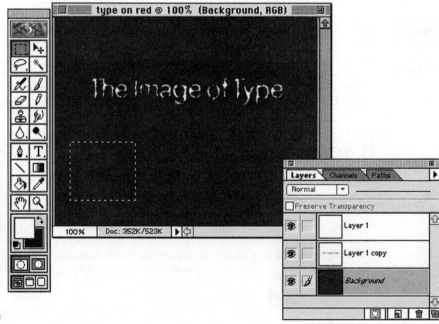

Figure 13-5:
Describe a
square of
about one
inch from
the rich, red
background
of your
image
editor file.

Checking it out

Back in HTMLville, your document looks much better. You added several steps, but the tighter end result is worth it.

Not only is executing this graphic more work, it also takes a few more steps to code it. Here's what you do.

1. **As before, open an HTML file, and give the child a name.**

```
<HTML>
<HEAD>
<TITLE>Type on the Web</TITLE>
</HEAD>
```

2. **Even though you now have a background image, you still assign a background color. That's so surfers already have something to see while they're waiting for the rest of the stuff to download.**

```
<BODY BGCOLOR="#BE1626" background="typeback.gif">
```

3. **Now your good ol' image, though this time you know that it's stuck on a background of its own.**

```
<P><CENTER><IMG SRC="type1.gif" WIDTH=288 HEIGHT=76>
        </CENTER></P>
```

4. **And then end HTML the conventional way.**

```
</BODY>
</HTML>
```

Really, you've only added one thing to the code: you've specified a background image. Figure 13-6 shows the result.

Figure 13-6:
The type lying over a background of its own background looks a lot better.

Setting Graphic Type Tips

The technique you just looked at will work in a number of situations. You can, for instance, lay the type over a textured background for an even deeper effect, as shown in Figure 13-7. Just be careful with those color and size combinations!

You can also use type from special programs dedicated to certain things, like FontFX or Aldus TypeTwister, just remember to watch the antialiasing.

It is also possible, while you're still in your image editor, to incorporate other images in the same file.

Figure 13-7: Incorporating images with your type is another option. It can add finish as well as functionality.

When Type Is an Image

Type created outside of HTML to be included in a Web page is handled in exactly the same way that a graphic is handled. From a technical standpoint, in fact, that type *is* a graphic.

That means that within HTML you use the exact same IMG and SRC tags you use for any type of graphic. And you can expect the same results.

Setting type in HTML

Not long ago, *setting type in an HTML editor* was an oxymoron. The Web was where type was mashed and strangled, not gentrified. It would be going too far to say that all of this has changed. But it's getting better.

The newer versions of the popular browsers have added font support. This comes via the non-HTML standard FACE tag, which is supported by both Netscape Navigator and Internet Explorer.

While you can specify a font using the FACE tag, you should still be cautious in using it.

Many people still use early versions of Internet browsers, versions so old that they don't support the FACE tag. Also, some fonts work on one browser but not both. This means that rather than adding control of the way your HTML will look, in some ways you're giving some of the control away because you can't be sure *exactly* how it will all come out in the wash when someone looks at the file.

Using the FACE tag

Whether the fonts you specify show up on the surfer's side depends on a couple of things:

- ✔ The browser being used to view the page
- ✔ The fonts the surfer has installed on his or her computer
- ✔ The default fonts you specify in your coding
- ✔ The default fonts the surfer has specified in his or her browser

All of these variables mean that using the FACE tag is sketchy, at best. That doesn't mean you shouldn't use it. Just that you should be aware that using it doesn't guarantee the look of your file.

Specifying fonts with the FACE tag

To create Figure 13-8, I used the FACE tag a lot. Let's look at how it was done.

1. Open an HTML file in the usual way, specifying a title as well.

```
<HTML>
<HEAD>
<TITLE>Let's look at fonts</TITLE>
</HEAD>
```

```
<P><CENTER><FONT SIZE="+2" FACE="Klang MT">Klang is
        another one of the Fonts that the Web likes. Not
        a favorite of mine: too hard to read.</FONT></
        CENTER></P>
<P><CENTER><FONT SIZE="+2" FACE="New Berolina MT">New
        Berolina is another one that gets installed a
        lot. And it's also difficult to read in a lot of
        places.</FONT></CENTER></P>
<P><CENTER><FONT SIZE="+2" FACE="Treefrog">Specifying a
        font like Tree Frog is not a good idea: how many
        people are likely to have this one installed?
</FONT></CENTER></P>
<P><CENTER><FONT SIZE="+2" FACE="Palatino">Palatino is
        another font that is already on a lot of
        people's systems, so seems a safe bet.</FONT>
</CENTER></P>
```

4. End the file in the usual way.

```
</BODY>
</HTML>
```

If I'm silly enough to put this page on a Web site exactly as it is, people without all of the fonts can see words: They just can't see them in the way I intended. *Especially* if I insist on using Tree Frog!

Some tips on using the FACE tag in HTML

✔ FACE is an option tag. That means it isn't actually included in the specifications for the current release of HTML, however it is supported by the major Internet browsers. That means that not everyone who sees your Web page will have a FACE-enabled browser. Figure 13-9 shows a non-FACE browser.

✔ The fonts that *are* supported depend entirely on the fonts installed on the surfer's computer. So it's good to use common fonts.

✔ When you use the FACE tag to specify a font, you have to remember to include whatever space is in the name. So "Arial Italic" must appear that way in your code and not "arialitalic" as other tags in HTML often have to be written.

✔ You can suggest default fonts with the FACE tag by using commas between font names. That would make the line of code look like: FACE="Arial, Palatino, Tree Frog." The browser would look for Arial first, Palatino next, and then Tree Frog. If it found none of them it would default back to the regular default font.

Working with Preformatted Text

One of the few HTML tags that sort of simplifies a page of text is is PRE.

The PRE tag stands for preformatted and solves many problems of text formatting. It enables you to write text perfectly, exactly the way you want it to display. It's like a printed version of words on a page, but breaking exactly where you want.

Figure 13-10: A stanza from a poem displayed with the <PRE> tag in place. The formatting I put in stayed put, and would at any size.

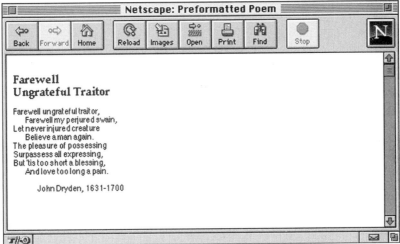

Figure 13-11: Same poem. Same file. But saved without the <PRE> tag. It even looks less like a poem than the one in Figure 13-10.

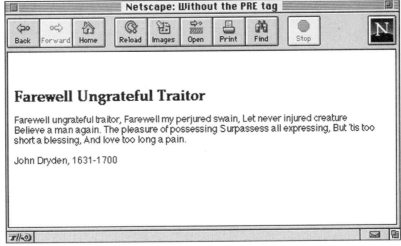

Using the PRE tag

The PRE tag is very easy to use. You just open it, <PRE>, before you start talking about fonts, and then close it, </PRE>, when you're done.

Following is the HTML mark-up for Figure 13-10.

Chapter 14

Background Beautiful!

Sometimes, the simple, stately gray of the standard-issue Web page is just what's called for. The thing is, those times seem less and less frequent. In a world where color is possible and photo backgrounds are doable, that natural gray seems ever less attractive.

The Background on Web Backgrounds

Back when Web pages were synonymous with Netscape and Mosaic, you didn't have a lot of decisions about your background. Would you like that in gray or gray (see Figure 14-1)? The message was the key, the graphics were a bonus, and the presentation was never questioned. It reminds me of the earliest cars. Those old Model T Fords came in black or black or maybe . . . black. But no one cared. It was just so durned novel to drive a horseless carriage. After the novelty wore off, we had our expectations. I want it in puce, with bucket seats, touch-control locks, and a makeup mirror for my poodle.

Of course, everyone knows that Internet time moves faster than regular time. Just like football time moves slower. It didn't take seven decades for us to get from Model T Web site to specifying what size canine would be using that mirror.

Figure 14-1:
The good ol'
gray on
gray of the
standard-
issue Web
page
background.
It's easy to
read, but
pretty
unexciting.

Web backgrounds do not add to the functionality of a Web page as much as a makeup mirror for a dog adds to a car, however it isn't that huge a leap, either. In an environment where visuals give friends and customers a real feel for their cyber "surroundings," it makes sense to use everything at our disposal to make their Web visit a comfy one.

Now that I've told you how wonderful backgrounds are, I must tell you how nasty they can be. Although, if you've spent any amount of time on the Web at all, you've probably already seen for yourself. Nothing's worse than arriving at a Web page — especially one you've spent some time surfing — only to find that you can't actually *read* anything because the background is so loud that it outshouts the text. Help!

The lessons of this story are clear:

- ✔ Use backgrounds only in moderation.
- ✔ Soft pastels beat screaming colors.
- ✔ Gentle, muted designs beat aggressive lapel-grabbers.

In design, less is often more. This is no less true in designing for the Web than it is in other disciplines.

Plain color or all the trimmings

When we talk about backgrounds on a Web page, we're really talking about one of two things:

✔ An image background specified in code

✔ A simple colored background

Either way, backgrounds are pretty easy. Much more so than that makeup mirror for the poodle.

Figure 14-2 illustrates an image background in code. This simple, tiled background was achieved by using a *clouds* filter in Photoshop and then dropping a shadow around a portion of the image. It gives the page a kick, but is also a classic example of what to be aware of with a Web page background. It doesn't take much for your background to compete with your message.

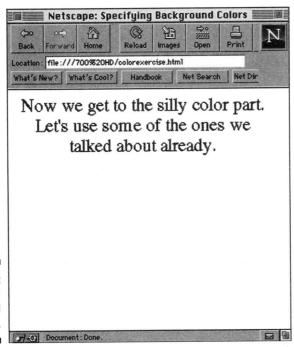

Figure 14-2: A classic code-based background.

Figure 14-3 shows how a colored background gives most pages a lift. Especially when the images used on the page share a background of the same color. It gives the appearance of the graphic floating over the background. A pleasing effect when properly done.

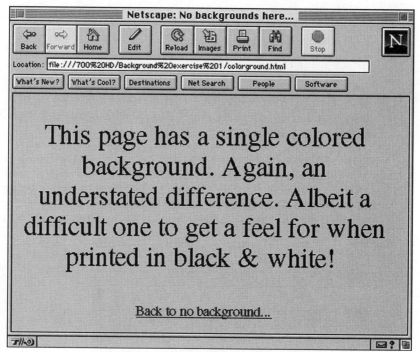

Figure 14-3:
A color-
screen
background.

Including a background image

Including backgrounds on your Web pages is startlingly easy. A simple piece of code makes it all happen.

To show just how simple, here is the exact HTML code that makes Figure 14-2 happen:

```
<HTML>
<HEAD>
<TITLE>Lovely Page With Background</TITLE>
</HEAD>
<BODY BACKGROUND="cloudshadow.gif">
<P><BR>
<BR>
</P>
```

```
<P><CENTER><FONT SIZE=+4>This page has a happy, tiled back-
          ground. See the difference?</FONT></CENTER></P>
<P><BR>
</P>
<P><CENTER><A HREF="colorground.html"><FONT SIZE=+2>This
          way to a simple, colored background...</FONT>
          </A></CENTER>
</BODY>
</HTML>
```

Making it happen step-by-step

As you can see, the business end is just five lines in.

1. **First, open the file in the traditional manner — begin the HTML file:**

   ```
   <HTML>
   ```

2. **Let it be known that this is a head.**

   ```
   <HEAD>
   ```

3. **Specify a title for the title bar.**

   ```
   <TITLE>Lovely Page With Background</TITLE>
   ```

4. **End the head.**

   ```
   </HEAD>
   ```

5. **Follow with the tag that makes the background happen.**

   ```
   <BODY BACKGROUND="cloudshadow.gif">
   ```

And that's it! As you can see, it's just one simple line of HTML code that installs the makeup mirror for the poodle.

The simple part is the HTML code

Of course, if it's just that simple, it wouldn't warrant its own chapter! But coding is the easy part. *Applying* that code is as important as actually using it.

Remember, not everyone can see your backgrounds. People using older versions of popular browsers — prior to Netscape 1.1 for instance — and those who surf using Lynx can't get the benefits of your backgrounds. Also, some people will see them differently than others. So try not to make the message depend on the background. Also, the KISS method of design applies doubly here. Keep those backgrounds simple and uncluttered so there is less room for misinterpretation.

Keep in mind that a background loads in the same way that any graphic file loads. A large background slows things down a lot. Sometimes unbearably! Try to keep the size of your background files really teeny so that visitors to your Web site can peek and run.

Setting Background Color

It's important to talk about background colors at this point because they play a vital role in working with backgrounds. I get really kick-butt in-depth with color for the Web in Chapter 15. But I'll sneak a little bit in here because it relates to background images.

Very briefly, the colors Web surfers see when they land on a page are determined by hexadecimal color values programmed into the Web page. Before you head for the hills at the first hint o' the dreaded "H" word (hexadecimal . . . yuck!) let me say quickly that Hex colors don't require algebra or a mail-order pocket protector.

What you *do* have to remember is that each of the 140 Hex colors recognized in HTML 3.2 have an RGB (red, green, blue) code and a really stupid corresponding name. For instance, 16 colors are considered universal — and these have the least stupid names. Just to give you an idea, here are a few codes and their names:

```
00FFFF is aqua
000000 is black
FFFF00 is yellow
```

Where we get into stupid-name-land is with the 124 extended colors. A few examples:

```
F0F8FF is aliceblue
FFEBCD is blanchedalmond
7FFF00 is chartreuse (and because I've never been able to
         get four artists in a single room to agree on
         the exact nature of chartreuse, this seems an
         especially silly one)
```

Let's quickly put some of this stupid color knowledge into practice.

To specify a colored background:

1. In your HTML editor, start a simple file.

```
<HTML>
<HEAD>
<TITLE>Specifying Background Colors</TITLE>
</HEAD>
```

2. Now you get to the silly color part. Use some of the ones I talked about already.

```
<BODY BGCOLOR="#f0f8ff">
```

This specifies that the background color be aliceblue. I don't know who Alice is. Judging by the coolness of the color, maybe she's some sort of ice maiden.

3. Now a little text — I centered mine, as you can see — just to make a bit of a complete file.

```
<P><CENTER></CENTER></P>
<P><CENTER><FONT SIZE=+3>Now you get to the silly color
          part. Use some of the ones talked about
          already.<FONT></CENTER>
```

4. Then close the HTML file, as usual.

```
</BODY>
</HTML>
```

As you can see, the only part relating to the background color is that single piece of code in step two. It's an easy and efficient way to add a background that is a little different than gray yet doesn't slow down your load time at all.

When you want someone else to do it

Lots of places on the Web feature archives of background images for you to download and use or customize. Here are a couple to get you started.

The Clip Art Connection at `http://www.ist.net/clipart/homepage.html` says that they want to become the world's largest bank of clip art for the Web, and their growing archive of backgrounds moves them towards that claim.

Rose's Background Archive at `http://www.wanderers.com/rose/backgrou.html` says that it's "The Largest Collection of Links for Backgrounds, Textures, Buttons, Bars, Rules, Icons, Ray Trace & Clip Art on the Internet!" Which makes both of these a good starting point!

Making a background from scratch

It's easier than making an angel food cake, but there are lots of steps. Follow me through making this silly one that ends up quite pretty.

1. **I used the Connectix Color QuickCam 2 to take a digital picture of a crumpled piece of tissue.**

2. **The tissue photo was saved as a TIFF and brought into Photoshop 4.0 where I cleaned it up a bit, cropping it tightly and adjusting the color, as shown in Figure 14-4.**

3. **I made a little HTML file around this background, just to see what it would look like if I used it in this form, as shown in Figure 14-5.**

Figure 14-5:
Using the
background
in its
current
form
produces
some nasty
tiling. In
fact, viewed
here in
Netscape,
this
background
looks pretty
much
exactly like
a tile you
may find
around
someone's
bathtub.

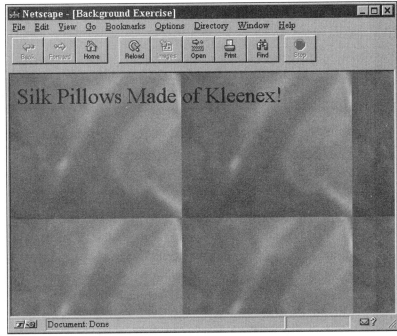

Figure 14-6:
In
Photoshop,
I create my
own tile
system. The
object is to
soften the
tiled look
that will
occur in
HTML
before it
starts.

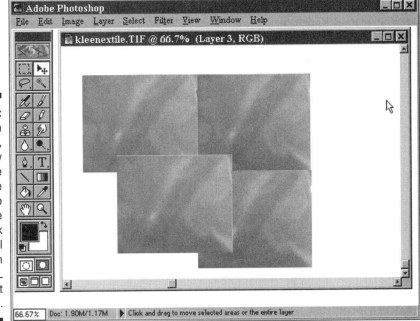

Fi

TJ

w

b

ot

r

a

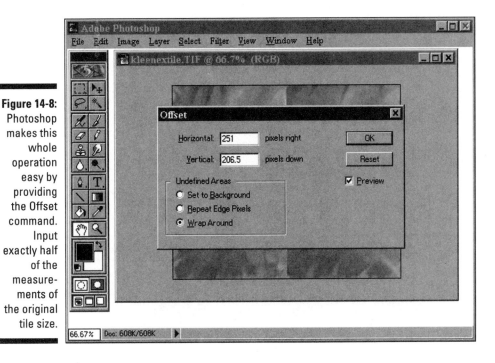

Figure 14-8:
Photoshop
makes this
whole
operation
easy by
providing
the Offset
command.
Input
exactly half
of the
measure-
ments of
the original
tile size.

The resulting tile will again be exhibiting hard edges at the joins. Use whatever tools you used the first time to make the joining areas more gentle. Remember to bring as many elements across the join as possible.

Back in Netscape, you can see that the tiling is still obvious, but with the manipulations, I managed to control the final look to a far greater extent. The tiles now have more of a look of belonging to each other. On close inspection, as shown in Figure 14-9, you can still see the join, but the overall result is far more acceptable.

A variation on the same theme

A tighter variation of the now familiar tissue is to make a smaller tile from the same image. Here I simply cropped to the center portion of the image; used the *offset* command again on the new, smaller image; blended the hard edges made by reoffsetting, and exported the whole shebang as a GIF.

The resulting tile is very similar to the previous one, but with a softer, tighter finish, as shown in Figure 14-10.

Figure 14-9:
The finished tile has a softer, more of a piece look than the original did.

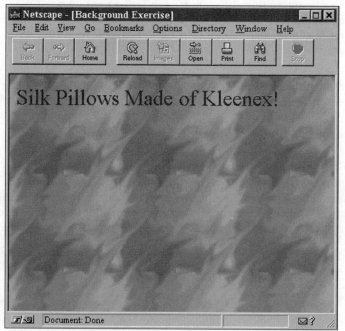

Figure 14-10:
Exactly the same, only different. Cropping to the center portion of the image, offsetting again, and then blending the results resulted in this tighter tile.

Applying the tiling procedure to your own images

The preceding steps and remembering a few simple rules will assure the success of your own tiles.

- ✔ Choose soft colors and pastels to avoid backgrounds that conflict with the type and images that your image will play background to.
- ✔ When blending between tiles in your image editor, remember to bring together as many common elements as possible to ensure the best join.

When you want to view changes in your HTML code in an Internet browser, remember to save the changes to your code before you look. The changes you've made aren't reflected until you've saved.

On the same line, an easy shortcut to seeing the changed file in the browser is to simply ask the browser to *Reload* in Netscape or *Refresh* in Explorer. This updates the screen to the most recently saved file without having to reload the file.

Connecting Images to Your Background

Sometimes, you want a graphic to float over the background. Maybe even cast a shadow on that background. It's an ever-so-casual look, when done properly, which really requires a lot of planning to make happen successfully. And though it needs to be properly thought out, it's really a very easy way to create an elegant look.

1. **In your image editor, create a simple tile.**

   For the one shown, I simply made a small square in Photoshop, filled it will a purple that was pleasant to my eye, and then used a texturizing filter to give it a simple sandstone finish and saved it as a TIFF, so I'd have it around for later steps.

2. **Sample a small square of the larger file and use the crop tool to create a small sample chip. Save this smaller piece as a GIF, as shown in Figure 14-11, to be your background tile.**

Figure 14-11:
A simple
background
image that
doesn't
show the
tiling HTML
gives it in
too obvious
a way. At the
back is the
larger TIFF
file. I used
that for later
steps. At the
front is the
tile that I
cropped out
of the larger
image and
saved as a
GIF. This
small one
is my
background
tile.

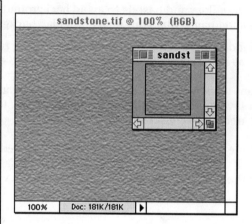

3. Using the BODY BACKGROUND tag in an HTML file produces a smooth, clean result with no visible edges, as shown in Figure 14-12.

4. Back in your image editor, open the larger TIFF file and lay some type or a graphic on it. That is, proceed as you normally would to create type, but using the background as your background, as shown in Figure 14-13.

5. This connection needn't be limited to type. You can connect any type of graphic to your HTML document using this technique, as shown in Figure 14-14.

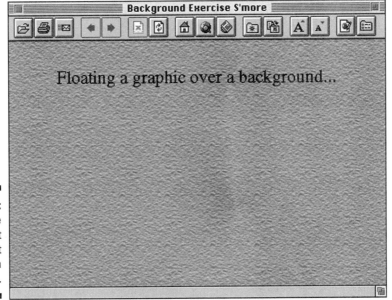

Figure 14-12:
The simple
tile doesn't
look tiled at
all in a
browser.

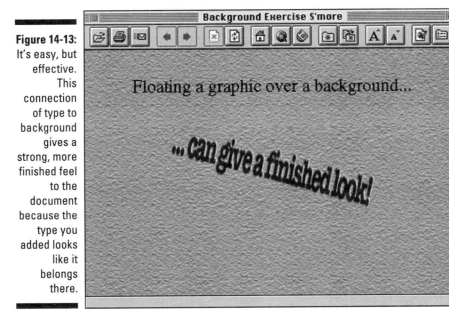

Figure 14-13:
It's easy, but
effective.
This
connection
of type to
background
gives a
strong, more
finished feel
to the
document
because the
type you
added looks
like it
belongs
there.

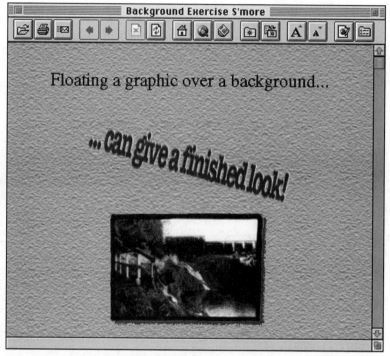

Figure 14-14:
Three
images to
make one
HTML file,
but the look
is very
finished and
smooth...
even for this
page that
doesn't say
much of
anything!

Background Check List

Here's a fast take on things to remember when creating background images:

✔ Don't dither. A dithered background looks particularly bad and should be avoided if you possibly can.

✔ Remember everyone. Make sure that the color choices you make look just as good (or almost so) on a low-end monitor with a cheap graphics card.

✔ Go for contrast. You really want to make sure that your text will read *over* the background, no matter what. This is why pastels and softer colors generally work better in backgrounds.

✔ Be redundant. When using the background tag in HTML, specify a background color as well. One that is complimentary to the background image is best. That's because the background color will show up with the file and Web visitors can be reading your text while waiting for the background image to show up. If the color of the text can't be read against the default gray background, you can lose some visitors.

✔ Go teeny. Make your background images as small as possible, especially when there are also other images on the page. A huge background file can slow the whole thing down unbearably.

✔ Use one background, many times. Using the same background throughout a Web site reduces the download time for Web visitors. That's because, as long as it's the same image file with the same name, the information is cached on the user's computer. Every time that background is encountered on that visit, it loads instantly.

Chapter 15

Crazy Color

● ●

In This Chapter

▶ Where to begin?

▶ How do computers see color on the Web?

▶ How are colors edited?

● ●

A few color issues stand out when looking at Web graphics. We need to look at these different angles carefully.

✔ Color from the aesthetic point. No rules here, but a few guides.

✔ Color from the technical point. You find rules here. The current Web palette limits our choices to colors that people can actually see, so it behooves us to know those colors and how to use them.

Both of these elements affect the way your graphics appear on the Web.

How Computers See Color on the Web

Four parameters define Web color:

✔ Monitor

Better quality monitors (read as more expensive) show better color. And, depending on the monitor, maybe even more colors.

✔ Video cards and boards

Here again, the better the stuff, the better the reproduction of colors.

✔ CPU

System performance dictates how much and how fast color details register.

✔ Web browser

216 colors are common to all graphical Web browsers. Each browser sees 256 colors, but only 216 are common to all major graphical Web browsers.

When a color is specified that the Web browser doesn't have, it will try to create that color by using its own palette. It'll use bits of this made-up color or colors to try and make up the colors it doesn't have. This is what is commonly known as "dithering."

While this sounds like — and can be — a good thing, sometimes the results aren't so great. In Figure 15-1, you can't see the subtle color shifts that have happened between the 256-color GIF on the left and the 8-color GIF on the right. What you can see is a slight unevenness of tone, especially in the region of her head and hair. Here, where there are a lot of different colors, the image has been dithered. While it's not problematic with this particular image, it is with other types of graphic.

Figure 15-1:
Dithering
can create
subtle color
shifts.

Controlling what you can

User hardware and software is out of your control, but the Web page palette isn't. Web graphics designers must keep tight control on their Web palettes to make sure that the subtleties of Web graphics can be seen by the largest number of people.

Remember the lowest common denominator. Even when your monitor sees millions of colors, many Web surfers can't. Limit your graphics to the 216 colors that everyone can see. You can use this color palette, saved as 216hexrgb.gif on the *Web Graphics For Dummies* CD-ROM, in a variety of ways. Each color chip incorporates both the HEX and RGB values so you can instantly reference the color, as shown in Figure 15-2.

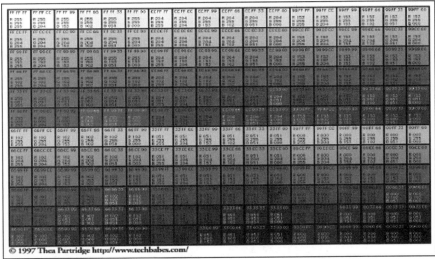

Figure 15-2:
The cross-platform, cross-browser color palette from the *Web Graphics For Dummies* CD-ROM.

Using the color palette

You can use the color palette to help create your Web graphics in a number of ways.

While creating the graphic

By importing the palette into a window in your image editor, you can use it on the spot to pick useable colors from the outset.

I like to have the palette in another open window in my image editor. It's inactive, behind my working window, with nothing really going on.

I use the eyedropper tool, as shown in Figure 15-3, to select the color I want from one of the palette's well-marked chips. I can then go ahead and use the selected color, knowing that it's one of the "safe" 216 cross-platform colors.

Like an interior designer

Having the color palette handy at all times lets you make use of it in the same way that interior designers use their color swatches. When you use the cross-platform colors as a springboard, you can't go far wrong.

In other words, let the palette inspire your creativity, not hinder it.

Figure 15-3:
By keeping
the color
palette in
an inactive
window on
your image
editor while
you work,
you can
use the
eyedropper
tool to
select
browser-
safe colors
while you
build your
image.

Like an architect

Use the color palette to help build the parameters of your Web site. For instance, it's a lot easier to look at one of the color chips and say: "I know, I'll make that background this lovely blue," and then type in the appropriate hex numbers, than it is to just keep on typing in hex numbers willy-nilly and then viewing them, hoping that the one you pick next is the right one.

In this way, you can much more easily specify background colors, as well as text and link colors because you know absolutely what they look like before you even begin. An added bonus: Because you see them together, you get a feel for which combinations work.

Working without a Net

I always think it's a good idea to know the basics, without any of the tools we develop to help us. In this context, the preceding color palette is certainly a tool. But what is it really made of?

aliceblue	F0F8FF
beige	F5F5DC
cadetblue	5F9EA0
crimson	DC1436
darkviolet	9400D3
gainsboro	DCDCDC
coral	FF7F50
dimgray	696969
gold	FFD700
linen	FAF0E6
orchid	DA70DG
seashell	FFF5EE

As you can see, many of these names aren't the least bit descriptive. And even the ones that may be really aren't. After all, coral can be a lot of colors. And so are seashells. And what color is gainsboro, anyway?

You can also see, between the dumb names and the confusing hex numbers, why lots of people look at alternatives to the traditional methods of Web color selection.

The difference between O and 0

Please remember that when you see a zero (0) in a hexadecimal number, it will always be a number, not the capital letter. You can be sure of this because the letter portions of this particular program only go up to F.

I wish it was always that simple!

Alternatives to Hex color

It's easy to see why so many designer types who get sick at the very first hint of math stuff have worked so hard to devise all sorts of alternate ways of dealing with hex color. I mean, the color part is fun. And the hex part pretty much isn't.

As we've seen, the color palette can handle this pretty neatly. You just point, click, and let an eyedropper tool select the right one for your work.

Hex color is also, I think, one of the reasons WYSIWYG HTML editors have become increasingly popular. There isn't one of these that handles code as efficiently as I can. And most of them add stuff I don't need. And sometimes, in frustration, I look at the code and get the page right by doing it quickly by hand.

And then there's color. The color portion of every WYSIWYG HTML editor I've ever worked with is just a delight, and the designer in me celebrated from first contact with the homey color wheel that let me do my selecting.

Using Color to Make Teenier Files

Almost every part of creating a Web graphic is about giving some of this to get some of that. It's a challenging game of give and take that feels really great when it comes together.

The give-and-take are about color, detail, and file size. Sometimes, you give up one to get another. Ideally, you balance everything to get something excellent.

Reducing a GIF file

It is possible to substantially reduce a file by using the color map and actually taking advantage of the reduced number of colors available. Using the minimum number of colors, you still produce a colorful graphic.

Let's look at all of this in action.

1. **Start with a color scan of a traditionally executed illustration.**

   Shown here in Photoshop format (though you're not working in Photoshop), the saved image is a very good representation of the original watercolor that hangs in my studio. The original wasn't huge (just 128K). The scan is in Figure 15-6.

Figure 15-6:
A good scan of a colored, non-photographic original.

2. **Working in DeBabelizer, choose Reduce the Colors from the Palette menu, as shown in Figure 15-7.**

   I asked for a target of 256 colors, just to get going. Also, I asked it to dither when remapping.

Fig
Th

Co
th

DeP

Fig
Th

col

re
DeP

3. **Undo the palette reduction and start again. Same image, same process. Again choose Reduce the Colors from the Palette menu.**

This time, take it a drastic jump down to 32 colors. The dithering is so dramatic it's yucky and certainly doesn't work for this image. It may for another image, so dithering shouldn't be ruled out for other different images. But for this one — to my eye — even though it's now down to 11K, you're still back to the drawing board. Figure 15-9 shows the results.

Figure 15-9:
The same process, with more colors out. This time, however, the dithering renders the result unacceptable.

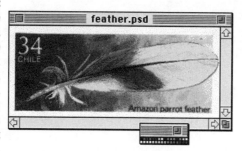

4. **Undo again and go from a different angle. This time, do things the easy way. Rather than messing with palettes at all, go straight to the file menu and choose Save As. You are given a dialog box, as shown in Figure 15-10. From the list of file types, choose GIF. For the number of colors choose 32 (5 bits) and select Save.**

Figure 15-10:
The Save As dialog box in DeBabelizer.

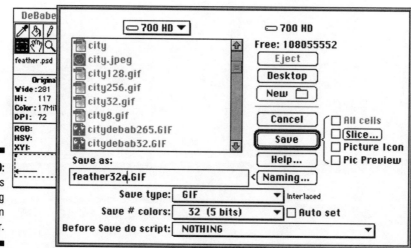

The resulting image is a slight improvement over the last, but the dithering is still pronounced and the file is bigger than the last at 22K.

5. **Back to the original Photoshop file. Still in DeBabelizer, choose Change Pixel Depth from the Palette menu, as shown in Figure 15-11. From the fly-out menu, choose 6 bits = 64 colors dithered.**

The file remaps quickly. Now you see a happy compromise (see Figure 15-12). At least, I did with this file. There is only a small amount of visible dithering, and this is concentrated in one area. To my eye, it's an acceptable amount. Most of the colors appear true, and the background looks really excellent, especially with a file that is now only 20K. This last permutation satisfies me on several fronts. The file appears acceptably true to the original and the file size is entirely acceptable. Which doesn't mean it can't be smaller. I always think it can — with further experimentation.

The preceding exercise was done in DeBabelizer. Doing it in a different image converter makes some of the commands slightly different, as well as some of the locations of various items and what they're called. What *remain* the same, from program to program, are the basics. It's always called remapping color, and dithering is always one of the options. You will, at some point, have the option of changing the depth of the pixel.

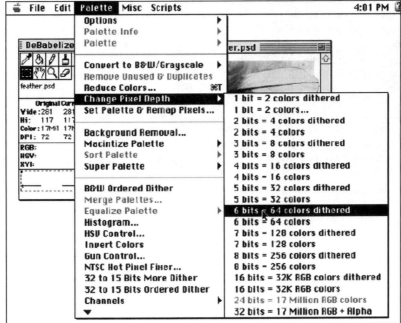

Figure 15-11: Choose Change Pixel Depth from the Palette menu.

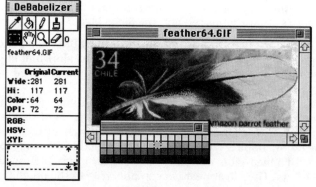

Figure 15-12:
Fourth time
a charm?
Not a rule,
but it
happens.

Don't be put off when the screens in your converter look different from the controls shown in this example. Although the results vary from program to program, the object of all of these converters is largely the same: to get you the best Web graphics possible.

Your Mileage Will Vary

And as I've said many times when talking about converting Web graphics, experimentation is key.

It's impossible to give absolute formulas that work every time for every image. This is because every graphic is different. Even graphics made in basically the same way require different color palettes and thus yield different results.

Another factor, of course, is the way your own hardware is configured and what software you use. Don't be afraid to try different things in order to see what works. After a while you get a taste for the winning combinations in your own work and will get to the great ones that much quicker.

Don't forget, all of these things make a workable Web graphic. Sometimes it's okay to settle for one that looks great but can be smaller. You can refine it after the page is in place.

Chapter 16

WYSIWOG = What You See Isn't (Always!) What Others Get

In This Chapter

▶ What do people see when they look at your images?

▶ Variables in online image viewing

▶ How platform affects image

▶ How monitor size and quality affects image

▶ How viewing software online affects image

▶ How to minimize the differences in online viewing

▶ How to check your work for multiple browsers

▶ Gamma correction

So you slave and sweat over the perfect Web graphics and — perhaps — the perfect Web site. You toil in your image editor to create zap bang graphics that you just *know that* everyone is going to love. They're beautiful and you feel they're the very best that you can do. And you're at your friend's house, and you ask her to load your Web page while you're there. And as you watch them load you feel your heart — so recently alight with pride — sink somewhere into the region of your boots. Because your beautiful, perfect pages and your lovingly created graphics all look like doo doo on your friend's system.

Seeing as They See

What do other people see when they visit your Web site? Always remember:

> ✔ Just because something looks great on your system doesn't mean it will look great anywhere else.
>
> ✔ When something looks great on your system, you can be sure that someone has their system configured in such a way that it is guaranteed to make your pages look yucky. It will almost seem like an evil plot.

Of course, it isn't an evil plot. It is, however, one of the hazards and sureties of designing for this medium. Computers bring variables. It's one of the things that computers all share: their differences. And even systems that *look* exactly the same on the outside may have really different pieces on the inside: pieces that will make your Web pages appear different from the way you conceived them.

How surfers see you

Some of these factors affect the way a surfer will see your images.

Platforms

No matter that our universe is rapidly moving to a cross-platform reality. In the now, many programs *work* the same way on a Mac and a PC — they'll use the same commands to access the same functions. However, intrinsic hardware differences guarantee surfers on different platforms see things differently. Period.

Monitor size and quality

Too many designers work on huge high-res monitors and then wonder why the average surfer sees something entirely different. In a perfect world, designers would be forced to work on systems of the same quality as the people who view the site. Or worse. Just to keep them designing with real people in mind. Meanwhile, many mortals suffer when viewing pages designed by Olympian Web designers.

Software

Netscape looks different than Mosaic than Cyberdog than Internet Explorer, and so on, *ad nauseum*. Even on the same computer with the same bits and pieces, each browser looks differently at the world.

Minimizing the differences

But wait! Before you go off in despair, all is not lost. All of this is really about realizing the differences and working within those parameters.

Monitors

If we already know that most of the browsing world surfs on a monitor somewhere under 15 inches, it behooves us as designers to have at least one 13- or 14-inch monitor somewhere on our system, if only to check our work after it's done.

The moral of the story? Check your work on various sizes and qualities of monitors.

Software

Don't fight the system. Accept it. Netscape, Microsoft, and everyone else refuse to make just one browser. Some would argue it would be like having only one flavor of ice cream. I say that each is trying to hold onto some silly, invisible edge. Whatever the case, you and I aren't going to change them. What we have to do is discover how to work with them. By checking your work on popular browsers, you'll make sure that your page looks good everywhere.

Fonts

The newest generation of browsers let the designer spec a limited number of fonts in HTML, which is very cool and opens some design opportunities that didn't exist before. However, it's fact that most surfers don't use the latest browser versions. Ever. So when you use these HTML fonts in your designs, make sure that you know exactly what it looks like with non-font supporting browsers.

Another thought on fonts. It is fact that font sizes specified in HTML on the Mac will appear bigger on the PC. This is a simple fact. So something that looks bold and elegant on a Mac can look childish and overdone on a PC. Another case for looking through more than one Window when you design in HTML.

Checking your work in multiple browsers

Looking at your work in more than one kind of browser is simple. First, you need to have at least two distinct types of browsers loaded on your computer; more if you have the space. At present, I have four. But you should at least have the most popular two: Netscape Navigator and Microsoft Internet Explorer.

With one of the browsers open to a browsing window, from the File menu choose Open File (Netscape) or Open (Explorer) and then navigate your way to the file you'd like to look at, as seen in Figure 16-1.

Figure 16-1:
In
Netscape,
select Open
File from
the File
menu. In
Microsoft
Internet
Explorer,
select Open
from the
same place.
All Internet
browsers
let you peek
at local files
in a similar
manner.

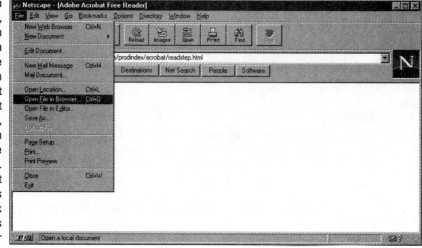

We'd all be a whole lot happier if everyone agreed on one Web browser. Which, of course, isn't going to happen. Even more than the differences in browsers, the fact that people choose different computers is pretty much out of our hands. The best course of action is just to accept the differences and work with them.

The fact that our work is being viewed on different platforms means it is seen differently by different people in different places. The only thing we can really do about it is try to make sure that it doesn't look *bad* on any of those systems.

Gamma Correction

I've talked enough about gamma correction in other parts of this book that I don't want to make your brain sweat with it all over again. Because it is brainsweaty stuff. If you missed that part, truck on back to the index and see where it is. Or if you just want a memory jog, here's the short 'n' sweet version.

gamma setting, so you can see what an image looks like on a PC. To set it back, simply do the same thing: Shift, Command and 9, and you return to your Mac's normal gamma.

The price of GammaToggle FKEY is pretty reasonable. Some call it freeware, but actually it is, says Gustafsson, ThankYouWare. In the Read Me file that Gustafsson includes with the software there is this note: "If you find it useful, all you have to do is say 'thank you.'"

So, "thank you," Roland! It's a great deal at twice the price!

In this part . . .

Lots of Web stuff is visual, and in the dinosaur days, that was good enough. Today's Web, however, is in constant multimedia motion, so it's good to know about these aspects.

There's no rule that says you *must* have audio on your Web site. Or that you *must* design for WebTV. However, it's certainly good to know where to start if you want to or have to. So here's where to start when *you* start making Web graphics sing and dance.

A

Figure 17-1:
I want my
WebTV!
Right now
the part of
WebTV that
most
everyone
can
experience
is the very
sexy Web
site at
http://www.
webTV.com.

But what *is* WebTV?

Boiled down, WebTV, as served up by the good folks at WebTV Networks, Inc., is a television-based online service. How you get it, as a consumer, is through a specially designed set-top box that becomes your — sort of — direct link to the Internet. Sort of.

Unlike lots of Internet schemes that include televisions, WebTV doesn't make use of coaxial cable as installed by the cable company. Instead, the WebTV stuff is piped in your good ol' television via a customized modem and your good ol' phone line. It's one of those plans so simple, you wonder why you didn't think of it.

What does this all mean to the designer?

The good folks at WebTV say that 95 million American homes can access WebTV. While that doesn't mean that all of those 95 million will sign up, it *does* mean that WebTV will be in lots of homes. There are no test areas, as in days gone by. And it means a whole new breed of people can see your stuff.

For instance, at present, it's reasonably okay to surmise a certain level of technological literacy when designing for the Web. Surfers must set up those beasts on their desks and then configure their Internet connection. With the potential hordes of WebTV users in the picture, this isn't true. It's as easy to connect WebTV as a cable box.

Monitors aren't televisions

Computer monitors are different from televisions. So what looks right on a computer monitor can be illegible on a television.

Big, bold graphics

Small type and lines aren't the only things likely to get lost to some WebTV viewers. Your graphics need to be big, bold, and punchy for full impact. As well, text in or over images — as in some image maps — needs to be carefully rethought.

And while bigger is better, for WebTV, actual file size is still a consideration. The specifications for the WebTV hardware call for a special 33.6 Kbps V.34bis modem. And it's special in the way it handles the phone, but not because of its speed. If anything, WebTV pages need to load *faster* than computer pages. Television viewers aren't used to waiting with their hands in their pockets.

Terminal realities

One of the things that WebTV happily forces away is the rule that all viewers view things differently. On WebTV, they don't. As shown in Figure 17-2, the WebTV terminal is a fixed size, 544 pixels by 378 pixels, which is only about 7.5 x 5.25 inches. In addition, the screen may be caused to scroll vertically but not horizontally. Also, a fixed title bar shows where on the Web someone is.

This means a radical rethinking of the way some designers work. In a world where no one can scroll off the screen to the left or right, all the salient information must fit within those limits. As designers, that means going back where we came from.

In many ways designing for WebTV demands all of the Web skills you're discovering now, only more of the same. Tighter, quicker, stronger.

544 Pixel Horizontal Width

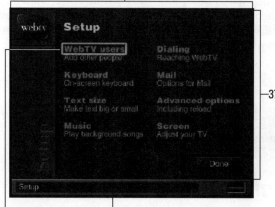

370 Pixel Vertical Height

Figure 17-2:
The WebTV
interface.

Title Bar - Displays the title of the current web page along with other useful information

Highlight the selected link

Inside Designing for WebTV

There is already a WebTV developers Style Guide at the WebTV site at
`http://webtv.net/primetime/`.

PDF and other versions of the WebTV Style Guide can be downloaded. On
the same site, Web designers can join a sort of developers club that entitles
them to several privileges, including the WebTV simulator, as shown in
Figure 17-3. It isn't cheap, but there's a T-shirt included somewhere.

Designing for WebTV

Though there is lots of information about designing for WebTV straight at
the source, here are a few points worth noting:

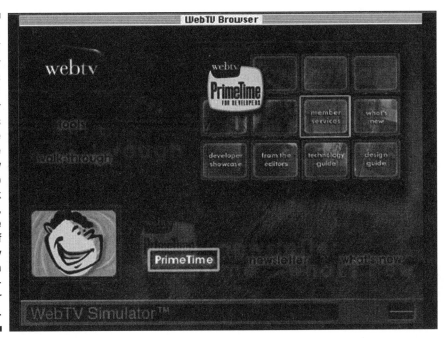

Monitors

Your computer monitor dispenses information differently than a television set. Televisions aren't ideal for small text, fine lines, or intricate graphics. When in doubt, go bold.

Download time

Being TV doesn't make it fast. You still need to make your graphics small so they download without overloading your pages with extraneous stuff.

Fixed terminal size

WebTV is viewed in an area about $7^1/_2$ x $5^1/_4$ inches, regardless of the size of the television it's viewed on. Also, the WebTV terminal doesn't allow for side-to-side scrolling. Web pages ideal for WebTV must be executed with pockets of that size in mind.

Color

All red or all white backgrounds should be avoided because they cause a bending effect. I hate this one, because I really like the look of an all-white background on my Web pages!

Image maps

Client-side image maps respond better to input from the remote control than server-side image maps. This is happy news, because client-side image maps are easier!

Limited stuff

Television audiences are used to looking at one focal point on their screen. Because of this, it may be a good idea to reduce the amount of overall *stuff* on your Web page to avoid confusion and oversaturation.

Forms

Avoid them. Too many form elements can be confusing to a user without a computer and keyboard in front of them.

Chapter 18

Sites and Sounds

In This Chapter

▶ How do your graphics sound?

▶ What is Web sound good for?

▶ When do I use sound?

*O*kay, so we're talking about Web graphics. Just what the heck does audio have to do with that?

Hear the Graphics?

Sometimes, it seems, the way things look just isn't enough. And, really, in an environment where it's cheap and easy to add sound to your Web page, maybe it isn't such a bad idea. Maybe.

For our home audience

If you're thinking that your pages may be of interest to WebTV viewers, sound can be a good thing, as well. Television viewers are, after all, used to hearing some type of soundtrack while they watch. Is a soundtrack for your Web page something you want to think about?

Physical limitations

In the strictest sense of the thing, it is possible to link a Web page to just about anything: not just other Web pages or graphics. The real limitation, of course, is not so much "What can I link to?" as it is, "Will anyone be able to hear (or see!) it when they get there?"

In terms of audio, then, it's important to do a bit of exploration before you commit to including it on a Web site.

Ask yourself these questions:

✔ How will I benefit from having audio on my Web site?

✔ Who will benefit from my having audio on my Web site?

✔ What are the most popular audio readers for the Web?

The first two questions can be answered in a bit of self-talk and can make the third question moot.

If you do get to question three, however, make sure that you're using the very latest of the newest technologies. At present, there are still lots of experiments with sound technology on the Web and we're not sure what is the best because this stuff changes almost weekly.

Curves Ahead

Sending sound on the Internet is still in its infancy. Even the stuff that is deemed to be good is not as stable or high quality as it can be. I expect that this will level out in the near future. Keep your eyes on the road as you progress through adding sounds to your Web pages. The best is yet to come.

What has taken so long?

Why is audio technology apparently so far behind various visual technologies on the Web?

We all know that the Web is pretty much a Johnny-come-lately in the technological world, so everything about it evolves while we all contribute to growing the World Wide Web.

While it grows, however, it's easy to see that some aspects are more natural than others. The Web was intended to transmit text and pictures, so visuals have seen the biggest leaps and can now enjoy the largest breakthroughs.

But it just happened that the Web sort of *erupted* in the era of multimedia. It was easy to see that the Web *could* be made to transmit sound and video bytes. Next — and we're still working on that particular next — it had to be convinced to do it elegantly.

Where is sound useful?

Certain situations make sound on a Web site especially useful, and some companies use their Web sites for sound-related activities. Indie record producers, for example, are making incredible inroads by including sound on their Web pages, which increases their potential audience in ways that weren't possible a few years ago, as shown in Figure 18-1.

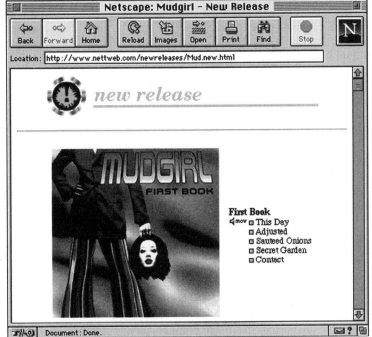

Figure 18-1: Independent record producers benefit from audio on their Web sites.

Who uses sound?

In these three cases, there's no other way that these companies can get the exposure and connectivity they enjoy on the Web:

- ✔ The music industry

  Record companies and others who would like to reach the largest number of people at the lowest possible cost.

- ✔ Software companies

  Especially those who sell games with startling audio effects. It's a cool thing to be able to demo how that exploding demon actually sounds.

✔ Radio stations

Live radio shows are increasingly common on the Web.

Background Sounds

The reality of adding sound to a Web page is much easier than whether it's a good thing and — provided it is — where to get the sounds.

You add a background sound to a Web page in much the same way you do a background image. And, really — when you think about it — is it that much different?

Well, it is, simply because the background sound tag isn't an HTML thang. Because of this, both Microsoft Internet Explorer and Netscape Navigator have come up with their own proprietary tags to make background sounds possible. The problem is, they came up with *different* proprietary tags. That means that when you want to include a background sound that most everyone can hear, you have to sort of double tag them. Let's look at them separately and then together.

Here's how you create a background sound in HTML that is readable in Internet Explorer.

1. **Start a file in the same way you would any other: by specifying codes for HTML and head.**

   ```
   <HTML>
   <HEAD>
   <TITLE>Background Sound</TITLE>
   </HEAD>
   ```

   Here I specified a white background — because I like them, but also so you can see how similar it is to the background sound tag.

   ```
   <BODY BGCOLOR="#FFFFFF">
   ```

2. **Now the background sound stuff. The LOOP tag tells it how often the browser should play the sound file, in this case a .wav.**

   With this particular setup, Explorer plays the sound five times and stops. I can make this number as big or small as I want. And if I want it to play endlessly, I can specify LOOP="infinite."

   ```
   <BGSOUND SRC="kitty.wav" LOOP="5">
   ```

The background sound tag can go either in the head, or after it. I prefer this configuration as it's a nice logical place right after the background color. Explorer doesn't seem to react differently either way.

3. **Now add some gratuitous stuff, just to make a for-real file with something in it.**

If nothing else, this gives you a real feel for where it all falls.

```
<H1><CENTER>A Background Sound Can Add an Interesting
           Texture to a Web Page</CENTER></H1>
</BODY>
</HTML>
```

Netscape Doesn't Freak on This Tag

Which is a good thing to know. Netscape Navigator doesn't balk when it hits one of Explorer's proprietary background sound tags. In fact, it doesn't even blink or shuffle its feet. It just keeps surfing blithely along. In fact, when you navigate on Navigator, you don't even feel the bump. Which is better than the crash you get with some browsers when you hit something they don't know about.

A background sound for both Internet Explorer and Navigator will play

We really only went through building a file around an Explorer-friendly sound so that you can see the break-off, the place where Internet Explorer and Navigator differ on this matter.

Navigator's code is a little more demanding than Internet Explorer's. Sheesh! Don't these guys talk about anything?

Now let's look at building a file with a background sound that both can hear.

1. **Open HTML in the usual way, leaving the background color from the last exercise.**

In fact, except for the few lines that pertain to Navigator, this code is entirely the same.

```
<HTML>
<HEAD>
<TITLE>Background Sound</TITLE>
</HEAD>
<BODY BGCOLOR="#FFFFFF">
```

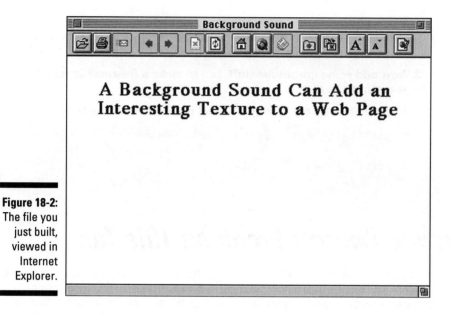

A Background Sound Can Add an Interesting Texture to a Web Page

Figure 18-2:
The file you just built, viewed in Internet Explorer.

2. **Here's the Navigator stuff, just in advance of the Explorer stuff you already looked at. Navigator likes the sound to be embedded. Thus, do it as follows.**

```
<EMBED SRC=kitty.wav" HEIGHT="1" WIDTH="1"
        AUTOSTART="true" HIDDEN="true">
<NOEMBED>
```

Set the height and width to one inch to make sure that the embedded sound takes up no visible space on the page. AUTOSTART starts the .wav file automatically, while HIDDEN="true" makes the LiveAudio control panel hidden from the surfer. The NOEMBED tag helps the browser choose an approach.

3. **Now the tag for Explorer:**

```
<BGSOUND SRC="kitty.wav">
```

4. **Now the whole EMBED deal is turned off with the /NOEMBED tag.**

```
</NOEMBED>
```

5. **Finish by adding the message and the end tags.**

```
<H1><CENTER>A Background Sound Can Add an Interesting
        Texture to a Web Page</CENTER></H1>
</BODY>
</HTML>
```

Finding Sounds

It's one thing to think about adding sounds to your Web pages and making them compliment your graphics, but where do you get the sounds to do this with?

In this Web graphics book, I don't go into this aspect in much detail, but a few pointers will help you get the sounds for your Web pages:

✔ Simple input device

Many multimedia computers have a simple microphone that lets you input sounds and then save them as one of the Web appropriate sound formats. This can be fun for simple voice exclamations and other short sounds.

✔ Making music

Musicians have given thought to this aspect. You can create your own music using computer software or a synthesizer. This can be fun for background music: your own composition!

✔ From CD

You can buy CDs of royalty-free music and sounds. Be careful here, though. Read the fine print properly. You don't want to put stuff on your Web site that can be someone else's property.

✔ The Internet

Many Web sites include audio clips of all sorts for you to download. Be careful, though. Before you put anything on your Web site, make sure that it's free of copyright so you aren't sued for using it!

Sometimes you don't want the sound to run in the background of your Web page. Sometimes, like a big graphic that people should be able to grab at will, you want to create a link to a sound file stored somewhere on your server.

In this case, the sound is handled with an HREF tag, like any internal link.

```
<A HREF="kitty.wav">
```

RealAudio

RealAudio is cool but out of the reach of many. To include RealAudio sounds on your Web site, your site has to be on a RealAudio server. Your visitors can hear your sounds with RealAudio Player software, as shown in Figure 18-3.

Chapter 19
The Day after Tomorrow

*F*uturizing is a risky business at the best of times. Even when you're talking about comparatively static technologies like the auto industry or the fall television lineup, there's a risk in opening your big mouth about what will be.

When discussing Internet-related technologies, however, the risk is multiplied by a factor of about a zillion. It just moves so darned fast.

This preamble is my convoluted way of letting you know that *I* know just how far out I'm sticking my neck on this one. The possibility of being wrong looms. However, the possibilities in general are just too tantalizing.

Here's my neck.

Information Appliances

It seems likely that household information appliances will change the way large companies approach their "Web campaigns." That is, in a society increasingly in love with Internet technologies, an inexpensive plug-and-play Internet computing device seems entirely likely. And it will probably provide some type of access to WebTV.

If, within the next five years, an Internet machine becomes as easy and accessible in your home as a television, then, well, it happens. And whether "the masses" have access to the Web — as is already happening — then the Web itself changes to reflect the people using it.

More people online means more traffic. It also means that the elitist crust of early users gets worn even more thinly. A few years ago, Internet users were hard-core geeks and ivory-tower academics. And they knew their way around. An increasing flow of new users means larger numbers, but it also means that a good percentage of these newbies can't negotiate a "back" button, let alone a complicated image map or a convoluted frameset.

As designers, then, it behooves us to continue to build logically flowing sites filled with graphics that make negotiating more easy.

Stuff That Looks Like It Did Before

This trend has already begun with technologies like Cascading Style Sheets and a continued interest in PDF. One of the continued restraints of designing with — heck! even *dealing* with — the World Wide Web is the fact that every piece of software interprets all your careful code (and to a certain degree, your graphics) in an entirely different way. This is frustrating for the designer, but it's just as maddening for the user who never *really* gets to see things the way the artist (that's you!) intended.

The powers-that-be know that this limitation exists, but what do they do about it? The fact remains, HTML and the Web were designed by and for physics geeks to share academic information and pictures. If the Web had been designed by advertising and television executives it would look quite different.

We've got what we've got, though. But what we've got is in constant flux. HTML 1.0 was a shadow of the present version of HTML, and each new version offers progressively more control to the designer. To keep track of these changes, check in periodically at http://www.w3.org/pub/WWW, which is where all such official notices originate.

In truth, the way to really make change happen would be to scrap the whole thing and start again with a system — both of code and graphics — that was truly designed to do what we are doing with it. The fact is, though, that scrapping and starting over isn't an option. So we keep hacking at the stuff we've got and hoping for the best.

I guess this one isn't a huge risk to me at all. Predicting change on the World Wide Web is like predicting that Popeye will eat more spinach. And then what happened?

Designers of Web graphics have to pay extra-special close attention to these innovations that will change the way our audience sees us. Cascading Style sheets will, I think, provide a lot of the answers after it's gained wider browser and user acceptance, so perk your ears when you hear anything about both it and other changes to HTML that affect how pages look.

The Automated Browser

There is growing demand (not by me!) for an Internet browser that is sent out all on its own; goes out, surfs, and brings stuff back for you to look at when you get a chance. Like a superduper Gopher on steroids.

Personally, the idea doesn't do much for me. Browsing without surfing would be sort of like swimming without getting wet. It can be fun, but it ain't swimming.

However, software companies are already responding to the perceived demand. Products like Lotus' Weblicator let people work with online material while they're no longer connected. The upside is no pesky connections and slow downloads to have to worry about, because everything is in the can. The downside is, there's no sense in falling off the 'Net in excitement because everything is in the can.

If surfers spend more time looking at our stuff offline, it behooves us to make sure that it's easy to figure out where they got it. It's not a bad idea, for instance, to try to squeak the page's URL, or at least the Webmaster's e-mail address, onto every single HTML page you do. That way, if someone prints your site and then moves on, they can reference where they got it.

Cyberspace Rip-Offs

This isn't exactly futurizing, either. It's one of those logical leaps that takes us smack dab into the middle of a conundrum. Artistic copyright has always been fiercely protected and jealously guarded, and all of this long before it was possible for every surfer and his Aunt Meg to siphon your good graphics directly from your computer to their computer. Heck! More than that, it's actually *impossible* for a browser to look at your stuff without moving it to their computer. That is, in fact, how the whole thing works.

Some unscrupulous people deliberately kife other people's work for their own gain. More often, the theft is unintentional, or at least innocent — people who honestly think that it isn't bad to use or borrow other people's work from the Web.

It's not okay to use other people's images on your Web site (or any place else, for that matter). It's also not okay to use someone else's images as part of something else, or to somehow manipulate someone else's copyrighted work into something even only partly recognizable.

Is an image copyrighted?

When you find an image you like on the Web and it doesn't say "royalty free, use at will" or words to that effect, then it's not okay to use it. Modern copyright laws are pretty universal about this sort of thing, regardless of the usage. The creator of the work is the copyright holder. Period. And it's not a very difficult thing to prove who the image's creator is. When you admire the work and would really like to use it, it's usually a pretty easy matter to contact the creator via e-mail. Whether they let you use it and for what fee is between you and them. Sometimes, creative people are so pleased that someone enjoys their work that they give permission to use it, provided you give them credit or provide a link to their page.

What about its source?

Borrowing or somehow manipulating the source code for someone else's home page is another matter entirely. Since the early days of the Web it's been a fairly accepted practice to save a page you like and would like to emulate as "source" from your browser.

How this is done is by choosing Save As from your Internet browser's active window, and choosing "source code" when given a choice between that and text.

You can then open the source code in your HTML editor or a word processor and borrow some of those good ideas to morph that page into something original.

Borrow is the salient word here, though. A few of my pages have been outright stolen in a really unpleasant way. A while ago I started receiving really strange e-mail from people I'd never heard of asking about their orders. I've never been involved in a mail-order business or anything involving delivery of orders.

I did an AltaVista search on my e-mail address and discovered the reason for the funny mail: Some noncreative person had "borrowed" the source code from one of my guest book pages. They didn't bother to change anything, including my e-mail address. They even stole my background image.

Fortunately for them, I was more amused than chagrined. I sent the company an e-mail that read something like, "Imitation is the highest form of flattery, but this is ridiculous."

There's a lesson in this

It can be very interesting to look at the source code of someone else's Web pages. It's possible to find a lot that way; to understand how the "wow!" gets put into a lot of pages. Sometimes, it's surprisingly simple. However, just taking stuff and not recreating it as your own is just theft. It can be hard to back a law suit against someone who does it, but it's still morally wrong. It's also so lacking in creativity as to be ridiculous, which leads me to a couple of points.

Previously created graphics are easy for their creators to identify. So be careful.

- ✔ Allow yourself to be inspired by others' artwork. Sometimes it's not as necessary to reinvent the wheel as we think.

- ✔ But don't borrow, steal, or otherwise take anyone else's artwork, ever. At least not without permission. This is not only morally and creatively wrong, it's also real easy to prove in court. Avoid stealing by not stealing.

HTML code is a little different from original artwork, but code is still subject to the principles of copyright. So respect the codewright's original work.

- ✔ Look at other people's source code in HTML to see how HTML works.

- ✔ But don't take anyone's HTML source code and whack it right into your own Web site. It's not only wrong, it can have embarrassing consequences (such as linking your site directly to the source of the code).

Part V
The Part of Tens

The 5th Wave — By Rich Tennant

"It says,' Seth- Please see us about your idea to wrap newsletter text around company logo. Production.'"

In this part . . .

Talk show hosts do it, teachers do it, even the evening news sometimes does it. We live in a society that loves lists.

I love lists as much as the next person, so I've made a few of my own. And I wrote this book, so I'm going to share them with you. Lists about Web graphics software and hardware, lists about solving problems and looking to the future.

I can rest now. I've made my lists. And it was good.

Chapter 20

Ten Technologies to Watch

*W*hen you signed up for this Internet thing, you knew you were going to have to stay on the edge of your seat if you didn't want to fall off. But did you understand how fast everything you knew would be ancient history?

Okay, that's an exaggeration. Things don't move quite that quickly, even on the Internet. But keep in touch with hot, new ideas over the horizon. If it's impossibly hot today, it may be common next month.

How Hot Is Hot?

With a little practice, you get a knack for separating the great ideas from the duds. Tomorrow's hot ideas solve today's problems. So we'll look at the hottest of the hot.

A lot of the hot new stuff in this section will lead you to a page or several pages somewhere on the World Wide Web Consortium's (W3C) Web site. The W3C is hosted by the Laboratory for Computer Science at MIT. These folks know their stuff.

If you want to visit the W3C's site directly, it's at `http://www.w3.org/pub/WWW/`.

Languages

Web designers and users need powerful languages that carry ideas to computers of every system and size. Keep an eye on developments of these languages and formats:

Java

Java has been around nearly as long as the Web itself, so maybe it isn't new technology, even if it is only a few years old.

On the other hand, Java technology is both accessible and understandable by a large portion of the Web community and — more importantly — actually does some useful stuff.

I'm not going to go into a long discussion on Java here. I've done it a bit elsewhere in this book and there are about a million books devoted to the subject. Java will continue to be hot, as will Java derivatives. But I think that, at this moment, Java isn't as hot as it will be. The time when Java does really good and useful things has yet to come — and it will.

Dynamic HTML

I saw an ad on my local cable station the other night promising that some boring-looking guy's show is interactive. Maybe he takes live calls?

I'm not implying that Dynamic HTML is boring, but calling it dynamic may be stretching the point. (Who says software developers need dictionaries, anyway?)

If the name is slightly misleading, the implementation is more so. There is not one, but *two* versions called Dynamic HTML. Netscape has one and Microsoft (you guessed?) has the other. Don't worry. There's been a lot of cross-platform collaboration in Dynamic HTML. What runs on one version runs on the other. Hurray! This says bright things for the future. Check these Web addresses for the latest:

```
http://www.microsoft.com/workshop/author/dhtml/

http://home.netscape.com/comprod/products/communicator
           features/Dynamic_HTML.html
```

VRML

Virtual Reality Modeling language is fun. It's also — after a long time coming — finally pretty hot. Hot enough that companies developing 3-D-type software are adding support for the technology as a matter of course. This development makes getting into VRML a whole lot easier. (Which is good. As I said, VRML is fun!)

There's more about VRML in greater detail in Chapter 10, but — for a quick recap — VRML is a set of standards for displaying 3-D virtual worlds on the Web. If the very thought of that doesn't make the back of your mouth dry, you haven't read as much sci-fi as I have!

VRML is pronounced "ver-mil," which I think gives it a sort of friendly, happy sound. It's something like a 3-D, graphical analog of HTML: a universal file format.

Like a lot of what is hot and new, the best of VRML is still to come. The standards (again, like HTML) are still evolving and its uses are still being discovered.

There are lots of places to look if you want to spend some time exploring VRML. Silicon Graphics maintains a strong interest in VRML. Check out their relevant site at `http://vrml.sgi.com`. A Yahoo search on the topic will also bring up screens and screens of the latest news in VRML.

PDF

PDF (Portable Document Format) has been durable enough and dynamic enough to stick around for a while. Recent developments make it more attractive than it's ever been. (There's more on it in Chapter 10.)

PDF gives you final control of the way your document will look when downloaded. You create documents in virtually any conventional page-layout program, such as QuarkXPress or Microsoft Word. Adobe Acrobat changes the output from your page-layout program to PDF format. Finished PDF files are added to your Web page; surfers download them and read them. What they see there is exactly the document you planned; all your fonts, graphics, and drop caps are exactly where you want them.

What's good about this is also what's bad. Detail means big files. That's a Bad Thing on the Web. Lots of people are too busy to read more than the front page of the newspaper. You're pushing your luck if you expect them to sit and wait so you can show off your typesetting skills.

All that has saved PDF from an ignominious end is the power of Adobe. Some months, I can't turn around without receiving yet another version of the Acrobat reader. In fact, there's a copy on the *Web Graphics For Dummies* CD-ROM, and there's an Acrobat reader in both Internet Explorer 4.0 and Netscape Communicator. So many copies of Acrobat in circulation means somebody, somewhere may read your file if they have the patience.

Cougar

If you're interested in HTML or you work with Web graphics, keep an ear to the ground for Project Cougar.

Cougar is the code name of the next version of HTML. It's being developed by the W3C HTML Working Group, which includes R&D minds from Adobe, Hewlett Packard, IBM, Microsoft, Netscape, Sun, and others.

Cougar is still very much a work-in-progress, but the work thus far looks interesting. Updates to HTML will make beautiful possible, if not easier to make.

Check out the W3C Web site at `http://www.w3.org/pub/WWW/` and follow the links to Project: Cougar for more detailed information.

Frontier

When I first saw Frontier four years ago, it was so advanced there weren't many uses. Apple aficionados will remember seeing it several years ago, booting it, and saying, "Oh. Cool." And then trundling off to more useful pastures. At the time there just wasn't a lot of use for an object-oriented scripting language. At least not for you and me.

Then the Web happened. And the world, it seems, caught up with Frontier. Or would, perhaps, if it stood still long enough for anyone to catch up with it.

An Apple thang for many years, the recent port to the Windows environment will bring many more users to Frontier. With those users will come an infusion of interest and more hands doing more stuff with Frontier and sharing their knowledge.

Essentially, Frontier is an automated Web site development tool. It will mostly be of interest to people responsible for managing mega-sites because it's technical enough to make even fairly accomplished geeks cross their eyes. Anyway, the management power that Frontier brings is pretty much wasted on smaller sites. Especially considering the learning curve.

However, learning curves have a way of getting shortened in the Internet environment once software developers jump in and start building tools to shorten it. And with the Windows port complete, I anticipate that that is just what will happen.

Meanwhile, check out the Web site at `http://www.scripting.com/frontier/` to learn more about Frontier. (Figure 20-1 illustrates the Web site.)

Technology on the March

There's more to Web mastery than flashy features. As the Web community grows, we can expect more needs to be addressed by software innovators and giants.

Site management tools

While site management tools aren't a totally new idea, packages that make it happen are still evolving. The best are still to come.

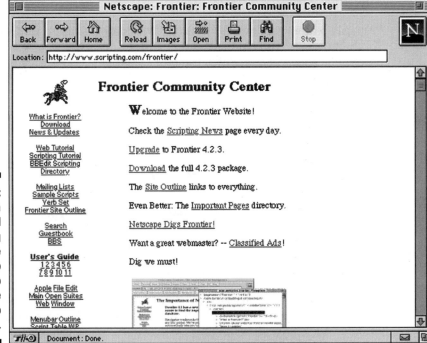

Figure 20-1: Frontier is a powerful scripting language intended to help manage mega-Web sites.

What's imperfect about the tools now, may well have little to do with the tools themselves, but rather with the way the whole thing is approached. Webmasters with rapidly growing sites understand the need for an electronic assistant.

For a six page Web site, management isn't an issue. A change that affects every single page can be made by hand. Large sites — a few hundred pages — can be halted by broken links if Webmasters aren't careful. How can something change — such as a corporate logo or the day and date — on every page without opening every file and changing things by hand?

Changes to the site aren't the only thing that will be expedited by Webmastering software. In the future, the best packages will guide Webmasters through every step of the process from start to finish. While today's management packages try to do everything Webmasters need, the technology is still very much developing.

Amaya

Amaya is also known as "the testbed client" to the W3C who is nurturing her. (And with a name like "Amaya" I find it difficult not to speak of the project in the feminine. Go figure.) Amaya is a Web client that acts as both a Web authoring tool and a browser.

Amaya's features include WYSIWYG HTML editing, support for Cascading Style Sheets, and full implementation of HTML. At present, you can't even download a beta unless you're running a UNIX box. However, a Windows version is expected (maybe by the time you read this!). There's no word — unfortunately — on the Mac port.

If you want more information on Amaya, see the newest entry in the browser wars for yourself on the Web at `http://www.w3.org/pub/WWW/Amaya`.

Cascading Style Sheets

This is a hot, hot one from our perspective as Web designers.

Cascading Style Sheets (CSS) finally control design elements we designers haven't controlled in HTML. Like style sheets in such traditional desktop applications as QuarkXPress and Word, cascading style sheets define fonts, line spacing, type color, and indentation. And you can redefine the look of every document that shares style sheets with one change. Anyone who has ever edited several hundred HTML documents to change a simple piece of stupid code appreciates the time savings from centralized changes.

As with so many hot, new things, support for CSS is not yet universal. Signs are positive and just about everyone who talks about these things is talking about CSS. Today, both Internet Explorer 4.0 and Netscape Communicator support CSS. Some of the HTML editing programs I talk about in this book support them as well. Others are likely to follow.

To show how quickly this stuff moves, work on CSS began at CERN in 1994. In December, 1996 it became a W3C recommendation. And now here we are, and acceptance is practically universal.

For now, I wouldn't rush out and add CSS to my skill set, but it's worth understanding. The W3C Web site will help with that. Check out the relevant CSS Web site at `http://www.w3.org/pub/WWW/Style/` for the complete specification and links to other CSS sites of interest.

Disabilities awareness

Since the advent of the personal computer, there has been growing use and awareness of the possibilities of the machine for disabled people. After all, in an environment that is largely driven by intellect — and certainly *not* by physical prowess — the division between those with disabilities and those without them becomes thinner. With our cooperation, those divisions will become thinner still. It's positively win-win.

Some of the things you can do to make your Web site friendly to people with certain disabilities are so strikingly simple it's too easy *not* to do it. For instance, imagine a blind person who relies on their computer reading things on-screen, hitting a graphic-heavy Web page with no words to be read. You know they'll be hitting the Back button pronto; there's simply no choice!

The easy solution is just to make sure you make good and sensible use of the ALT tag to plug in bits of text that could help those who couldn't actually *see* your graphics find their way around. Since it's not only blind people who surf around not looking at graphics, this makes doubly good sense.

Making the Web accessible for people with disabilities is an interesting challenge. And it's something a lot of people are thinking about and bringing things to.

For instance, the W3C has a very healthy Web area that focuses just on this issue. You can see it at `http://www.w3.org/pub/WWW/Disabilities/` which is a portion of the site completely given over to studying about Disabilities Developments on the World Wide Web.

Chapter 21

Ten Pieces of Software You Need

In This Chapter

▶ Image editors

▶ Image mapping

▶ HTML generators

. . . .

*T*he more you look for cool stuff to help you make Web graphics, the more stuff you'll find. This is one of the irrefutable laws of Web graphics design. You could just keep buying and downloading stuff on a daily basis for, well, for a really long time — and still not have all of the really interesting and excellent stuff that is available to you, regardless of platform.

There is so much truly excellent stuff that a mind can start reeling. In fact, mine does all the time. I keep no less than six image converters on my computer, ready to go at any time to tweak images in just the right degree. Likewise, I have several image editors, several animation programs, various VRML packages, and the list goes on.

If I reduced my system to ten crucial applications, I'd have the software that's described in this chapter.

Share the Wealth

I love shareware. And Web graphics is one area where you can find all sorts of really wonderful shareware, because the people who made it are passionate and connected.

Remember, please, shareware doesn't mean free. It means you get to try the software at no cost. But if you like it, either buy the full version or pay the shareware fee requested. It's usually inexpensive. I've seen shareware authors ask for something as small as a postcard from wherever you are up to a few dollars ($20 is common).

Properly paying the people who write shareware has a wonderful ripple effect. It makes them want to write more!

Image Editors

Web graphics designers need to create and change all kinds of electronic images. Start with these and you won't go wrong.

Adobe Photoshop

Platform: Macintosh, Windows 95, NT, and 3.11

Photoshop is my main Web graphic creation tool. Most Web designers agree that Photoshop is the program they can't live without, for lots of really good reasons. Photoshop does many tasks really well, so it's useful at every stage of graphics.

- ✔ Painting
- ✔ Editing
- ✔ Converting

It's the industry standard in a field it pretty much created. What others do, Photoshop generally does better.

Photoshop has one drawback. It's expensive. But the people who find a way to buy it seldom seem to regret their decision.

Photoshop doesn't need any plugs from me. I wish I could tell you about a hot new program. Try as they may, the pretenders haven't been able to even come close. Have a look at Photoshop in Figure 21-1.

```
Adobe Photoshop
345 Park Avenue
San Jose, CA 95110-2704
http://www.adobe.com
```

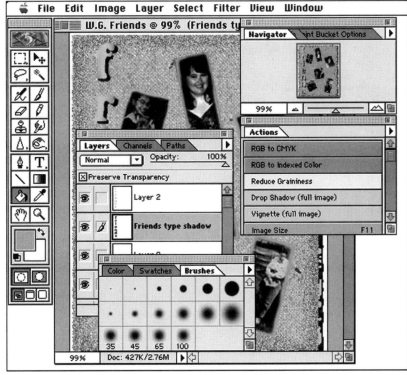

Figure 21-1:
Photoshop's
quality and
versatility
keeps it at
the top of
the heap.

PaintShop Pro

Platform: Windows, Windows 95, NT

If anything gives Photoshop a run for its money, it's PaintShop Pro. And the
money is much less. The latest version, Version 4 is recommended for
Windows 95 and NT, while Version 3 is still available for Windows 3.1x.
Considering how much PaintShop Pro costs, it's an impressive package.
More impressive, Jasc Incorporated (the people who make PaintShop Pro) is
dedicated to software distribution policies that have made Netscape a real
force. You can download a full trial version of PaintShop Pro 3 from the Jasc
Web site, along with demos of other Jasc software products. All the demos
do the full spiel of stuff, but they only work for 30 days unless you buy a
license: plenty of time to decide if you want to bite on this value-packed
package.

PaintShop Pro isn't available for Macintosh, and I don't expect it soon. With
Macs still the beasts of choice in most design studios, this has probably
held back the program. All that aside, PSP is well worth a careful look if you
think you can't fork over the bucks for Photoshop.

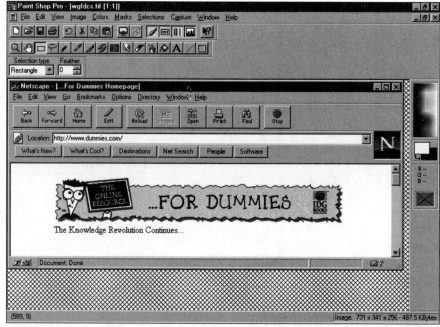

Figure 21-2:
PaintShop
Pro offers
really
fabulous
features for
a teeny
price.

```
Jasc Incorporated
11011 Smetana Road
Minnetonka, MN 55343
http://www.jasc.com
```

Graphics Utilities

You aren't the only person who has ever said, "Gee, I wish I had a tool for this." Resourceful programmers have been creating special software that simplifies every step of graphics. Here are some of the best.

DeBabelizer and DeBabelizer Pro image converters

Platform: Macintosh, Windows 95, NT 4.0

DeBabelizer has been the image converter of choice for Macintosh users as long as people have been making Web graphics. More recently, Equilibrium — the company that makes the package — added DeBabelizer Pro, with support for the Windows platform. DeBabelizer Pro is called an *auto-mated graphics processor,* which confuses the issue, I think. But DeBabelizer still converts images, remaps palettes, and eliminates palette conflicts.

I've always liked how smart DeBabelizer is about conversions. It converts TIFF files to any Web format with the least amount of fuss: wonderful when you're doing lots of conversions for a Web site. DeBabelizer and DeBabelizer Pro do other things as well. Animators and those who work with digital video will find uses for it, but it's the Web stuff that keeps me sold. (See Figure 21-3.)

Figure 21-3: DeBabelizer and its new-fangled cousin DeBabelizer Pro make short work of image conversions.

```
Equilibrium
Three Harbor Drive, Suite 111
Sausalito, CA 94965
http://www.equilibrium.com
```

WebPainter animation tool

Platform: Windows 95, NT, Macintosh

Every now and then a program comes your way that isn't necessary, but you find you wouldn't want to do without. When it comes to Web graphics, WebPainter is like that. I mean, no one needs Web animations, right? But they're fun to do and fun to enjoy. WebPainter makes them easy, too. Actually, it's so easy to do animations in this program you can almost do them by accident. (This interface is shown in Figure 21-4.)

In a pinch, WebPainter can double as an image converter, but only in a pinch, as it doesn't do this very well.

The full version of WebPainter also ships with a Sizzler editor for "streaming file formats" and a streaming media player. Overall, these are well documented and easy to use programs at a reasonable price.

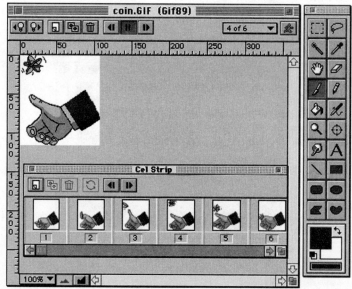

Figure 21-4:
WebPainter makes GIF animations so easy, you can get yourself in trouble.

```
Totally Hip Software, Inc.
P.O. Box 4160
VMPO
Vancouver, B.C. Canada V6B 3Z6
http://www.totallyhip.com
```

WebMap and Mapedit image mapping utilities

Platform: Windows 95, Windows NT (Mapedit), WebMap (Macintosh)

It's exciting to find shareware programs as powerful as WebMap and Mapedit. I've lumped them together because both do the same thing. They do the exacting job of calculations for image maps fast.

I won't say I prefer one, because each exploits the full power of its Windows or Macintosh platform. Both are brilliant pieces of software. Other packages make image maps, but these are the most popular for their platforms — for good reason.

Mapedit can be downloaded at: `http://www.boutell.com/mapedit/mapedit.html`.

Figure 21-5: Both WebMap (shown) and Mapedit simplify the image mapping process. The fact that both programs are shareware is a happy bonus.

ColorFinder color utility

Platform: Macintosh

The worst thing about this utility is that it's only available for the Macintosh. If anyone comes across a similar PC utility, please let me know.

Other than that (huge) shortcoming, ColorFinder has everything going for it. It's one of those programs that is delightful to discover and use.

First, it's free. (Free is good.) Second, it's teeny. The program itself is 44K and it requires only about 100K of system memory to run.

Developed by Acme Software, ColorFinder was the result of an inspired midnight hack after Wayne had spent too many hours determining text and background colors.

ColorFinder offers an eyedropper to "grab" color information from anywhere on the screen — even the desktop — and then converts that information into hex colors that plug into your source code, as shown in Figure 21-6.

Figure 21-6:
Simply
move the
ColorFinder
eyedropper
tool over
the color
you'd like to
sample.
Poof!
Instant hex
colors!

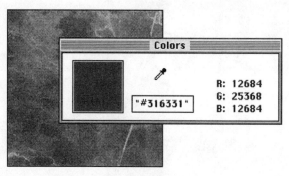

```
ACME Software
http://www.acmetech.com/freewares.html
```

Image Alchemy imaging utility

Platform: DOS, Macintosh, OS/2, and "all flavors of Unix"

Image Alchemy is one of those imaging utilities that have been around for a while and has only become useful to a large group since the advent of the Web. As such, it has the comfortable "feel" of tried and true software. There aren't many bells and whistles (and no hint of a wizard anywhere), but lots of pure processing power. The interface is practically nonexistent. Even the toolbar seems different from other programs. Alchemy let's you process images with a minimum of fanfare. And it works as well as programs that cost a lot more.

The downloadable demo version is slightly crippled but fully functional. You can use the demo to process files for the Web, but the demo limits the size of the files you start with. The allowed size, however, gives designers a good taste of this efficient program.

Usually, I use Image Alchemy as an image converter. It converts over 75 image formats and it's quite happy to bring in a file in Photoshop format and convert it to JPEG, PNG, or GIF.

A major drawback for many users is that it is not intended to run under Windows 95. It does run under MS-DOS, OS/2, SCO Unix, BSD, Linux, the Mac OS and others, so the lack of a Windows 95 version does not seem to be an unintentional oversight. If you're not a Windows 95 user, it's well worth checking out.

```
handmade software incorporated
48860 Milmont Drive, Suite 106
Fremont, CA 94538
1-800-252-0101
http://www.handmadesw.com
```

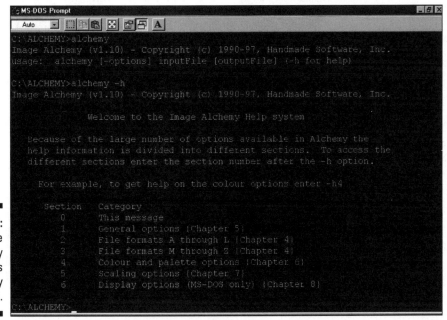

Figure 21-7:
The Image
Alchemy
interface is
startlingly
simple.

HTML Editors

Adobe PageMill 2.0

Platform: Macintosh, Windows

PageMill 2.0 is good, basic software that does all the stuff you need without a lot of fanfare. I like that. If you know your way around HTML at all, you can build a Web page in PageMill quickly without stopping to RTFM. To me, that's a high recommendation.

The latest version of PageMill is a vast improvement over Version 1.0. PageMill 2.0 supports tables and other HTML basics, but also because it didn't allow an easy peek at the code. For me that meant that any time I actually wanted to look at the HTML that PageMill was producing for me, I had to drag it into a "real" HTML editor to give it the final once-over. Version 2.0 has solved this, however, with a handy command to view the source code: all at the touch of a couple of keys.

There are lots of things that make PageMill a good choice for me. It's easy to use and workability high among them. But the thing that pleases the designer in me the most is really silly: I can, in PageMill, pick colors with all the ease with which I do it in QuarkXPress or Photoshop. A touch of a couple of keys, a color wheel and I've selected my colors: no changing background colors. It's all right there and waiting.

```
Adobe PageMill 2.0
345 Park Avenue
San Jose, CA 95110-2704
http://www.adobe.com
```

BBEdit

Platform: Macintosh

Want bells and whistles? Want a Web page that almost makes itself? Don't get BBEdit. This Web page building program has been around almost as long as there's been a Web. Formerly known as "Bob's HTML Editor," BBEdit is one of the more solid and durable HTML editors available for the Mac platform.

Figure 21-8:
If you must
have a
WYSIWYG
HTML
editor,
Adobe
PageMill 2.0
is easy to
use. Basic
Web pages
practically
make
themselves.

Notice that I haven't referred to a version number in the introductory information? That's because BBEdit gets updated pretty regularly: both the freeware version you can download on the Web (known as "BBEdit Lite"), and the "full" version available at a software store near you. The main difference between the commercial version and the shareware version seems to be that the one you buy in a box is the very latest, while the one you can download is a full version behind. Web designers who can't wait generally buy the newest, and there are many people who'd rather buy than wait.

I won't wax poetic about BBEdit's features, simply because it doesn't have many. What it offers is a reliable window to your HTML. This is one of the programs that I can't be without. No matter which HTML editor I've started in, I have a last peek at the code in BBEdit before I actually upload the page to a Web site.

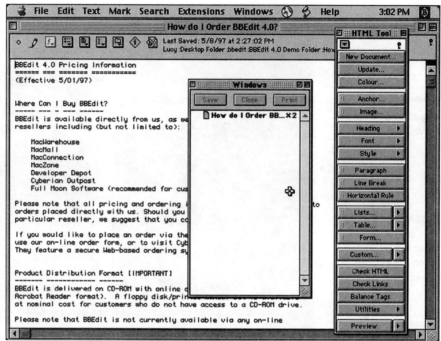

Figure 21-9:
BBEdit is
the Chevy
of HTML
editors.

CMed

Platform: Windows 95, Windows NT 3.51 and later

CMed is not a WYSIWYG HTML editor. Nor, would purists call it a strictly basic text-entry-only editor. What you see is code (not a graphical representation of your site), but an intuitive series of menus lets you input code with a couple of keystrokes.

All of this makes CMed a good choice for the new HTML coder, because CMed has both the space to learn what's actually going on and the convenience of having some of the repetitive steps done automatically.

Another nice part of the CMed story is that this functional, sturdy editor is shareware. The shareware version entitles you to 30 days to play with the program and see if you like it. After that, you're required to register CMed for $25.

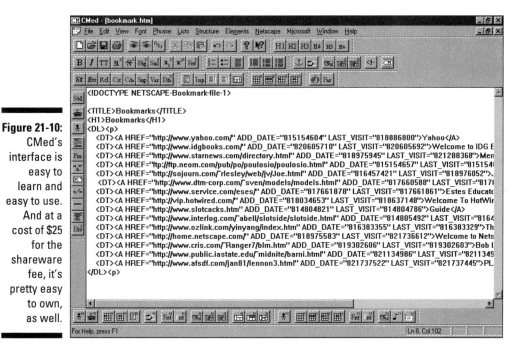

Figure 21-10:
CMed's interface is easy to learn and easy to use. And at a cost of $25 for the shareware fee, it's pretty easy to own, as well.

Matheson's Software Development
P.O. Box 625
Newman, W.A. 6753
Australia
http://users.highway1.com.au/~cmathes/

Chapter 22

Ten Tools for Better Web Graphics

In This Chapter

▶ The ultimate Web graphics creation computer

▶ Speedy system hardware

▶ Time-saving accessories

Some things are absolutely essential for effective Web graphics. Skills you have to know. Equipment you have to have. Other things that are cool to know and have. The machine you do all this on has the same qualities. And, again, the fact is you *can* make Web graphics on a basic computer. I even know people who have done it blind on 80386 computers with no graphics card. But this is *not* the ideal condition.

Let's explore the ideal condition. If you build the ultimate Web graphics system, what does it include?

Gobs of RAM

In the not-so-distant future, everything on your computer will run in high RAM. I've been saying this for a number of years, but we're only now starting to see machines that reflect this. I have no less than three close friends whose main computers sport no less than 100 megabytes of *RAM*. Lots bigger than the hard drives I enjoyed so much a few years ago! None of my own computers has more than 32MB of RAM, but I can dream, can't I?

Any time you're doing anything graphical, you're hogging RAM. To begin designing Web graphics without pulling hair, plan on having at least 16MB of RAM. And more is better. When I'm working, I usually have several programs open. I jump from an image editor, to my favorite converter, to e-mail. That demands large quantities of RAM. And having more makes the jumps faster.

RAM is a small part of the cost of a system, so this part of the wish list is easy. It'll get harder from here.

A Big Hard Drive

The ultimate Web graphics machine sports no less than 1GB of hard storage. That sounds like lots, but you need it. Each graphic file needs space, and you need space for every version of every file you save.

There's little worse than working with a large, complex image and suddenly getting memory error messages. Then you crash and have to restart (possibly losing work!). Or you have to stop — in the middle of a brainstorm! — to decide which files you're going to kill. Oooh, ick!

The ultimate Web graphics machine has at least a gig of hard storage, maybe more. Fortunately, hard storage — like RAM — has gotten a *lot* cheaper in recent years. Which makes me think of my friend Mark, who was the first among my geek friends to get a hard drive back in the Good Ol' Days. Mark saved and scrimped for months to buy his 5MB hard drive for his Apple II. It was such a huge event that we had a party around it. None of us could imagine a time when a 5MB hard drive wouldn't be the answer to anyone's storage dreams.

Think big, buy cheap. A bigger, faster, cheaper drive is always just around the corner.

Back Up to Beat the Band

Think about making copies of your files. Good Web graphics are teeny — the teenier, the better. But the files we need to create those teeny Web-published files can be *huge*.

My personal Web site has some 22K files. The originals are 2MB or larger. If you even faintly expect you may need to rework your Web graphics, you should keep your originals and the intermediate stages. So you need to be able to take files off your system.

If your work is for clients, most want delivery on some sort of disk. A high-capacity backup system beats splitting your graphics files onto standard disks for shipping. And it's a given that most clients are only marginally computer literate, so one disk will be easier for them, too.

Choose a backup device that's popular with designers and service bureaus in your area. It's easier for you if someone else already has the hardware to read your disk. These things tend to have a regional and time sensitive flavor, but some backup formats are enduring. I still deliver a high percentage of client stuff on 44MB Syquest disks from a drive not less than five years old. (Syquest was state-of-the-art when a lot of bureaus were buying equipment, so almost everyone has one.) If your work goes to clients and service bureaus, consider what they can handle when you choose hardware.

Fast Internet Connection

If you have a 14.4 Kbps modem, you're probably already thinking about a 28.8. If you have 33.6, you're probably thinking ISDN. If you're sharing a T1, you're probably thinking about hogging the whole thing to yourself. Really, faster is never fast enough and too fast hasn't been invented yet.

A fast Internet connection can be dangerous for Web graphics designers. Keep a modem around that represents the speed that the masses move. As I write this, most people are still using 14.4 and 28.8 Kbps (Kilobits per second) modems. If you settle into the blinding fast speed of a T1 ISDN connection, you can forget how quickly (or rather, how *slowly*) the masses travel. And a slow graphic invites early bail-outs. If your audience leaves, you've lost before you got started.

On the other hand, a really fast Internet connection makes *your* job a lot easier. You can upload files to networked servers faster. A fast connection also makes it easier to stay current by surfing everyone else's site. But remember the dangers before modeming off into the sunset.

Big Monitor

Why is bigger always better with computers? No matter your monitor, spending a lot of time designing on it will make you want a bigger one. Better still — and if your hardware configuration will allow it — a second one, so that you can check graphics on one while the other is in use.

Here again, as with the faster Internet connection, consideration for users serves designers well. While a bigger monitor is delightful, most surfers are on a 14- or 15-inch monitor. It's maddening for someone with a small monitor to arrive on a Web page designed for a 17-inch monitor. Or — worse still — designed with no one but the designer in mind.

When you think of it, a good designer works for the middle ground. The successfully designed chair, for instance, isn't one that's designed for the seven-foot basketball player or the diminutive jockey, but rather one that works for almost *everyone*. (Having it work well for absolutely everyone may be too much to ask!) Keep that principle in mind while designing Web pages and Web graphics. If a graphic looks good on a 14-inch monitor, it will look stunning at 17 inches. The reverse isn't always true.

Scanner

The ultimate Web graphic designing system *must* have a scanner. Not to say that you can't design Web graphics without one. You can. But a scanner will help your creativity and enrich your designs. If you're designing for money, you won't want to leave home without one!

There are the obvious uses for scanners, of course. Logos from business cards, photos, pencil sketches, and any other flat art that needs to be changed to an electronic file. A scanner can also double as a camera, if the products you're shooting are small. But there are more subtle uses, too.

One of my favorite Web backgrounds started life as a crumpled brown paper lunch bag. I crumpled it again — creatively, I think — scanned it, and manipulated it in Photoshop. Voila! Instant original background.

Anything that fits on a scanner *bed* (the glass part, like a photocopier) is fodder for a Web designer. When you shop for your scanner, keep this in mind:

- ✔ Get the largest scanner bed you can afford that fits in your office. The larger it is, the more stuff you'll be able to scan. Seriously. As I said, doing product shots in your studio is a boon to the Web designer. And entirely possible with the right scanner.

- ✔ Get color. Even if you see the deal of a lifetime on a black-and-white scanner (they're still out there), don't be tempted by anything less than full, living color — the livelier, the better.

- ✔ Look for software bundles with your scanner. The right software makes a big difference to the value and performance of your system. For example, some scanners include software that adds scanner controls to Photoshop, so you don't have to jump between applications. In other cases, scanner manufacturers simply negotiate volume deals with software manufacturers and pass the saving on when you buy the scanner. You may find that $300 extra buys a thousand dollars of software.

Watch out for *limited* versions of software in scanner bundles. The "LE" version of Adobe Photoshop, for example, doesn't have all the functions of the full $600 package. (Photoshop LE is still a good thing. If you have Photoshop LE, Adobe usually offers an upgrade to the big tamale at a friendly price.)

✔ Don't sweat scanner obsolescence. Scanners evolve more slowly than other pieces of hardware. I bought my scanner several years ago and the same model is still that company's top-of-the-line model. In fact, you may be able to find a used scanner that still has the same performance as a new one.

✔ Insist on compatibility. Scanner manufacturers are a hungry bunch. You should have no problem finding a scanner with the cables and software for your system. Don't be persuaded into a unit that *may* work with your system. Someone down the street will sell you a perfectly tailored scanner. Hold out for the right one!

Faster CPU

Uh-oh. You knew this one was coming, didn't you? And this is also a cross-platform thing. It doesn't matter whether you're a Windoze enthusiast or a Mac geek, designing Web graphics is guaranteed to make you want a faster system. If not now, at some point you'll think, "My system is a turtle!"

So what's ultimate? How about, as fast as you can afford. As fast as this year's (and this month's, and this week's) model is, *next* month's software will make it seem slower. And the faster the machine that you have processes everything, the more quickly you'll get through your work.

Bottom line? A Pentium-100 is the least that could be considered "optimum" at present on the PC front. A Pentium-200 would be even better. For the Mac-aholics, go for the PowerMac from the start. You'll be glad you did.

On the other hand, if you already have a machine, don't despair. You can still do everything you need to do on your 486-50 or your Centris 650. Just don't call it the ultimate system. At least you'll have time to read this book while you wait for redraws and long saves.

CD-ROM Player

If this seems like a no-brainer to you at this point, skip this part, because you've probably already got a CD-ROM tucked away somewhere and don't need any convincing.

Unlike the bad ol' days, when software shipped on disks, nowadays even small programs arrive on CD-ROM. Some of them are too durned big to fit on less than 20 disks, and some marketing managers understand that users like CD-ROMs. Whatever the case, the days when a CD-ROM unit was a luxury are over.

Web designers have even more need for a CD-ROM drive. If you want a library of images — clip art and photographs — at hand, then CD-ROM is the best way. CDs don't take much room, and are a relatively cheap medium for companies to distribute.

So CD-ROM units are important to Web designers mainly for two reasons:

- Swapping 72 bazillion disks to install software is no fun.
- One CD-ROM can hold more clip art than 500 floppy disks.

For Web graphics, extreme CD-ROM speed isn't necessary. After software and art is installed on the hard drive, the CD-ROM isn't important. Gamers and multimedia mavens need the fastest CD-ROM they can get, because they use the CD-ROM the whole time the computer is running. (If you design by day and play games at night, buy the fastest CD-ROM drive you can afford.)

If your demands on a CD-ROM player are only those of a designer, then you can get by with a pretty slow (read that c-h-e-a-p) one. A 2X (double-speed) or 4X (quad-speed) CD-ROM drive will be fine.

Unlimited Power

If there's anything worse than working for hours on a really special file and then losing it to an unexpected power surge, I'm not quite sure what it is. Power losses were expected not so long ago. Now, we have ways of dealing with the unpredictable power-outs that can steal our data.

If you live where power surges are frequent, you've probably already thought about preventing the juice from being sucked out of your computer. People who live in rural areas are used to dealing with power losses. But sometimes even city dwellers have to put up with power problems. An ounce of prevention is worth a pound (or more!) of cure.

Protection against power problems is as near as your computer store. At the very least, a good quality surge protector will prevent your computer's brains from being blown out in the event of a really drastic power surge.

Most surge protectors only last through one big surge. What they do, basically, is absorb the blast that your computer would have taken. It's easier to replace a $26 surge protector than a $3,000 computer, but it's still a pain (I *hate* unplugging all that stuff!) and it mounts up if you live where surges are common.

A more expensive *and* permanent alternative is to blow the wad on a gen-u-wyne Uninterruptible Power Supply. Check the specs carefully to make sure a UPS does what you need it to do. If a UPS costs less than $100, it's probably a zap-it-once surge protector. A proper, for-real, Uninterruptible Power Supply will set you back between $200 and $300.

If you're willing to spend the money, what you're looking for is a device that swallows surges, smoothes microspikes in your electricity (a process called *conditioning*), and powers your system for a few minutes — giving you time to power down — in a total loss of power.

Digital Camera

The photobug in me especially likes this one. The latest generation of digital cameras makes this a fun way to get photos inside your PC. There's something immensely power-bestowing about going from idea to finished photo in a couple of steps. And since, with Web graphics, we're already by-passing the smarties at the print shop, it seems kind of fitting.

A digital camera can perform the obvious very easily, such as taking photos of friends, family, pets, and company employees in order to add them to a Web page. You can also use them to take pictures of products to add to an online catalog. Or even to input pictures of *stuff* to be manipulated into backgrounds.

In terms of cost, you can go in cheap with something like the Connectix QuickCam that costs less than a lot of software packages, right up to the professional digital photography systems that will put you back the price of a summer home. And there are lots of options between.

Unlike some of its more expensive brethren, the QuickCam is pure peripheral and can't function without being directly connected to your computer. It's the price you pay for not paying a big price. It comes in two basic flavors: color and black and white, and the price you pay is reflected in the choice. Color costs more.

There are some real neat pluses to the camera being part of your system. Setup is easy. The hardware portion installs with a couple of easy-to-follow instructions. As simple as a keyboard installation. There isn't even an "on" button, because the camera powers off of your computer. The software portion installs and plays as easily as any photo manipulation software. The big negative is that you can't just grab the camera and take it down to the beach (unless your computer is a laptop, and that would make the system hard to fit in a beach bag anyway).

For the price, the photos are amazingly sharp and the color is good. But the color isn't perfect. I save photos I want to keep as TIFFs and then color-correct them in Photoshop. You can use any image-editing program. The Web page in Figure 22-1 is built around a photo of my parrot (Fred) and me captured with a Connectix QuickCam2, saved as a TIFF, and then massaged in Photoshop. The beauty of digital imaging is its speed — from concept to this Web page, about 30 minutes. And Fred isn't nagging me to finish his Web page!

Figure 22-1:
A digital camera makes it easy to add snapshots to Web pages.

Chapter 23

Ten Online Resources for Web Graphics

. . . .

. . . .

*O*ne of the very best sources of information on all types of Web weaving, is the Web itself. The Internet continues to provide an ever-growing and ever-changing array of *stuff*. Sometimes the trick isn't finding something on-topic — it's narrowing the field of what's available down to what's good!

Keeping all of this under consideration, how can one possibly be expected to narrow down all of this exciting stuff to just ten? Or — in arrogance — claim that the ten I've chosen here are *the* ten? In actuality, then, this is a listing of ten sites on the Web that I've either found extremely useful, or sites that I thought would be good jumping off points on your search for higher ground. But to select tensites out of a possible bazillion was pretty tough. If you figure I really missed the boat and you know of a site that really should be included in the next edition, I'd love to hear about it. Drop me a note at scrybe@istar.ca and tell me about it.

All disclaimers aside, then, let's have a peek at ten Web sites of use to the designer of Web graphics.

The World Wide Web Consortium (W3C)

http://www.w3.org/pub/WWW/

The W3C is hosted by the Laboratory for Computer Science at MIT and its purpose is to "develop common protocols for the evolution of the World Wide Web." That means that this site is filled with a lot of stuff that can make your head hurt when you look at it too closely and too long, but it's also a powerful resource when you're trying to keep current with what's going on — now and in the future — with the Web.

The W3C acts as a repository of information about the Web. As well, this is the place to find the latest changes to various standards and protocols relating to the World Wide Web.

This is not a "happy happy, let's learn together" type of site. It's geared to the very top level of users, and there's some stuff there that even that elite group doesn't get. There is also, however, pockets of really basic information. The real plus is, everything I've seen there is *correct* information. Something you don't find on all sites. In addition, you find (but you have to look hard) lots of really great off-site links to stuff like HTML editors, graphics converters, and other stuff of interest to Web designers.

If there is a definitive Web authority, W3C is it.

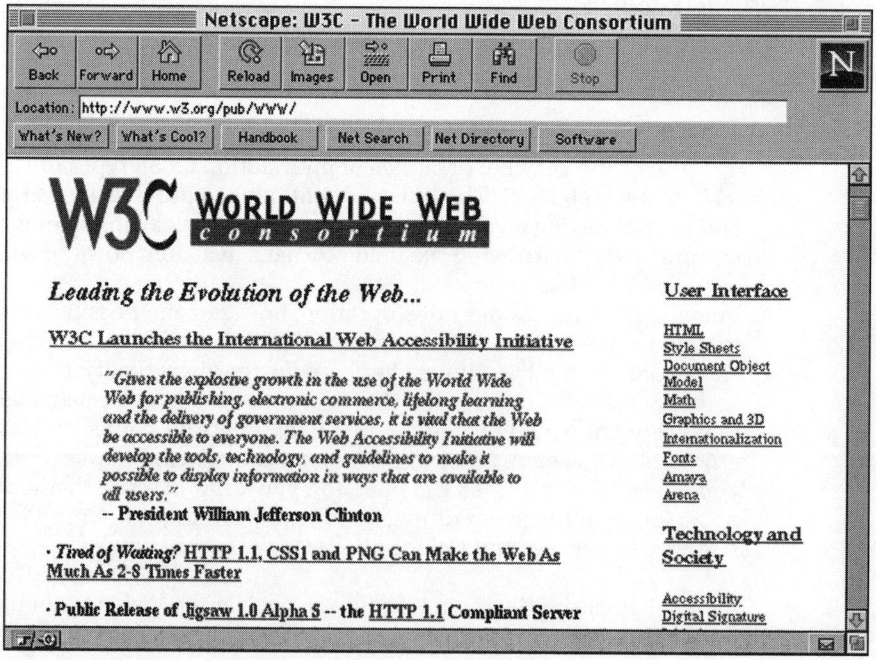

Figure 23-1:
The technical level is inarguably at the high water mark, but there's an awful lot of useful and up-to-the-minute stuff at the W3C site at http://www. w3.org/pub/ WWW/.

Netscape: W3C – The World Wide Web Consortium

Back | Forward | Home | Reload | Images | Open | Print | Find | Stop

Location: http://www.w3.org/pub/WWW/

What's New? | What's Cool? | Handbook | Net Search | Net Directory | Software

W3C WORLD WIDE WEB *consortium*

Leading the Evolution of the Web...

W3C Launches the International Web Accessibility Initiative

"Given the explosive growth in the use of the World Wide Web for publishing, electronic commerce, lifelong learning and the delivery of government services, it is vital that the Web be accessible to everyone. The Web Accessibility Initiative will develop the tools, technology, and guidelines to make it possible to display information in ways that are available to all users."
-- President William Jefferson Clinton

· *Tired of Waiting?* HTTP 1.1, CSS1 and PNG Can Make the Web As Much As 2-8 Times Faster

· **Public Release of Jigsaw 1.0 Alpha 5** -- the HTTP 1.1 Compliant Server

User Interface

HTML
Style Sheets
Document Object Model
Math
Graphics and 3D
Internationalization
Fonts
Amaya
Arena

Technology and Society

Accessibility
Digital Signature

The HTML Writer's Guild

`http://www.hwg.org/`

As the name suggests, The HTML Writer's Guild is an organization of Web weavers. Since the organization — like the medium — is fairly new, their Web site tends to go through lots of changes, but the stuff there is always well tended and carefully selected.

There are, of course, lots of sections specifically related to the Guild and its business, but many helpful links also connect to all sorts of Web resources and information on various Web technologies.

The HTML Writer's Guild is an international organization with a growing membership, and their Web site reflects the very serious way in which they take themselves. However, don't be fooled by the lack of blinking lights and winking eyes. The site is worth a careful look when you're looking for that certain something that evades you.

Figure 23-2:
The HTML Writer's Guild Web site looks a bit stuffy at first take, but push on anyway. There's a real wealth of heavily vetted information here when you take the time to surf through properly.

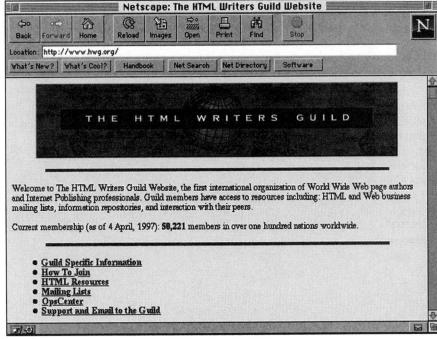

Yahoo!

```
http://www.yahoo.com/Computers_and_Internet/Internet/
                World_Wide_Web/Authoring/
```

Just say "Yahoo!" And don't let the convoluted Web address through you off. Yahoo! delivers on material relating to Web graphics.

What's here is a pretty mixed bag of all that is of interest to designers of Web graphics — everything from GIF conversions to JavaScript info. It's all here.

As usual with Yahoo!, beware of link rot. These days Yahoo! seems to dish up as many as 1/3 of links that don't work. When you can get past the frustration of looking forward to seeing a page that just doesn't exist — at least at the URL they've listed — you find some pearls among all the rocks. Just don't slip on the oysters.

Figure 23-3:
Just say
"Yahoo!"
But say it
gently.
Yahoo!
continues
to be a
valuable
source of
information,
as long as
you don't
mind a bit of
link rot
with your
information.

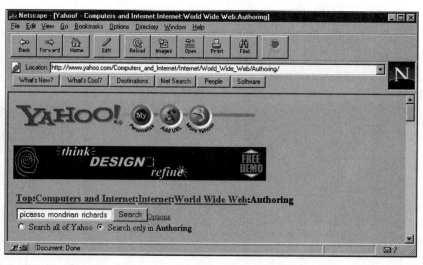

Techbabes

http://www.techbabes.com/

As the name suggests, at its heart, the Techbabes site is about women online. But the resources here are valuable no matter what your gender.

In addition to links to a diverse collection of Web design sites, Techbabes also features a good selection of original material on a wide variety of topics, all relating to building Web sites around powerful graphics.

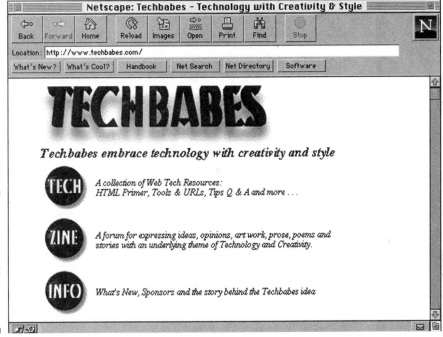

Figure 23-4:
A growing collection of tips and links at http://www. techbabes. com/.

GifWizard

http://www.gifwizard.com

This isn't a bunch of links, but this resource is so useful for Web graphics designers that it merits mention. GifWizard is a free online resource that optimizes your GIFs. This can be especially satisfying for those who have already put GIF files on a Web site, but suspect that the job may have been done better by someone else. Or *something* else.

To use GIFWizard, type in a URL in the allocated spot, answer a few questions, and then go for a soda. GIFWizard does its stuff, right then, while you're online.

After a few minutes, you see a message like Figure 23-5, letting you know the size of files it has Wizarded for you. It shows thumbnails of the files, with the largest possible size savings available for the file. Clicking on one of the thumbnails brings you to a detailed report for that GIF variations of the file with different schemes for saving file space, as well as where you can go to download your newly-processed GIF.

All pretty slick, and it's free.

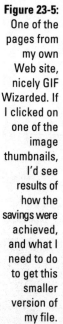

Figure 23-5: One of the pages from my own Web site, nicely GIF Wizarded. If I clicked on one of the image thumbnails, I'd see results of how the savings were achieved, and what I need to do to get this smaller version of my file.

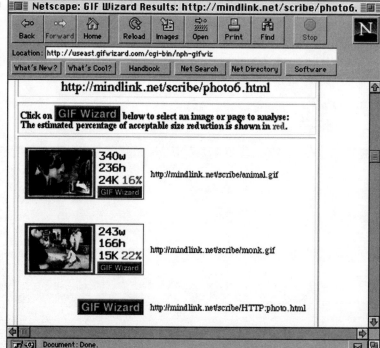

A Couple of Cows and a Place Just for Downloads

Here's where I sneak two resources into one heading, but they sort of go together for me. When you're looking for stuff — shareware, freeware, and demo versions of helpful software — several sites rule.

Bookmark both of these sites for times when you're looking for something special and you're not quite sure where to start.

Download.com

```
http://www.download.com
```

Tucows.com

```
http://www.tucows.com
```

The Internet Design & Publishing Center

```
http://www.Graphic-Design.com/
```

Not only is it a treat to look at, but *The Design & Publishing Center* is a great tool for designers of Web graphics. Reviews of the latest programs, tricks, tips, and other good stuff.

This is a good starting point for hard to find, medium-to-expert level advice and information.

The Pixel Foundry

```
http://the-tech.mit.edu/KPT/
```

Served out of the MIT tech server, The Pixel Foundry was the original home of Kai's Power Tools.

The site is a no less powerful one for designers, these days. All sorts of tips, tricks, and techniques, as well as links to some other really top notch sites.

Figure 23-6:
The Pixel
Foundry is
home to all
manner of
techniques,
tricks, and
tips, as well
as a super
jumping-off
spot to
other sites
online that
concern
themselves
with the
graphics of
the Web.

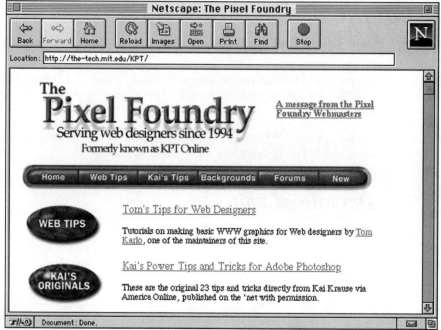

The Bandwidth Conservation Society

http://www.infohiway.com/faster/

You just can't help but like the name of this one. Though I guess when there can be a society to promote polenta (and there is!), there can be one to conserve bandwidth.

In the name of conserving said bandwidth, this site gives lots of good advice and lessons to creating small and gorgeous graphics.

Figure 23-7:
Don't you
love an
organization
called the
Bandwidth
Conservation
Society?
You can
almost
imagine
them
walking
with
plaques
that read,
"Save our
backbone"
and "Teeny
graphics
unite!"

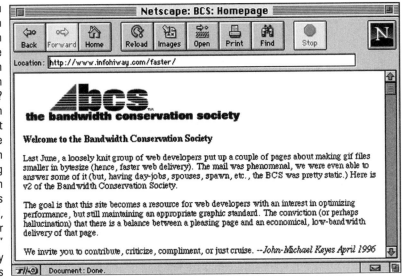

The Newbie's Net Guide

http://www.newbies-netguide.com/index.html

Like the name says, this site has a little bit of information about almost everything to do with the Internet.

The HTML authoring index, at the same site at http://www.newbies-netguide.com/web_pa~1/webpgidx.html has lots of articles and information on HTML and Web graphic specific subjects.

Chapter 24

Ten Common Problems

In This Chapter

▶ Why do my Web pages look different on other computers?

▶ How can I make Web pages load faster?

▶ Do I have rights to my own work?

You've built your Web page, and everything is going great. Or not. If you're not happy with your Web page, you'll probably find the reason in this chapter.

My Web Page Looks Different on Someone Else's Computer

There's a couple of reasons for this, and some easy solutions. But all the reasons arise from the nature of the medium and the many variables involved.

One thing that causes this to happen is looking at a Web page on different browsers. Different browsers — like Netscape, Explorer, and others — can look at the same thing quite differently. To confuse things more, different versions of the *same* browser can look different again.

Obviously, it would be impossible for you to look at your graphics on every browser on every platform. However, you should try to keep at least the last couple of versions of the more popular browsers on your system so you can view your files and correct potential problems *before* you upload your files to a Web site.

The other thing that makes Web pages look different is varying platforms. Files that look great on a Mac look dark on a PC. That's because the PC views the world in an entirely different way. This is called gamma and is discussed in-depth elsewhere in this book. These gamma differences are solvable, however, and can be avoided entirely when anticipated in the design stage.

Figure 24-1 compares Macintosh and PC images.

Figure 24-1:
An image corrected for Macs on the left and PCs on the right.

I Don't Have Time or Resources to Check My Page on a Lot of Machines and Platforms

There a couple of online syntax checkers intended just for this purpose. And they're cooler than cool. All you do is surf there, input the URL of the page you'd like to check, and then cool your jets for a couple of minutes while the syntax checker does its work. If all of that isn't cool enough, these syntax checkers were developed just for this purpose and the ones that I know about are free.

The Real Time Validator is at

```
http://ugweb.cs.ualberta.ca/~gerald/validate/
```

Browser compatibility information and disability access can be found at Bobby's site at

```
http://www.cast.org/bobby/
```

DR HTML is at

```
http://www2.imagiware.com/RxHTML/
```

Even when you have the time and resources to check your stuff out on your own computer, these validators find stuff you can't spot. Plus, it's free and fun!

I Keep Trying to Zip (or Stuff) a JPEG File, and It Just Doesn't Get Smaller

That's the nature of the beast, I'm afraid. You can even say that a JPEG has been previously stuffed.

You see, properly it's called "JPEG compression" because a JPEG file is already compressed. That's part of what happens when you convert it into a JPEG.

This is also the reason that JPEG is a crummy format for a lot of purposes besides Web exhibition. I've opened a few in QuarkXPress and lived to regret it. Quark opens them just fine, but you can go for a soda while you wait for a big one to display on screen.

The thing that saves JPEG from certain death on the Web is in both the way it displays and the teeniness of the files. That big JPEG I opened in Quark was over a meg. The JPEGs we encounter every day on the Web generally are a bazillion times smaller — 6 and 10K are quite common.

I've Seen "Natural Size Flag" in Some Source Code

To make a huge simplification, it means you've been working in a WYSIWYG HTML editor — or someone has.

As far as I know, that "Natural Size Flag" is a proprietary Adobe PageMill tag. PageMill likes to stick it in when no one is looking. The best thing to do when you see it is just rip it out. You certainly don't need it, and it can even confuse some browsers because it most definitely isn't an HTML tag.

Decoding WYSIWYG coding

WYSIWYG HTML editors stick bits of code in when no one is watching. You can even be tricky and take it out when you're in text mode, but switch back to WYSIWYG mode and then switch back again and it's there again, as though you'd never taken it out in the first place.

Personally, I don't like extra bits of code in *my* code for no reason. The old adage, "when in doubt, take it out" works for me here. After I've done any "coding" in a WYSIWYG editor, I always do a final pass through a text-only HTML editor — one that I know doesn't mess with my code — to take out all the extra bits that don't need to be there.

I Want to Use a Thumbnail of a Large JPEG, but It Looks Really Yucky Small

Sometimes, big images — big on the screen and the hard drive — really can't take being reduced. Maybe the colors are too varied or the picture demands too much detail. One solution is to use just a portion of the image for your thumbnail. This can give the feel of the image you're showing, without subjecting it to extreme reduction.

I Really, Really Want to Use a Large Graphic on My Web Page

Well, don't.

When you really must use a large graphic, try burying it under a warning link. Show a little bit of the huge graphic or a miniature and link to a separate page with the gigantic graphic.

When I hit pages like that, I like to know in advance how big the big image will be. When I'm interested, I may hang around for something that's 180K, but there's not a lot that can make me wait for half a meg. When you include the image size on the page that has the warning link, surfers can make the decision for themselves.

My Mondo Kewl Background Images Look Gross on My Friend's Computer

Background images are a double-edged sword at the best of times. This is one of the reasons: Carefully used and skillfully created, a background image can add a lot to a site. But background images often aren't that well designed or considered. So use background images with caution.

The problem, however, sounds like it may have more to do with the way the background was created than with the way it was used. Computer designers sometimes forget that the whole world doesn't have the latest computer systems. A background designed on a 24-bit screen can be impossible to see on a 256-color system.

The simplest answer is to not use backgrounds at all. When in doubt, leave it out.

However, when you really want to use a background but are not sure how it reads on inexpensive systems, set your monitor to 256-color — or less — and check the background — and your text and images — in low-res mode.

I Want to Make My Page Transmit As Quickly As Possible

One thing you can do to minimize download time is to go back to mechanics and think about how the whole thing actually works.

When a surfer's browser asks a server for a page, the server's job is to deliver it. What a lot of people don't realize is that the server can only dish it up in chunks of four. That is, each time the server is accessed, it can only deliver four separate chunks of information. So trip one is the code (or part of it, when it's long), the background image, and a couple of graphics. When there are more than four elements, the surfer must wait for the server to even begin in order to finish uploading the page to the browser.

So you can expedite the whole thing by producing small graphics and limiting your designs to three graphics on a page. That way, at least your visitors have a whole page to watch with big graphics or slow connections.

Oh, and make your graphics smaller.

I Built an Image onto a Background Tile and It Worked Fine Until I Resized It

You broke a rule. One that can't be broken. You simply can't resize an image that's built onto a background after it's been converted to a Web format. The success of the effect of floating an image over a background relies on the image's background being the same as the page's background, if you follow.

Resizing the image after the fact causes the background to be stretched and pulled as well. The result is that your background appears broken.

Don't despair, though. There's a fix for this. Whether it's an easy fix depends on how much you like your image editor and how far along you kept your backups. To resize the image, you need to go back to the stage prior to conversion to Web format. You need to resize the image part without resizing the background, which means going back to a stage before flattening layers (if you worked in a program like Photoshop that has them).

In any case, it's usually a better idea to do your resizing in your image editor, rather than resizing via HTML tags. Pages load faster when your images are already the size they're meant to be.

How Can I Protect My Ideas and Images from Being Stolen after They're on the Web?

Theft is a funny thing on the Web, a whole new deal. It's almost like you start out stealing stuff and then work your way back from there.

Let me explain. Every time you look at someone's Web page, your browser actually downloads all the information from that page onto your computer. It has, in fact, been stolen. Or more accurately, borrowed, because the assumption is that it's not going to be kept.

But the very fact that it's so easy brings a whole new set of problems. I honestly believe that most people are basically honest critters and don't mean to steal your stuff. On the other hand, the few unscrupulous ones cause us some concern, especially when it's so easy to use graphics from Web sites.

Some people also borrow images from other people's Web sites just because they don't know any better. They've heard that the Internet is free and that everything is owned by everyone. And in some ways, all of this is true, except when it comes to matters of copyright law — which is quite clear on the ownership of things you've created, even in electronic space.

There's really nothing you can do to prevent theft (or even innocent borrowing) of your work. However, you can catch it and prove it.

At present, there is a movement in the online world to stop borrowing, stealing, or otherwise using other people's images. As a product of this, several digital watermarking schemes are available.

A digital watermark marks an image in a way that is invisible to the naked eye, but that can be instantly detected by a watermark reader and certain software packages. When I open an image that has been digitally watermarked in Photoshop 4.0, a copyright symbol appears in the title bar, as shown in Figure 24-2.

If you further crop or resave this image — even in a different format — the copyright symbol is still visible. Also, the copyright is registered to the user — when my image gets separated from my name, someone can find me again by consulting the DigiMarc Web site to find the artist.

You can discover more about DigiMarc on line at `http://www.digimarc.com`.

Figure 24-2:
You can tell that this image has been watermarked by the DigiMarc System by the copyright symbol just left of the file's name in the title bar.

Chapter 25

Ten Tips for Creating Eye-Catching Graphics

I've talked a lot throughout this book about stuff you can do to make tight, good, and elegant graphic images for your Web pages. Now, I'll set apart ten things that greatly contribute to making the ultimate in eye-catching graphics.

The Case of the Disappearing Web Graphic

Color plays an ever-important role in your Web graphics — color and the schemes you play those graphics in.

There can be few things worse than spending a lot of time creating a tight, tiny, and gorgeous graphic of which you're really proud, only to have it melt away into a background it doesn't jump out from.

Here are a few tips to avoid this:

✔ Get out your old color chart, or invest in a new one if you don't have a color chart stuck in a box somewhere. Sometimes it's hard to remember that green is the opposite of red, for instance, and putting them together makes for easy reading. On the other hand, a dark green and a light green of different chromas make it hard to see much of anything at all.

✔ Keep your backgrounds clean and uncluttered. There's nothing like a bold pattern to suck all the snap out of the lovely graphic you lay on it. The best backgrounds for graphics often include either no texture or pattern, or else have such a subtle pattern that they don't detract from the overall snap of the finished page.

JPEG or GIF?

In general,

✔ Use the GIF format when you're making a graphic that is largely bit-mapped or uses large chunks of solid color or blacks and whites.

✔ Choose JPEG when your image is photo-based or you need to shrink a huge image.

Photograph

JPEG is your best first shot. The format lends itself to the efficient compression of lots of tones and gradients.

Photo-illustration

JPEG here, too. The illustration elements are less important than the tones and gradients of the photographic base.

Bitmap

GIF images are small and fast.

Animation

GIF89a is the only currently popular format that saves multiple images in one file.

Transparency

GIF supports transparency and that gives you the most control over transparent elements.

View while downloading

Choose "progressive" JPEG or "interlaced" GIF. Both of these formats download a bit at a time, almost giving the impression of animation while the viewer watches (in browsers that support this feature).

File size

JPEG most often produces the smallest files, especially while using maximum compression.

Flatten?

While working in an image editor, you are most often given the option to "flatten" the image. Take it before saving the file as a GIF or PNG. Flattening the image actually reduces the depth of the colors, creating a smaller final file without affecting the overall look of the image much at all.

On the other hand, an image that you intend to save as a JPEG benefits from *not* being flattened. Reducing the color depth compromises the JPEG compression technique.

Experiment?

Building wonderful Web graphics means exploiting the freedom to experiment and fool around with all the possibilities to get just the right combination of effects.

There are so many variables in graphics. They're as unique as the people who create them. It's impossible to think about every possibility and say, in an unqualified way, "Do this in that situation." What I can say — and I've said lots! — is feel free to play with all of the tools at your disposal. And feel open to saving many versions of the same file and even — and especially in the beginning — opening those files after they're saved and looking at them. Examine what's good and bad about each before you decide which one will actually grace your Web page.

Converting an existing image into an acceptable Web graphic is easy-cheesy. Doing it the very best way requires patience, discovery, and lots of playing with your tools. Give yourself permission to experiment! Figure 25-1 shows that you should give yourself permission to play. What's going to make the best combination of compression, format, and bit-depth? It depends entirely on the nature of the image you're working on.

Figure 25-1: Saving many versions of the same file and then looking to see what gave you the best result is not that time-consuming and can really help you get a feel for what works. Especially in the beginning.

Resize Before You Upload

When possible, make your document the size you want it to be *before* you upload it to a Web site. That is, resize in your image composer, not in HTML.

There are two reasons for this. Resizing in HTML makes your document slower to download. That's because the server is doing some size translations while it brings up your image. Also — and more importantly for our purposes — resizing an image in HTML can make you end up with a really yucky looking graphic.

Figure 25-2 is a classic example of why resizing in your image editor is an infinitely better idea than resizing in HTML. Both of these graphics are the same file, sing.gif. The one on the left, however, has been resized in HTML. The one on the right is the size that the file was saved at in the image editor. The graphic on the left looks staircased and bitmapped and, well, yucky. While the one on the right — remember, it's the same file — looks great.

Figure 25-2:
A good case for doing the groundwork before you get to HTML.

Include ALT Tags

What happens when someone visits your Web site without using a graphical browser? Or when your images just don't load? Can surfers still navigate your site?

The ALT tag ensures that visitors who — for whatever reason — can't see your good graphics still have a clue about what's going on. Figure 25-3 shows how ALT tags look in place of graphics.

Figure 25-3: What happens when one of your graphics doesn't load? When you use the ALT tag in HTML properly, people can still negotiate your site.

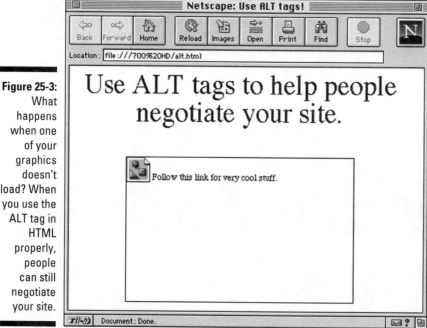

Using the ALT tag

Let's look at how it's done.

1. Open your HTML file in the usual way.

I specified a light background just so you can see everything real well on the printed page.

```
<HTML>
<HEAD>
<TITLE>Use ALT tags!</TITLE>
</HEAD>
<BODY BGCOLOR="#ffffff">
<P><CENTER><FONT SIZE=+4>Use ALT tags to help people
        negotiate your site.</FONT></CENTER></P>
```

2. Here's where you get to the image-specific stuff.

```
<P><CENTER><IMG SRC="follow.gif" WIDTH="301"
        HEIGHT="185" ALIGN="BOTTOM" ALT="Follow this
        link for very cool stuff."></CENTER>
```

As you can see, the ALT command is very simple to use. It sneaks right in with all of the image-specific commands. You can either describe what *would* happen if the graphic were there, or what *should* happen now that the surfer has arrived.

3. Then end your file in the usual way.

```
</BODY>
</HTML>
```

Another good reason to include the ALT tag

 Increasingly, people with disabilities find that the Internet is an incredibly powerful resource for finding information. The Internet, don't forget, is that fabulous equalizer and many people who feel challenged in other aspects of their lives feel freedom and equality on the 'Net.

As a designer, you can help by making your site as friendly as possible to all people. The ALT tag helps.

For example, some sight-impaired people have computers that *speak* your site aloud to them while they surf. ALT tags help the blind negotiate your site as you intended, even without your graphics.

Remember, the most effective sites work on many levels.

Use Your Cache

After a browser downloads an image from your Web site, the graphic is in the browser's cache — kind of like the computer's cash on hand — for the duration of the visit. In very simple terms, every time the computer needs that same image, it loads spanky-fast because it's already on the client's end.

Now that *you* know that, you can see why it's a good idea to trade on that knowledge. Anything that makes your pages load faster — or even *seem* to load faster is a Good Thing. Learning a few caching tricks is a good idea.

✔ Recycle images as much as possible. This means the exact same image used in the same size and saved as the exact same name on different pages. Every time visitors need this image, it's already in their cache and loads — from their own hard drive — at lightning speed.

✔ Sometimes you can tile frequently used images with new ones for a whole new image — or just to show off.

You accomplish this by jamming the <IMG> tags next to each other without a break. Because of this, the images look like one continuous graphic, as shown in Figure 25-4.

Figure 25-4: Sometimes you can tile several images together. When you use this technique with images that the browser has already cached, it can give a look of freshness to a new page without adding to download time at all.

Here's how you do it.

1. **In a regular HTML file, open an HTML file and assign that file a title and a background color, as shown in the following code example.**

```
<HTML>
<HEAD>
<TITLE>Two Images for the Price of One...</TITLE>
</HEAD>
<BODY BGCOLOR="#ffffff">
```

2. **Image tags work in the usual way, except there is no space between them. In this example, the size has been specified, but you can do it without that, as well.**

```
<IMG SRC="opera.gif" WIDTH="262" HEIGHT="232"><IMG
       SRC="opera8.gif" WIDTH="262" HEIGHT="232">
```

3. **The HTML file is closed as usual.**

```
</BODY>
</HTML>
```

Watch Your Colormaps

Remember, for cross-platform color you're really limited to 216 safe colors. Get a good handle on what they are and how to secure them. There are times when a dithered image — one that has invented itself from colors the browser *thinks* are right — is okay. Sometimes, dithering just isn't kosher. For instance, dithered backgrounds hardly ever work. Make sure that you've used one of the 216 colors in your colormap, as shown in Figure 25-5, while working with backgrounds.

Interlace

Saving your GIFs as Interlaced doesn't actually make anything go more quickly. It does give people downloading your file the feeling that things are going more quickly. This is because a file that has been interlaced downloads a bit at a time. Visitors to your Web site can watch something while waiting for your interlaced files. Surfers waiting for non-interlaced files to download look at a big hole until the whole download is done. Figures 25-6 and 25-7 illustrate an interlaced image that is partially and fully downloaded.

Figure 25-5:
The 216 colors of the cross-platform color map. When you use these colors to build your graphics and backgrounds you're safe. Go out of the palette and you run the risk of dithering.

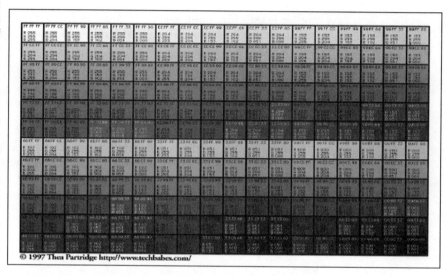

© 1997 Thea Partridge http://www.techbabes.com/

Figure 25-6:
The interlaced GIF as it downloads. It looks pretty sketchy while it's happening, but the surfer can see that something *is* happening.

Figure 25-7:
The same image as Figure 25-6, only this time it's fully downloaded. Giving the surfer something to look at while they wait can sometimes stop them from surfing off elsewhere.

Understand HTML Tags

This is true even when you always use a WYSIWYG HTML editor. Knowing what stuff actually does helps you get the most from the Web graphics you work so hard to create!

Here are some of the basics:

- ✔ IMG always stands for image, and lets the browser know that some type of graphic is incoming.
- ✔ SRC stands for source, which tells the browser just where that graphic is coming from, because images need not always be located in the same place as the HTML code.
- ✔ ISMAP tells the browser that this particular graphic is an image map.
- ✔ USEMAP tells the browser that the image map is client-side, so information about where you can go on the map is found right here, thank you.
- ✔ ALT is for displaying the *alternate* text that is only shown when, for some reason, the graphic itself doesn't show up.

Understanding image-related HTML codes helps you solve problems when they occur. Just as important, it helps ensure that your Web graphics appear in the best light possible.

Chapter 26

Ten More Useful Programs

- -

- -

*T*hroughout this book, I use various software packages and computer platforms to show how it's done. To be honest, I have my favorites — programs so useful, I seldom go a day without booting them at least once.

In the ever-changing world of Web graphics, it's important to stay on your toes. Watch for new programs and technologies that will help your work. I think the most useful programs probably haven't been invented yet. When they are, I'll be in line to try them!

The programs in this chapter are among the latest and best tools for Web Graphics. Some are free, or almost free. Others will set you back several hundred dollars. What do they have in common? They're handy to have around for use with Web graphics.

TextureMill

Platform: Macintosh

Sometimes the very best finds are so affordable and underpromoted that it's a wonder we find them at all. TextureMill is like that.

Slick and tiny, TextureMill weighs in at just over 500K. Even crummy games can take ten times that much disk space, so something this useful and this small is refreshing.

As the name implies, TextureMill helps you build textures; you can form the textures into backgrounds. An incredibly simple interface allows you to make over 400 patterns from the 20 base patterns included. After you pay the $20 shareware fee, you get another 80 patterns. These 100 base patterns let you make over 2,000 pattern variations.

```
Deep Devices
P.O. Box 620038
Newton Lower Falls, MA 02162
```

Corel WebMaster

Platforms: Windows 95 or Windows NT 4.0

Corel WebMaster wins in the "if I could only have one package" category. It has to. There's just so much there!

In the tradition of CorelDraw, the WebMaster package is stuffed full of programs to do virtually everything necessary to create and manage Web pages.

You expect a Web site management tool and a Web page creation tool, and both are here, with all the bells and whistles you can imagine plus a few more. Also included are an image editing program, a vector-based drawing program, an animation program, a program to help you publish database information on a Web site and a VRML modeling program.

The whole thing combines the rock-solid Corel feel and a very sensible approach to integration.

It's worthwhile mentioning that WebMaster doesn't rely on CorelDraw graphics in any way. It's quite possible to use WebMaster without running CorelDraw.

If there's a downside to this package, it's that no Macintosh version is available. Considering the number of Mac-based Web designers, I think Corel should reconsider.

```
Corel Corporation
http://www.corel.com
```

Adobe Illustrator

Platforms: Macintosh, Windows 95, Windows NT

Illustrator is worthy of mention because many designers — especially on the Mac platform — run Illustrator with Photoshop.

Illustrator has a long history as a Macintosh favorite. It is probably Photoshop's acceptance on the PC platform for Web creation that finally prompted Adobe to release a Windows version of Illustrator.

Whyever Adobe has added Illustrator to the Windows repertoire, Illustrator remains a popular partner for Photoshop. In its vector-y way, Illustrator creates drawings as sheets and lines that can be stretched and remolded until you're satisfied, then imported into Photoshop.

```
Adobe
345 Park Avenue
San Jose, CA 95110-2704
http://www.adobe.com
```

CorelDraw 7

Platforms: Windows 95 & NT 4.0

If I'm going to talk nice about Illustrator, it only seems fair I mention CorelDraw as well. Especially as Draw7 is just so darned impressive.

In the first place, CorelDraw comes in a much bigger, heavier box than Illustrator. Draw7 is so heavy because much more comes in the package. Corel is famous for packing so many useful goodies in their boxes. Draw7 is no exception. In fact, it exemplifies the rule.

As it happens, the Draw7 package is especially useful for the Web designer. Looking at the program, I don't think this is an accident. The package incorporates three important elements:

- CorelDraw, which supports the full range of Web graphics.
- Corel Photo-Paint 7, which offers the tools associated with Photoshop (including Kai's Power Tools, Digimarc digital watermarking, and support for Internet graphics).
- Dream 3D 7, which adds the tools to form 3-D images, such as the Internet standard VRML.

The fact that CorelDraw is an impressive draw tool in its own right — one that just seems to keep getting better — almost seems a bonus.

There are only a couple of downsides to CorelDraw 7:

✔ CorelDraw 7 is not a program for lightweight systems. Corel recommends a Pentium 120 PC, with 32MB RAM, and a minimum of 40MB of free hard drive space to hold Draw7.

✔ The Mac version of CorelDraw isn't anywhere in sight.

```
Corel Corporation
http://www.corel.com
```

GIF Construction Set

Platforms: Windows 3.1, 95 & NT

GIF Construction Set has a lot of really cool features for building various types of GIF animations that users of various levels of experience can take advantage of. However, the part of GIF Construction Set I really love is the Animation Wizard.

The Animation Wizard almost makes it possible to create a Web animation with your eyes closed. In fact, the Wizard in this program makes animation so simple, it's almost easier than loading a Windows program.

All you need to bring are the GIFs. The Animation Wizard strings them together — in seconds, you can be looking at your own little animation.

Too cool for school!

GIF Construction Set is shareware with a registration fee of $20.

```
Alchemy Mindworks Inc.
P.O. Box 500
Beeton, Ontario, Canada
LOG 1A0
```

FontFX

Platforms: Windows 95, Windows NT 4.0

FontFX doesn't do much at all. And what it does isn't just for Web graphics. However, it does this one thing so well (for so little money) that it's entirely worthy of mention.

FontFX lets you take any words, put them into any font, and then do amazing 3-D tricks with them. Just what looks absolutely smashing on a Web page — and hardly anywhere else.

FontFX offers a plethora of lighting, rotation, and camera effects that make type cool. A whole pile of templates guides you through custom files around your own type. (I built the graphic in Figure 26-1 in about 15 seconds with an existing template.) Because FontFX exports GIFs, it was also very easy to save it for a Web page. I dumped it into an HTML file and gave it a black background. Voilà! Instant logotype for the Web.

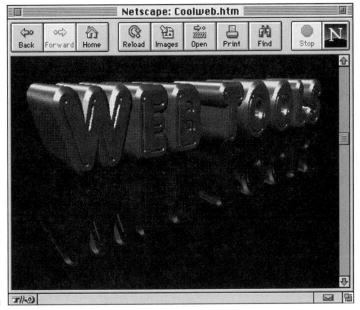

Figure 26-1:
I was able to create this type very quickly in FontFX.

```
DCSi
3775 Iris Avenue, Suite 1B
Boulder, CO 80301
http://www.dcsifx.com
```

Microsoft FrontPage

Platforms: Windows 95, Windows NT, Power Macintosh

Microsoft infiltrates all aspects of computing. In PCs in the 90s, it's impossible to turn around without smacking into a Microsoft application. Truth is, the quality of Microsoft offerings varies wildly.

FrontPage is at the top of Microsoft software. If your system runs under Windows 95 or Windows NT, there are worse choices.

Microsoft packs a lot into the slim FrontPage box. They call it "Professional Web Site Publishing Without Programming." That's really not far off. The FrontPage Web module encourages management of the Web site without much effort on the part of the user. If you follow instructions from the beginning, you're thinking about the totality of your Web site from the very beginning.

The FrontPage Editor makes a Web page easy to start, even if you barely know what a Web page is. FrontPage guides you through a lot of the tough spots. It's also possible (a big point for me) to edit the HTML code directly.

However, FrontPage Editor adds proprietary tags willy-nilly. There's no guarantee that FrontPage code will work in other HTML editors.

One of my favorite parts of FrontPage has nothing to do with FrontPage. Bundled with the program (casually, like an aside) is an elegant image editing program, Microsoft Image Composer. It's curious to me that you can't buy Image Composer all by its lonesome. You can download a trial version of Image Composer at the Microsoft Web site, and it's thrown in with a couple of Microsoft's Web-specific packages, such as FrontPage.

It wouldn't surprise me to see Image Composer on its own at some future point. It deserves the distribution. Image Composer is designed for exactly the task of this book: creating Web graphics. It's super-easy to use and handles most common graphic formats, such as TIFF, GIF, JPEG, and Photoshop.

```
Microsoft
http://microsoft.com/frontpage/
```

ClarisWorks 4.0: Internet Edition

Platforms: Macintosh, Windows 95

ClarisWorks is an all-things-to-all-basic-computing-dudes package. But it's a happy package — thorough in its own way and very easy to use.

I also like how well all the pieces fit together. ClarisWorks jumps from the word processor to the spreadsheet program to the database. None have much to do with designing Web graphics, but it's good to have around if you ever do anything besides design stuff.

The "Internet" part of this particular ClarisWorks software is extremely tough. In addition to Claris Home Page (which is also covered in this chapter), ClarisWorks includes Netscape Navigator and a couple of electronic versions of Internet reference books, such as the Internet Yellow Pages. Everyone (or at least, a whole lot of someones) bundles Internet Explorer at the drop of a hat, so it's nice to see Netscape sneak in there once and again.

ClarisWorks: Internet is not to be confused with FrontPage, or even considered for the same thing. ClarisWorks is powerful program for writing and recordkeeping.

```
Claris
5201 Patrick Henry Drive
Box 58168
Santa Clara, CA 95052-8168
```

Claris Home Page 2.0

Platforms: Macintosh, Windows 95, Windows NT

An elegant interface places Home Page among the top of the WYSIWYG HTML editing contenders. Like PageMill, the interface seems to have been created with the graphic artist in mind: Anyone who has worked in other types of design programs will immediately feel somewhat comfortable with this program. All of those features — and more — make Home Page a great choice. But, to my mind, the thing the really sets it apart isn't what it does, it's what it *doesn't* do.

Claris Home Page 2.0 creates clean HTML code without adding its own little quirks. As far as I can tell, it has no proprietary tags at all. Most WYSIWYG HTML editors add silly bits of proprietary code that no one outside of the software publisher understands — flotsam and jetsam that aren't part of HTML 3.2 and don't seem to do much of anything. The HTML code that Home Page produces is easy to paste into other applications.

```
Claris
5201 Patrick Henry Drive
Box 58168
Santa Clara, CA 95052-8168
```

HotMetal Pro 3.0

Platforms: Macintosh, Windows 3.x, Windows 95, Windows NT

Of all the HTML editors, HotMetal Pro 3.0 wins in the icon department. If you judge a program by the number of icons in the menubar, HotMetal wins. There are rows upon rows of them — almost everything, it seems, can be accessed from an icon in the main window. If you get past the bristling banks of icons, HotMetal Pro 3.0 is an incredibly powerful HTML editing tool.

HotMetal Pro 3.0 is what I call a hybrid HTML editor. It's not a straight code input-style editor, but it's not *exactly* WYSIWYG either. That said, many people are comfortable with the way HotMetal Pro works. You can turn the tags on or off, but you can't see straight code (which I like to see).

Of the WYSIWYG editors, HotMetal Pro 3.0 is the most proficient at working with files created by *other* WYSIWYG HTML editors.

HotMetal was one of the first WYSIWYG HTML editors and the program retains a strong following because it has its familiar features and the latest bells and whistles.

```
SoftQuad
20 Eglinton Ave. West
Toronto, ON Canada M4R 1K8
http://www.softquad.com
```

Part VI
Appendix

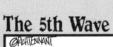

In this part . . .

The glossary will help you fight your way through the jargon jungle. Think of it as subtitles for computerese.

Glossary

Amaya

The W3C's "testbed client" is both a graphical Internet browser and a Web authoring tool.

Applet

An application written in Java meant to be downloaded on an Internet browser and executed on a remote computer.

ASCII

American Standard Code for Information Interchange. Standard code for representing characters as binary numbers. ASCII is most often referred to as plain text, in contrast to formatted text, which makes use of special characters and formatting commands.

Au

An audio format commonly found on the Internet.

bandwidth

The volume of information per unit of time that a computer, person, or transmission medium can handle.

Binhex

Binary Hexadecimal. A way of safely transporting non-text files from one computer to another.

bit depth

The number of data storage bits available to describe each point of a bitmapped image.

browser

A program that lets you look at the Internet's World Wide Web in a graphical way. Mosaic was the first Web browser of import. Current field leaders Netscape Navigator and Microsoft Internet Explorer are both interpretations on that same original theme.

Byte

Combinations of bits (ones and zeros) that stand for characters. There are 256 combinations from 00000000 to 11111111 in base 2.

Cascading Style Sheets

Also known as CSS. An HTML extension that allows more designer-friendly formatting of Web documents created in HTML.

CD-ROM

Compact Disc Read Only Memory. The CD-ROM can store up to 650MB of computer information for your computer.

CGI

Common Gateway Interface. The protocol that tells the Web server how to deal with other pieces of software on the computer.

CGI-bin

What else? The place on a Web server where the CGI scripts are stored. I always imagine a rat-proof, stainless steel storage compartment. They don't really look like that at all.

CGI Script

Scripts that are stored on a server that are necessary for interactive forms and server-side image maps.

clickable image map

See *image map.*

client-side image map

An image map where all of the map-relevant information is stored right in the Web page's own HTML code.

Cougar

The code name of the yet-to-be-released version of HTML.

download

To receive data or code from another system. The opposite of upload.

Ethernet

A type of Local Area Network (LAN) for interconnecting computers and peripheral devices at high speed.

FAQ

Frequently Asked Questions or a list of answers to the same.

file server

A computer whose function is the storage of files for a network.

file transfer protocol

An Internet service that allows the transfer of files between different computers.

freeware

Software that can be used and distributed without charge.

GIF

Graphic Interchange Format. One of the most popular methods of graphics compression used to transfer images over the Internet.

graphical browser

A Web client, such as Netscape or Explorer, that displays graphics and HTML coded files. See also *browser.*

GUI

Graphical User Interface.

hexadecimal

A notation for writing code in base-16. For example, 0E in hexadecimal is equal to 15 in everyday base-10 notation.

home page

The first or main document in a Web site.

HTML

HyperText Markup Language. The styles and markup tags used to create Web pages.

HTTP

HyperText Transfer Protocol. The way hypertext files are moved on the Internet.

HyperText

The linking technology on which the Web is based. The "hot" links you click on to get somewhere else on the Web.

image map

More than one hypertext link embedded in a single graphic. Clicking on an area in the graphic links you to a related hypertext page.

inline image

A graphic on a Web page that is automatically called when the page is loaded.

interlaced GIF

A GIF image that has been saved in such a way that it displays gradually while being downloaded.

Internet

The largest computer network in the world. All having in common the TCP/IP protocol for transferring files.

Internet Explorer

One of the more popular graphical browsers for the World Wide Web. Internet Explorer is made by Microsoft. Though it was a relatively late arrival on the browser scene, it's become popular very quickly.

intranet

A closed network used for distributing information throughout a corporation or other organization. The protocols used are based on TCP/IP.

IP

Internet Protocol. The most important protocol on which the Internet is based. It allows the transfer of packets of information on multiple networks.

ISDN

Interactive Services Digital Network. The way to download big files faster! A special type of telephone line that allows Internet connections at very high speeds.

Java

A programming language developed by Sun Microsystems that supports the creation of small programs — called applets — that can be seamlessly downloaded from a Web page and executed on a browser.

JPEG

Joint Photographic Experts Group format. A format common for displaying photographic-quality images on the Web.

K

Kilobyte. The symbol for the unit used to measure the computer's memory. 1K is equal to 1,024 characters.

LAN

Local Area Network.

link

A hyperlink connection between two separate files or locations from a Web site.

Lynx

A text-only browser. A Web client not intended to display graphics. Most common in the UNIX environment.

MIME

Multipurpose Internet Mail Extensions. The standard way that browsers attach files to e-mail.

Mosaic

The original graphical Web browser. The browser that all current Web browsers are based on.

Netscape

One of the more popular graphical browsers for the World Wide Web. Netscape Navigator is the name of the browser component. Netscape Communicator is the communications suite introduced in 1997 that includes the Navigator browser portion.

PDF

Portable Document Format. A format that retains the fonts formatting of the original layout, regardless of distribution method or platform: including the Web.

Plug-in

A small application that works within a larger application to add features and functionality to the existing program. For example, Adobe Photoshop has many plug-ins available that allow it to use third party scanners, apply special filters, and so on.

PNG

Portable Network Graphics. Pronounced "ping." A non-proprietary GIF-like format for displaying Internet graphics. PNG does not, however, support multiple frames in the way that GIF does for animations.

RAM

Random Access Memory. This is the area in memory that the computer reserves for its operator's uses.

RealAudio

An application that lets you hear sound from the Internet.

server

The computer where your Web pages live. The server is connected via TCP/IP to the Internet, and other browser-equipped computers come to see your Web pages. The server serves them up.

server-side image map

An image map where all of the map-relevant information is stored on the server, rather than right in the Web page's own HTML code, as is the case with client-side image maps.

shareware

Software that the author makes available on a free-to-try basis. You try it and — if you like it — you send the author the amount requested directly.

software

The set of programs that tells a computer what to do.

SGML

Standard Generalized Markup Language. The specification that describes the content and structure of a document. HTML is a subset of SGML.

tag

An element in HTML that holds the business end of a Web page. The secret stuff no one sees on your Web page unless they look at your source code.

TCP/IP

Transmission Control Protocol/Internet Protocol. The suite of protocols that make the Internet possible.

thumbnail

A small representation of a larger image. On the Web, the thumbnail can serve as a preview to a large graphic.

transparent image

An image with an opaque background that appears to float on the Web page. Of the presently popular formats, only GIFs can have a color made transparent.

UNIX

The operating system that was important in the development of the Internet and still plays a major role on many systems. UNIX was developed at Bell Laboratories in the early 1970s, replacing an earlier system called Multics.

upload

To transfer data or code to another system. The opposite of download.

URL

Uniform Resource Locator. The specification for identifying and locating any file on the Web.

VRML

Virtual Reality Modeling Language. Pronounced "ver-mil." VRML is a set of standards for creating virtual 3-D worlds on the Internet.

W3C

The World Wide Web Consortium. The governing body of all things HTML. We're not worthy!

Web authoring

The word *author* "verbed" once again. The creator of Web pages.

Web client

An application program that accesses Web pages and downloads information.

Webmaster

Alternately, Webmistress. The big cheese boss of a Web site. The person whose e-mail address is listed on a site as the person to send complaints to.

Webmistress

See *Webmaster.*

Web Page

A complete HTML document with tags linking it to other pages on the Web.

Web site

The sum total of a bunch of Web pages relating to the same topic, organization, or person.

Web surfer

A visitor to a Web site.

World Wide Web

Alternately the Web or WWW. The hypermedia-based system carried by the Internet for locating and accessing various Internet resources.

Appendix
What's on the CD-ROM

*T*he *Web Graphics For Dummies* CD-ROM included with this book includes several utilities and software demos for making Web graphics on the Mac and Windows platforms.

Like the book, the *Web Graphics For Dummies* CD-ROM is cross-platform. Readers using the disc on a Mac will see only the Mac files. Likewise, PC users will only see those files intended for the PC. And everyone can see the CD-ROM files that relate directly to exercises in *Web Graphics For Dummies*. Because the exercise files are in popular graphical and Web formats, these files are platform-independent. (One of the benefits of Web technology.)

The programs on the *Web Graphics For Dummies* CD-ROM are shareware, limited-time trials, or demonstration versions that allow only a certain amount of functionality so that you can try before you buy. The programs selected for inclusion on the *Web Graphics For Dummies* CD-ROM run the gamut of Web graphic tasks. There are programs to create and convert graphics; prepare GIF animations; produce image maps; prepare HTML code and some that are just cool to have around but are difficult to categorize.

Most of the software on the *Web Graphics For Dummies* CD-ROM is discussed elsewhere in the book, in addition to the coverage included in this chapter. In fact, this chapter can be a reference for you while you read the book. When a software package is described in the book, check this appendix to find if it's incorporated on the CD-ROM.

Shareware Nag Screen

Shareware doesn't mean *free*. It means you get to *try* the software at no cost. If you like it, please buy the full version or pay the shareware fee asked for. Usually, it's cheap. Some shareware publishers ask for something as small as a postcard from wherever you are. The few dollars they may ask is usually more than fair ($20 is common), especially when you consider that you aren't taking a risk — you've already tried the product.

Installing from the CD-ROM

In this chapter, I cover each program on the *Web Graphics For Dummies* CD-ROM, what the programs do, and how to get the software up to speed. But don't forget to read the special README files that help get you started. Most of the software packages have their own README files. Each was created by the software company that provided the software. You can find the latest about possible system conflicts, custom installation routines, and instructions for obtaining full versions or registering your software if you choose to use it after the trial period. Also, make sure you read the software's instructions before you run it.

This chapter is only an introduction to each program included on the *Web Graphics For Dummies* CD-ROM. Neither the author nor IDG Books Worldwide warrants the performance or suitability of the software on the *Web Graphics For Dummies* CD-ROM. But you save lots of time by installing the software from the CD-ROM instead of downloading from the Web so you can make your own judgment.

As always when purchasing software, your decisions about Web graphics software must be made carefully and with respect for your experience and comfort with the program or class of software. My needs are as likely to be different from yours as my computer system (or my car) is from yours. The more programs you try, the more educated your purchasing decision.

Cross-Platform Folders

These folders include files for *Web Graphics For Dummies* that can be read with both Windows and Macintosh computers.

README

This text file can be opened in any word processor and contains pretty much the same stuff you're reading now. It's just a good idea to have the file in both places.

Author

These files relate to the text in the book. These are mostly TIFF and GIF files that are asked for in certain exercises in the indicated chapters in the book.

The exception is the file called hexrgb.GIF, which is shown in Figure A-1. This is a cross-platform color chart that guides you to browser-correct colors for your Web page. You can use this chart to choose colors that look the way you intend in Microsoft and Netscape browsers on both Windows and Macintosh.

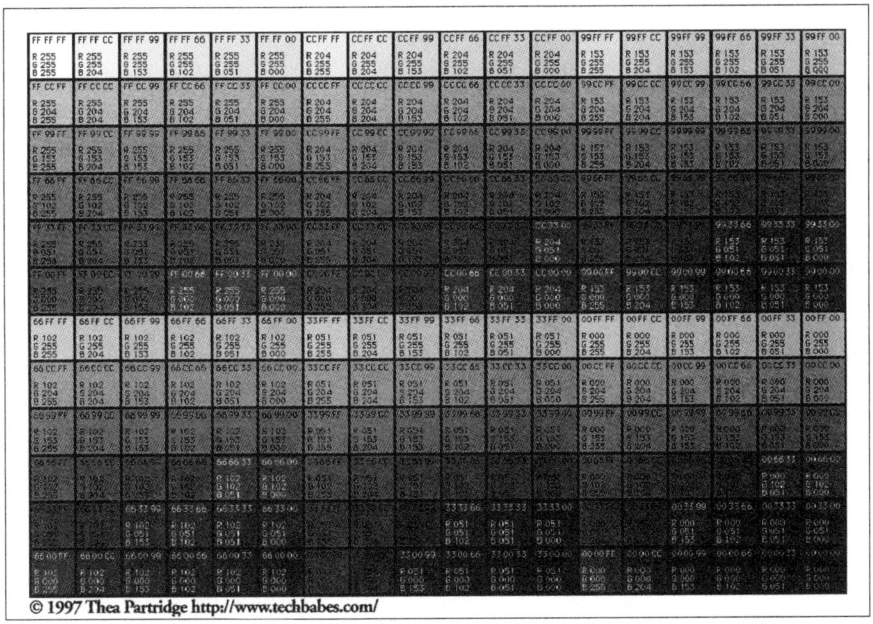

Figure A-1:
The 216-color cross platform color palette is on the *Web Graphics For Dummies* CD-ROM as hexrgb.gif. It's a lot more colorful in person!

© 1997 Thea Partridge http://www.techbabes.com/

Windows Programs

The Windows files included should all install nicely from their own directories on the disc. Don't forget to read each file's README or instruction files before working with each new program.

DeBabelizer Pro

This directory contains a demo of Equilibrium's DeBabelizer Pro. While DeBabelizer is an amazingly powerful graphics processor, it's a little tough to get the full feel for that with this demo. That's because the Equilibrium logo is embedded into anything you work on. That means this demo is of limited usefulness, as you can see in Figure A-2. It gives you a good feel for the interface and some of the program's possibilities, but it's tough to really see what the program can do while you keep staring at someone else's logo emblazoned all over your work. (Why can't everyone just get the whole 30-day demo thing worked out?)

Figure A-2: It's tough to get a really good feel for the capabilities of DeBabelizer Pro from the demo. You see *its* logo onscreen every time you do anything.

If you're thinking about purchasing this really excellent program, the demo gives you a good feel for the interface and how all the controls work, just don't plan on using any of the files you create unless you really, really like the company's logo . . . and even then, get permission first.

To install the DeBabelizer demo, launch the setup file from on the *Web Graphics For Dummies* CD-ROM.

You are prompted when the InstallShield Wizard is activated. Click Next to keep things hopping, but first stop and read what you're promising when you get to the DeBabelizer Pro Demo license agreement. If you agree to the terms, click the Yes icon to continue installation. If you don't agree, click No; the installation terminates.

The installer asks you where you want the demo installed on your hard drive. If you have a special place on your hard drive for demo software or graphical aids, use the Browse button to tell the Wizard where you want the program to be installed. Otherwise, the Wizard indicates a Destination Directory — most likely, near the base directory on your C: drive — where the file is installed. If you're okay with the default location, click Next to move to the next installation stage.

Next, you are offered three types of installation.

- *Typical* installation includes all the files you need to run the demo.
- *Compact* installation limits files to the very minimum needed to run the demo. Choose this option only if you are concerned about space on your hard drive.
- *Custom* installation is for advanced users; you specify exactly which files you want installed, if you think you know best.

Unless you are an advanced user with some customizing mandates, choose *Typical* and then click Next to continue the installation.

If you are a Windows 95 user, you are prompted for where you'd like the program's icons to show up on My Computer, as well as what you want the folder called. The default is Equilibrium, the name of the company that makes DeBabelizer. You may find it easier to locate the program if you replace the word *Equilibrium* with *DeBab* Demo or something else that immediately grabs your attention.

If everything went all right — it usually does, because DeBabelizer is a very cooperative install program — a screen tells you so and what to do next. Click OK to exit the installation routine and return to Windows.

The DeBabelizer Pro demo is now ready to run. Launch it the same way you launch other Windows programs.

Acrobat Reader

This directory contains Adobe Acrobat 3.0, Adobe's PDF reader. Installation software is included for both Windows 95 and Windows 3.1. Even if you don't plan on using Acrobat right now, remember that you have it here. When you get your hands on a PDF file, it's good to know how to look at it.

While the reader is free, if you want to create PDF files you must buy Acrobat. Purchase instructions are included with the Acrobat reader. They're in a PDF file, though, so you must install the reader to read the instruction!

To install the Acrobat Reader, simply launch the setup file in the appropriate folder. The setup files included are smart enough to install the Reader with very little help from you. (I like programs that do that!)

The first screen informs you that you're launching a self-extracting EXE and asks whether you want to continue. To continue, click the Yes icon.

The InstallShield does all of the necessary unpacking and organizing, and doesn't bother you again until it's time for a copyright notice and a warning to close all other Windows applications before continuing.

After reading the copyright information, click Next to acknowledge the notice and continue to the next window.

Now, the by-now-familiar License Agreement. It's always good to read these. You are, after all, installing software onto your computer that — strictly speaking — isn't yours. It's good to know just what you're promising!

If you agree, click Yes to continue to the next screen. If you don't, click No and the install is terminated.

On the next screen, the installer asks you where to install the demo. If you have a special place on your hard drive for demo software or graphical aids, use the Browse button to tell the Wizard where you want the program to be located. Otherwise, the Wizard indicates a Destination Directory — most likely, near the root directory of your C: drive — where the file is placed. If you're okay with the default location, click Next to move to the next item.

While the installer actually goes through installation, you're treated to a little Acrobat commercial. If you haven't seen it before, pay attention. These little install plugs impart all sorts of interesting tidbits.

If everything went okay, the next screen tells you and also lets you know that you can see a README file if you want to. Click Finish to continue. The README file appears on your screen in NotePad automatically.

The README file is worth a quick read. It contains late breaking news about Acrobat, its use and installation, and important advice on how to proceed after starting Acrobat. Read it before continuing.

After you exit the README file and NotePad, you get a dialog box telling you that installation is complete. Click OK to complete the installation and return to Windows.

You launch Adobe Acrobat in the same way you would any other dedicated Windows program. The interface is shown in Figure A-3.

Figure A-3:
Adobe
Acrobat
Reader 3.0
looking at
the PDF
file that
describes it.
It's actually
a pretty
interesting
document.

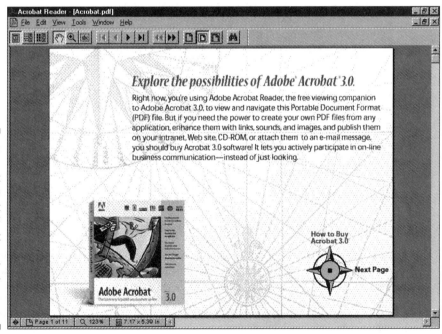

FontFX

This directory contains the very cool font manipulation tool FontFX. This is a working demo, and registration information is included in the package.

To install the FontFX demo, launch the setup icon in the FontFX directory on the *Web Graphics For Dummies* CD-ROM.

The first screen informs you that you're launching a self-extracting EXE and ask whether you want to continue. To continue, click the Yes icon.

The InstallShield does all of the necessary unpacking and organizing. It won't bother you again until it's time for the copyright notice and a warning to close all other Windows applications before continuing.

After you read the copyright information, click Next to acknowledge the notice and continue to the next Window.

On the next screen, the installer asks you to tell it where you'd like the demo to be located. If you have a special place on your hard drive for demo software or graphical aids, use the Browse button to tell the Wizard where you want the program to be located. Alternately, the Wizard indicates a Destination Directory — most likely pretty high up on your C: drive — where the file is placed. If you're okay with the default location, click Next to move to the next item.

Next you are offered three types of installation.

- ✔ The *Typical* installation gives you all the files you need to run the demo.

- ✔ The *Compact* installation gives you the very minimum number of files needed to run the demo. You would only choose this option if you have a very teeny or overfull hard drive and are concerned about space.

- ✔ *Custom* is for more advanced users and lets you specify exactly which files you want used.

Unless you are an advanced user and have some customizing mandates, you can choose *Typical* and then click Next to continue the installation.

At this point, the FontFX demo installation program offers to install the Adobe Acrobat reader. If you've already installed it, select No to continue.

Next you get a dialog box letting you know that the setup is complete. Click OK to exit back to Windows.

The FontFX demo is now ready to run. Launch it the same way you would any other dedicated Windows program. The interface is shown in Figure A-4.

Figure A-4:
The Font FX
demo:
ready to
create
interesting
font effects
for your
Web site.

HotMetal

Okay, so there's no folder for HotMetal on the *Web Graphics For Dummies* CD-ROM. HotMetal's demonstration program is designed to run from the root directory of a CD-ROM, so the HotMetal demo doesn't like being stuffed into a tidy HotMetal folder.

To view the HotMetal 3.0 automated tour on a Windows 95 system, launch Hmdemo32.exe from the root directory of the *Web Graphics For Dummies* CD-ROM. You don't get a trial version from the *Web Graphics For Dummies* CD-ROM, but you can see a thorough demonstration of HotMetal's features.

The HotMetal demo takes you on an automated tour of the HTML editor HotMetal 3.0, which will at least give you enough information to let you decide whether you want to

 ✔ Visit the the HotMetal Web site at http://www.softquad.com to download a working 30-day trial.

 ✔ Hop along to your friendly neighborhood computer store to buy the latest version.

Mapedit

This directory contains the very popular image map building tool Mapedit. It's a shareware program. If you like the program, you're required to register it after 30 days. The timed demo stops working after the month is up if you don't register Mapedit.

To install Mapedit, launch the appropriate icon in the Mapedit directory. You first get a dialog box asking you where you'd like to install Mapedit. The default is in a Mapedit directory in the Program Files directory, so — unless you prefer a special directory for this type of program — the default is quite acceptable.

The next dialog box informs you that Mapedit has been installed. If you're a Windows 95 user, you're asked whether it's okay for the installer to place a program group flag on your start menu. Since this makes it easier to find, this seems like a good idea. If you don't want it to install the program group on the Start menu, select No. The install will be completed, but you won't have a Mapedit icon on your Start menu.

The next dialog box informs you that the installation was successful and asks whether you want to start Mapedit. Select Yes if you want to look at this image mapping tool right away. Select No if you have other installs to perform before you restart your system.

PageMill

This directory contains an install for the working demonstration version of Adobe's WYSIWYG HTML editor, PageMill. While it's a fully functional demo, and you can try all of the cool things that PageMill does, the demo stops working 30 days after installation.

Please note that Adobe's implementation of 30-day-trial protection for PageMill is *very* sensitive to previous installations of PageMill and other Adobe products. Even if you don't remember PageMill on your system, this version may decide you've already had your 30-day trial period.

PaintShop Pro

This directory contains an install for a working demo of the full featured image editor and converter, PaintShop Pro. This is another timed demo. If you like the program, you must register it — at a very reasonable price — to receive a registration "key" that lets you keep the working version on your computer.

To install PaintShop Pro, select the setup icon from the appropriate directory.

In short order, you're prompted for a location for PaintShop Pro's files to be installed. If you have a special area on your hard drive where you like this type of file to be installed, it's easy to negotiate your way there. However the default location — in a special PaintShop Pro directory in your program's file directory — should be satisfactory in most cases. Click Next after you decide.

The next screen asks whether you want to backup any files that are replaced during the installation. In general, when working with Windows, it's a good idea to select Yes and do the backup any time you see this sort of prompt: Just in Case. If you don't need them, you can always toss them out after. Better safe than reformatting. Make your decision, then click Next.

If you're a Windows 95 user, you're asked whether you want shortcuts for PaintShop Pro added to your Start menu. Personally, I like this sort of shortcut because programs are easier to find from the Start menu. Make your decision, and click Next.

After you see the Ready to Install! Screen, you have your last chance to abort the install procedure. This always cracks me up — if I'm this far, why bail now? Click Start Install to (ahem) start the install.

While the program is installing you see some interesting factoids about the program on your screen as shown in Figure A-5. But not for very long: for a program this comprehensive, it takes a surprisingly short time to load.

The last screen of the install allows you a couple of options:

- ✔ View the Readme file.
- ✔ Run Paint Shop Pro.

My money is on the former. Get the latest scoop from the Readme file before you start PaintShop Pro and go to work, as shown in Figure A-6.

Figure A-5:
The Paint
Shop Pro
installer is
very cheery
about
letting you
know when
things are
done
properly.

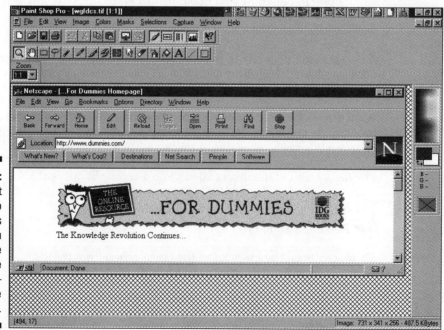

Figure A-6:
The Paint
Shop Pro
demo lets
you
manipulate
and save
graphics —
even create
them.

WebPainter

This directory contains an install for a working demo of WebPainter for Windows. WebPainter is a full-featured tool for creating GIF animations.

The demo version on the *Web Graphics For Dummies* CD-ROM is limited. It lets you use all of WebPainter's features to create GIF animations, and you can even save them. However, it will only let you export the first three frames of an animation file. (You can still create cool little animations with three frames.) Best of all, you get a real feel for the program to know whether you want to buy it.

To install WebPainter for Windows, launch the set up icon in the WebPainter directory of the *Web Graphics For Dummies* CD-ROM.

When you see the License Agreement dialog box, take the time to read the file. It's good to know just what you're promising when you install the software. Click the OK button at the bottom of the dialog box to indicate agreement with the terms and conditions set out there.

The installer next asks you where you'd like the WebPainter demo to be located. If you have a special place on your hard drive for demo software or graphical aids, use the Browse button to tell the installer where you want the program to be located. Alternately, choose the default Destination Directory, which is a directory called WebPainterDemo within the Program Files directory. If you're okay with the default location, click Next to move to the next item.

Windows 95 users are now asked whether they want WebPainter icons added to their Start menu. This can be a good idea as it doesn't take much room, but sure makes things easier to find if you use the Start menu much at all.

Next you get a dialog box letting you know that the setup is complete. Click OK to exit back to Windows.

The WebPainter demo is now ready to run. Launch it the same way you would any other dedicated Windows program.

Macintosh Programs

The Macintosh files included on the *Web Graphics For Dummies* CD-ROM should all install nicely from their own directories on the disc. Don't forget to read each file's README or instruction files before working with each new program.

ColorFinder

This directory installs ColorFinder: one of those fun-to-find programs that make the Web such a charming place. Here's the deal: one talented programmer wanted to be able to sample a color from anywhere on his Mac and have a program tell him what the corresponding hex color was. Since the program he wanted didn't exist, he wrote it. And since it was written, he shared it. As Wayne of acmetech.com writes in his README file, "ColorFinder is free. You can do anything you want with it except charge money for it. Enjoy." This so much evokes the spirit of the Web that I have to share it — and the program — with as many people as possible.

Thanks, Wayne.

ColorFinder is so refreshingly simple to use, you don't even have to install it. To use the program, simply drag the ColorFinder folder directly onto your hard drive. The result is shown in Figure A-7.

Double-click the ColorFinder icon to launch the program when you want to use it.

If you don't have much space on your hard drive, but want to check out ColorFinder, you can run it directly from the *Web Graphics For Dummies* CD-ROM, simply by double-clicking it as though it were on your hard drive. That's because ColorFinder is ready to use without installation.

Figure A-7:
Installing
ColorFinder
is as easy
as dragging
it to the
folder
where you
want it.

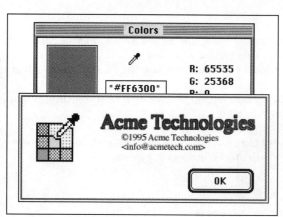

DeBabelizer

This directory contains a demo of Equilibrium's DeBabelizer Toolbox 1.6.5. The demo is limited — you can get a feel for the program and the interface, but you won't be able to save anything. Also, some of the formats that DeBabelizer can process aren't available on the demo version.

The DeBabelizer 1.6.5 demo does not require unpacking or installation. To use the program, simply drag the DeBabelizer 1.6.5 Demo folder directly onto your hard drive.

Double-click the DeBabelizer®1.6.5 DEMO icon to launch the program when you want to use it. (It stamps DEMO on your images, as shown in Figure A-8.)

If you don't have much space on your hard drive and want to check out DeBabelizer, you can run it directly from the *Web Graphics For Dummies* CD-ROM. Just double-click it like a program on your hard drive.

Figure A-8: The Debabelizer toolbox stamps the word "demo" firmly on your work. You get the feel of the program, but actually doing any work with the demo is out of the question.

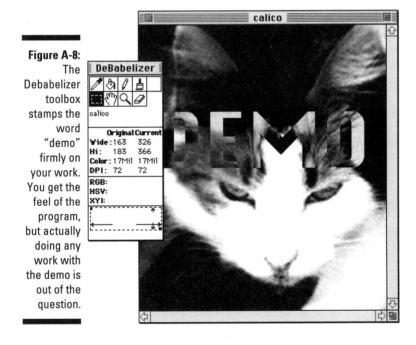

GammaToggleFKey

This is another one of those "spirit of the Net" programs. GammaToggleFKey is a simple, elegant little hack that lets you toggle your Mac screen to PC gamma and back again. It's so teeny, you hardly know it's on your hard drive. (Does 2K sound teeny enough?) GammaToggleFKey was written by Roland Gustafsson, who calls the program ThankYouWare. "If you find it useful," writes Gustafsson, "all you have to do is say 'thank you.'"

GammaToggleFKey is cleverly disguised as a font suitcase. That means you just drag it to the right location — your system folder. The system takes care of the rest by plunking it into the correct place.

Because this is a toggle key, not a program, make sure you read the README file for complete operating instructions. Until you use its key combination, you won't even know GammaToggleFKey is installed on your system.

PageMill

This directory contains an install for the working demonstration version of Adobe's WYSIWYG HTML editor, PageMill. While it's a fully functional demo, and you can try all of the cool things that PageMill does, the demo stops working 30 days after installation.

Please note that Adobe's implementation of 30-day-trial protection for PageMill is *very* sensitive to previous installations of PageMill and other Adobe products. Even if you don't remember having PageMill on your system, this version may decide you've already had your 30-day trial period.

Acrobat Reader 3.0.1

This install program contains Adobe Acrobat 3.0, Adobe's PDF reader. Even if you don't plan on using Acrobat right now, make a mental note of where you have it. If you get your hands on a PDF file, it's good to know how to read the file.

While the reader is free, if you want to actually create PDF files you must go the whole step and buy Acrobat. Instructions for purchasing Acrobat are included with the Acrobat reader.

To install the Acrobat reader, launch the Install Acrobat Reader 3.01 icon from the *Web Graphics For Dummies* CD-ROM. (The icon is shown in Figure A-9.)

Figure A-9: Double-clicking on the install icon launches the install program.

Install Acrobat Reader 3.0.1

After you're into the install, the first decision you make is whether you accept the terms of the licensing agreement. Read this carefully and then click Accept if you do. Accepting the terms causes the install to continue. Declining terminates the installation process.

The install dialog box appears in order to give you some choices about where you'd like Acrobat Reader to be located. You can click Switch Disk to indicate the hard drive (if you have more than one) where you'd like the Reader installed. You can click Select Folder if there's a specific target folder you'd like the Reader located in after the install is complete. If you're not sure, don't despair: it's a simple matter to move it around by dragging after the install is complete. Click the Install button to continue.

The next dialog box lets you know that your computer will be restarted after the install is complete. This is all right, as long as you don't have any unsaved windows open! If you have windows open, you can cancel and go back and close them.

When the install is successful, a dialog box appears to tell you so. It also lets you know that you can either restart your computer now or continue to install other programs. (I like to restart after each install. That way, if trouble develops I know when it started.)

After you restart, you can launch Acrobat from its application icon on the hard drive you specified.

WebPainter

This install program contains an install for a working demo of WebPainter for Windows. WebPainter is a full-featured tool for creating GIF animations.

The demo version included on the *Web Graphics For Dummies* CD-ROM is limited. It lets you use all of WebPainter's features to create GIF animations, and you can even save them. However, it will only let you export the first three frames of an animation file. You can still create cool little animations that are quite useable. Best of all, you get a real feel for the program to know whether you want to buy it.

To install WebPainter, launch the Install WebPainter Try Out icon from the *Web Graphics For Dummies* CD-ROM. You are then presented with the WebPainter README file. This is a great idea — a conveniently placed README that's hard to ignore. Read it before continuing.

The install dialog box offers you some choices about locating the WebPainter demo. Click Switch Disk to indicate the hard drive (if you have more than one) where you'd like WebPainter installed. You can click Select Folder in the hard drive dropdown list if there's a specific target folder where you'd like WebPainter located after the install is complete. If you're not sure, don't despair — it's a simple matter to move WebPainter by dragging after the install is complete.

Click the Install button to continue. When the install is successful, a dialog box appears to tell you so. You are now ready to launch the WebPainter demo from the application icon on the hard drive you specified.

TextureMill 1.1

TextureMill is a lovely, elegant, and reasonably priced program that lets you build gorgeous backgrounds for your Web pages . . . or whatever. The version on the *Web Graphics For Dummies* CD-ROM works completely. After you register the program, however, you can create many more cool backgrounds. Registration information is included with the program.

TextureMill does not require an install to work. You can launch it directly from the *Web Graphics For Dummies* CD-ROM to try it.

To have TextureMill handy on your system, simply drag the TextureMill 1.1 *f* folder onto your hard drive in the location of your choice. Launch the program by double-clicking on the application icon within the folder.

WebMap

WebMap is the image mapping utility of choice for the Macintosh. It's small, handy, and cheap.

The program is shareware. Developer Rowland Smith says simply on his very discreet nag screen, "If you like this program and use it, please send $20 for its continued development." A modest request for so useful a program.

WebMap does not require unpacking or installation. To use the program, simply drag the WebMap folder directly where you want it on your hard drive. Double-click the WebMap 1.0.1 application icon to launch the program when you want to use it.

It's important to read all of the README files that ship with WebMap. There are some known system conflicts, so it's best to know what they are *before* you start using the program.

Index

(continued)

(continued)

(continued)

Notes

Title	Author	ISBN	Price
The Internet For Macs® For Dummies® 2nd Edition	by Charles Seiter	ISBN: 1-56884-371-2	$19.99 USA/$26.99 Canada
The Internet For Macs® For Dummies® Starter Kit	by Charles Seiter	ISBN: 1-56884-244-9	$29.99 USA/$39.99 Canada
The Internet For Macs® For Dummies® Starter Kit Bestseller Edition	by Charles Seiter	ISBN: 1-56884-245-7	$39.99 USA/$54.99 Canada
The Internet For Windows® For Dummies® Starter Kit	by John R. Levine & Margaret Levine Young	ISBN: 1-56884-237-6	$34.99 USA/$44.99 Canada
The Internet For Windows® For Dummies® Starter Kit, Bestseller Edition	by John R. Levine & Margaret Levine Young	ISBN: 1-56884-246-5	$39.99 USA/$54.99 Canada

MACINTOSH

Mac® Programming For Dummies®	by Dan Parks Sydow	ISBN: 1-56884-173-6	$19.95 USA/$26.95 Canada
Macintosh® System 7.5 For Dummies®	by Bob LeVitus	ISBN: 1-56884-197-3	$19.95 USA/$26.95 Canada
MORE Macs® For Dummies®	by David Pogue	ISBN: 1-56884-087-X	$19.95 USA/$26.95 Canada
PageMaker 5 For Macs® For Dummies®	by Galen Gruman & Deke McClelland	ISBN: 1-56884-178-7	$19.95 USA/$26.95 Canada
QuarkXPress 3.3 For Dummies®	by Galen Gruman & Barbara Assadi	ISBN: 1-56884-217-1	$19.99 USA/$26.99 Canada
Upgrading and Fixing Macs® For Dummies®	by Kearney Rietmann & Frank Higgins	ISBN: 1-56884-189-2	$19.95 USA/$26.95 Canada

MULTIMEDIA

Multimedia & CD-ROMs For Dummies® 2nd Edition	by Andy Rathbone	ISBN: 1-56884-907-9	$19.99 USA/$26.99 Canada
Multimedia & CD-ROMs For Dummies® Interactive Multimedia Value Pack, 2nd Edition	by Andy Rathbone	ISBN: 1-56884-909-5	$29.99 USA/$39.99 Canada

OPERATING SYSTEMS:

DOS

MORE DOS For Dummies®	by Dan Gookin	ISBN: 1-56884-046-2	$19.95 USA/$26.95 Canada
OS/2® Warp For Dummies® 2nd Edition	by Andy Rathbone	ISBN: 1-56884-205-8	$19.99 USA/$26.99 Canada

UNIX

MORE UNIX® For Dummies®	by John R. Levine & Margaret Levine Young	ISBN: 1-56884-361-5	$19.99 USA/$26.99 Canada
UNIX® For Dummies®	by John R. Levine & Margaret Levine Young	ISBN: 1-878058-58-4	$19.95 USA/$26.95 Canada

WINDOWS

MORE Windows® For Dummies® 2nd Edition	by Andy Rathbone	ISBN: 1-56884-048-9	$19.95 USA/$26.95 Canada
Windows® 95 For Dummies®	by Andy Rathbone	ISBN: 1-56884-240-6	$19.99 USA/$26.99 Canada

PCS/HARDWARE

Illustrated Computer Dictionary For Dummies® 2nd Edition	by Dan Gookin & Wallace Wang	ISBN: 1-56884-218-X	$12.95 USA/$16.95 Canada
Upgrading and Fixing PCs For Dummies® 2nd Edition	by Andy Rathbone	ISBN: 1-56884-903-6	$19.99 USA/$26.99 Canada

PRESENTATION/AUTOCAD

AutoCAD For Dummies®	by Bud Smith	ISBN: 1-56884-191-4	$19.95 USA/$26.95 Canada
PowerPoint 4 For Windows® For Dummies®	by Doug Lowe	ISBN: 1-56884-161-2	$16.99 USA/$22.99 Canada

PROGRAMMING

Borland C++ For Dummies®	by Michael Hyman	ISBN: 1-56884-162-0	$19.95 USA/$26.95 Canada
C For Dummies® Volume 1	by Dan Gookin	ISBN: 1-878058-78-9	$19.95 USA/$26.95 Canada
C++ For Dummies®	by Stephen R. Davis	ISBN: 1-56884-163-9	$19.95 USA/$26.95 Canada
Delphi Programming For Dummies®	by Neil Rubenking	ISBN: 1-56884-200-7	$19.99 USA/$26.99 Canada
Mac® Programming For Dummies®	by Dan Parks Sydow	ISBN: 1-56884-173-6	$19.95 USA/$26.95 Canada
PowerBuilder 4 Programming For Dummies®	by Ted Coombs & Jason Coombs	ISBN: 1-56884-325-9	$19.99 USA/$26.99 Canada
QBasic Programming For Dummies®	by Douglas Hergert	ISBN: 1-56884-093-4	$19.95 USA/$26.95 Canada
Visual Basic 3 For Dummies®	by Wallace Wang	ISBN: 1-56884-076-4	$19.95 USA/$26.95 Canada
Visual Basic "X" For Dummies®	by Wallace Wang	ISBN: 1-56884-230-9	$19.99 USA/$26.99 Canada
Visual C++ 2 For Dummies®	by Michael Hyman & Bob Arnson	ISBN: 1-56884-328-3	$19.99 USA/$26.99 Canada
Windows® 95 Programming For Dummies®	by S. Randy Davis	ISBN: 1-56884-327-5	$19.99 USA/$26.99 Canada

SPREADSHEET

1-2-3 For Dummies®	by Greg Harvey	ISBN: 1-878058-60-6	$16.95 USA/$22.95 Canada
1-2-3 For Windows® 5 For Dummies® 2nd Edition	by John Walkenbach	ISBN: 1-56884-216-3	$16.95 USA/$22.95 Canada
Excel 5 For Macs® For Dummies®	by Greg Harvey	ISBN: 1-56884-186-8	$19.95 USA/$26.95 Canada
Excel For Dummies® 2nd Edition	by Greg Harvey	ISBN: 1-56884-050-0	$16.95 USA/$22.95 Canada
MORE 1-2-3 For Dummies®	by John Weingarten	ISBN: 1-56884-224-4	$19.99 USA/$26.99 Canada
MORE Excel 5 For Windows® For Dummies®	by Greg Harvey	ISBN: 1-56884-207-4	$19.95 USA/$26.95 Canada
Quattro Pro 6 For Windows® For Dummies®	by John Walkenbach	ISBN: 1-56884-174-4	$19.95 USA/$26.95 Canada
Quattro Pro For DOS For Dummies®	by John Walkenbach	ISBN: 1-56884-023-3	$16.95 USA/$22.95 Canada

UTILITIES

Title	Author	ISBN	Price
Norton Utilities 8 For Dummies®	by Beth Slick	ISBN: 1-56884-166-3	$19.95 USA/$26.95 Canada

VCRS/CAMCORDERS

Title	Author	ISBN	Price
VCRs & Camcorders For Dummies™	by Gordon McComb & Andy Rathbone	ISBN: 1-56884-229-5	$14.99 USA/$20.99 Canada

WORD PROCESSING

Ami Pro For Dummies®	by Jim Meade	ISBN: 1-56884-049-7	$19.95 USA/$26.95 Canada
MORE Word For Windows® 6 For Dummies®	by Doug Lowe	ISBN: 1-56884-165-5	$19.95 USA/$26.95 Canada
MORE WordPerfect® 6 For Windows® For Dummies®	by Margaret Levine Young & David C. Kay	ISBN: 1-56884-206-6	$19.95 USA/$26.95 Canada
MORE WordPerfect® 6 For DOS For Dummies®	by Wallace Wang, edited by Dan Gookin	ISBN: 1-56884-047-0	$19.95 USA/$26.95 Canada
Word 6 For Macs® For Dummies®	by Dan Gookin	ISBN: 1-56884-190-6	$19.95 USA/$26.95 Canada
Word For Windows® 6 For Dummies®	by Dan Gookin	ISBN: 1-56884-075-6	$16.95 USA/$22.95 Canada
Word For Windows® For Dummies®	by Dan Gookin & Ray Werner	ISBN: 1-878058-86-X	$16.95 USA/$22.95 Canada
WordPerfect® 6 For DOS For Dummies®	by Dan Gookin	ISBN: 1-878058-77-0	$16.95 USA/$22.95 Canada
WordPerfect® 6.1 For Windows® For Dummies® 2nd Edition	by Margaret Levine Young & David Kay	ISBN: 1-56884-243-0	$16.95 USA/$22.95 Canada
WordPerfect® For Dummies®	by Dan Gookin	ISBN: 1-878058-52-5	$16.95 USA/$22.95 Canada

Title	Author	ISBN	Price
DATABASE			
Access 2 For Dummies® Quick Reference	by Stuart J. Stuple	ISBN: 1-56884-167-1	$8.95 USA/$11.95 Canada
dBASE 5 For DOS For Dummies® Quick Reference	by Barrie Sosinsky	ISBN: 1-56884-954-0	$9.99 USA/$12.99 Canada
dBASE 5 For Windows® For Dummies® Quick Reference	by Stuart J. Stuple	ISBN: 1-56884-953-2	$9.99 USA/$12.99 Canada
Paradox 5 For Windows® For Dummies® Quick Reference	by Scott Palmer	ISBN: 1-56884-960-5	$9.99 USA/$12.99 Canada
DESKTOP PUBLISHING/ILLUSTRATION/GRAPHICS			
CorelDRAW! 5 For Dummies® Quick Reference	by Raymond E. Werner	ISBN: 1-56884-952-4	$9.99 USA/$12.99 Canada
Harvard Graphics For Windows® For Dummies® Quick Reference	by Raymond E. Werner	ISBN: 1-56884-962-1	$9.99 USA/$12.99 Canada
Photoshop 3 For Macs® For Dummies® Quick Reference	by Deke McClelland	ISBN: 1-56884-968-0	$9.99 USA/$12.99 Canada
FINANCE/PERSONAL FINANCE			
Quicken 4 For Windows® For Dummies® Quick Reference	by Stephen L. Nelson	ISBN: 1-56884-950-8	$9.95 USA/$12.95 Canada
GROUPWARE/INTEGRATED			
Microsoft® Office 4 For Windows® For Dummies® Quick Reference	by Doug Lowe	ISBN: 1-56884-958-3	$9.99 USA/$12.99 Canada
Microsoft® Works 3 For Windows® For Dummies® Quick Reference	by Michael Partington	ISBN: 1-56884-959-1	$9.99 USA/$12.99 Canada
INTERNET/COMMUNICATIONS/NETWORKING			
The Internet For Dummies® Quick Reference	by John R. Levine & Margaret Levine Young	ISBN: 1-56884-168-X	$8.95 USA/$11.95 Canada
MACINTOSH			
Macintosh® System 7.5 For Dummies® Quick Reference	by Stuart J. Stuple	ISBN: 1-56884-956-7	$9.99 USA/$12.99 Canada
OPERATING SYSTEMS:			
DOS			
DOS For Dummies® Quick Reference	by Greg Harvey	ISBN: 1-56884-007-1	$8.95 USA/$11.95 Canada
UNIX			
UNIX® For Dummies® Quick Reference	by John R. Levine & Margaret Levine Young	ISBN: 1-56884-094-2	$8.95 USA/$11.95 Canada
WINDOWS			
Windows® 3.1 For Dummies® Quick Reference, 2nd Edition	by Greg Harvey	ISBN: 1-56884-951-6	$8.95 USA/$11.95 Canada
PCs/HARDWARE			
Memory Management For Dummies® Quick Reference	by Doug Lowe	ISBN: 1-56884-362-3	$9.99 USA/$12.99 Canada
PRESENTATION/AUTOCAD			
AutoCAD For Dummies® Quick Reference	by Ellen Finkelstein	ISBN: 1-56884-198-1	$9.95 USA/$12.95 Canada
SPREADSHEET			
1-2-3 For Dummies® Quick Reference	by John Walkenbach	ISBN: 1-56884-027-6	$8.95 USA/$11.95 Canada
1-2-3 For Windows® 5 For Dummies® Quick Reference	by John Walkenbach	ISBN: 1-56884-957-5	$9.95 USA/$12.95 Canada
Excel For Windows® For Dummies® Quick Reference, 2nd Edition	by John Walkenbach	ISBN: 1-56884-096-9	$8.95 USA/$11.95 Canada
Quattro Pro 6 For Windows® For Dummies® Quick Reference	by Stuart J. Stuple	ISBN: 1-56884-172-8	$9.95 USA/$12.95 Canada
WORD PROCESSING			
Word For Windows® 6 For Dummies® Quick Reference	by George Lynch	ISBN: 1-56884-095-0	$8.95 USA/$11.95 Canada
Word For Windows® For Dummies® Quick Reference	by George Lynch	ISBN: 1-56884-029-2	$8.95 USA/$11.95 Canada
WordPerfect® 6.1 For Windows® For Dummies® Quick Reference, 2nd Edition	by Greg Harvey	ISBN: 1-56884-966-4	$9.99 USA/$12.99/Canada

For scholastic requests & educational orders please call Educational Sales at 1. 800. 434. 2086

FOR MORE INFO OR TO ORDER, PLEASE CALL ▶ 800 762 2974

For volume discounts & special orders please call Corporate Sales, at 415. 655. 3000

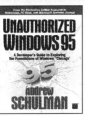

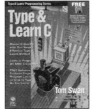

Order Center: **(800) 762-2974** *(24 hours a day, seven days a week)*

5/8/97

Quantity	ISBN	Title	Price	Total

Shipping & Handling Charges

	Description	First book	Each additional book	Total
Domestic	Normal	$4.50	$1.50	$
	Two Day Air	$8.50	$2.50	$
	Overnight	$18.00	$3.00	$
International	Surface	$8.00	$8.00	$
	Airmail	$16.00	$16.00	$
	DHL Air	$17.00	$17.00	$

*For large quantities call for shipping & handling charges.
**Prices are subject to change without notice.

Ship to:

Name _____

Company _____

Address _____

City/State/Zip _____

Daytime Phone _____

Payment: ☐ Check to IDG Books Worldwide (US Funds Only)

☐ VISA   ☐ MasterCard   ☐ American Express

Card # _____ Expires _____

Signature _____

Subtotal _____

CA residents add
applicable sales tax _____

IN, MA, and MD
residents add
5% sales tax _____

IL residents add
6.25% sales tax _____

RI residents add
7% sales tax _____

TX residents add
8.25% sales tax _____

Shipping _____

Total _____

Please send this order form to:

IDG Books Worldwide, Inc.
Attn: Order Entry Dept.
7260 Shadeland Station, Suite 100
Indianapolis, IN 46256

Allow up to 3 weeks for delivery.
Thank you!

IDG Books Worldwide, Inc., End-User License Agreement

READ THIS. You should carefully read these terms and conditions before opening the software packet(s) included with this book ("Book"). This is a license agreement ("Agreement") between you and IDG Books Worldwide, Inc. ("IDGB"). By opening the accompanying software packet(s), you acknowledge that you have read and accept the following terms and conditions. If you do not agree and do not want to be bound by such terms and conditions, promptly return the Book and the unopened software packet(s) to the place you obtained them for a full refund.

1. **License Grant.** IDGB grants to you (either an individual or entity) a nonexclusive license to use one copy of the enclosed software program(s) (collectively, the "Software") solely for your own personal or business purposes on a single computer (whether a standard computer or a workstation component of a multiuser network). The Software is in use on a computer when it is loaded into temporary memory (RAM) or installed into permanent memory (hard disk, CD-ROM, or other storage device). IDGB reserves all rights not expressly granted herein.

2. **Ownership.** IDGB is the owner of all right, title, and interest, including copyright, in and to the compilation of the Software recorded on the CD-ROM ("Software Media"). Copyright to the individual programs recorded on the Software Media is owned by the author or other authorized copyright owner of each program. Ownership of the Software and all proprietary rights relating thereto remain with IDGB and its licensers.

3. **Restrictions on Use and Transfer.**

   (a) You may only (i) make one copy of the Software for backup or archival purposes, or (ii) transfer the Software to a single hard disk, provided that you keep the original for backup or archival purposes. You may not (i) rent or lease the Software, (ii) copy or reproduce the Software through a LAN or other network system or through any computer subscriber system or bulletin-board system, or (iii) modify, adapt, or create derivative works based on the Software.

   (b) You may not reverse engineer, decompile, or disassemble the Software. You may transfer the Software and user documentation on a permanent basis, provided that the transferee agrees to accept the terms and conditions of this Agreement and you retain no copies. If the Software is an update or has been updated, any transfer must include the most recent update and all prior versions.

4. **Restrictions on Use of Individual Programs.** You must follow the individual requirements and restrictions detailed for each individual program in the "Using the CD-ROM" section of this Book. These limitations are also contained in the individual license agreements recorded on the Software Media. These limitations may include a requirement that after using the program for a specified period of time, the user must pay a registration fee or discontinue use. By opening the Software packet(s), you will be agreeing to abide by the licenses and restrictions for these individual programs that are detailed in the "Using the CD-ROM" section and on the Software Media. None of the material on this Software Media or listed in this Book may ever be redistributed, in original or modified form, for commercial purposes.

5. **Limited Warranty.**

   (a) IDGB warrants that the Software and Software Media are free from defects in materials and workmanship under normal use for a period of sixty (60) days from the date of purchase of this Book. If IDGB receives notification within the warranty period of defects in materials or workmanship, IDGB will replace the defective Software Media.

   (b) **IDGB AND THE AUTHOR OF THE BOOK DISCLAIM ALL OTHER WARRANTIES, EXPRESS OR IMPLIED, INCLUDING WITHOUT LIMITATION IMPLIED WARRANTIES OF MERCHANTABILITY AND FITNESS FOR A PARTICULAR PURPOSE, WITH RESPECT TO THE SOFTWARE, THE PROGRAMS, THE SOURCE CODE CONTAINED THEREIN, AND/OR THE TECHNIQUES DESCRIBED IN THIS BOOK. IDGB DOES NOT WARRANT THAT THE FUNCTIONS CONTAINED IN THE SOFTWARE WILL MEET YOUR REQUIREMENTS OR THAT THE OPERATION OF THE SOFTWARE WILL BE ERROR FREE.**

   (c) This limited warranty gives you specific legal rights, and you may have other rights that vary from jurisdiction to jurisdiction.

6. **Remedies.**

   (a) IDGB's entire liability and your exclusive remedy for defects in materials and workmanship shall be limited to replacement of the Software Media, which may be returned to IDGB with a copy of your receipt at the following address: Software Media Fulfillment Department, Attn.: *Web Graphics For Dummies*, IDG Books Worldwide, Inc., 7260 Shadeland Station, Ste. 100, Indianapolis, IN 46256, or call 800-762-2974. Please allow three to four weeks for delivery. This Limited Warranty is void if failure of the Software Media has resulted from accident, abuse, or misapplication. Any replacement Software Media will be warranted for the remainder of the original warranty period or thirty (30) days, whichever is longer.

   (b) In no event shall IDGB or the author be liable for any damages whatsoever (including without limitation damages for loss of business profits, business interruption, loss of business information, or any other pecuniary loss) arising from the use of or inability to use the Book or the Software, even if IDGB has been advised of the possibility of such damages.

   (c) Because some jurisdictions do not allow the exclusion or limitation of liability for consequential or incidental damages, the above limitation or exclusion may not apply to you.

7. **U.S. Government Restricted Rights.** Use, duplication, or disclosure of the Software by the U.S. Government is subject to restrictions stated in paragraph (c)(1)(ii) of the Rights in Technical Data and Computer Software clause of DFARS 252.227-7013, and in subparagraphs (a) through (d) of the Commercial Computer–Restricted Rights clause at FAR 52.227-19, and in similar clauses in the NASA FAR supplement, when applicable.

8. **General.** This Agreement constitutes the entire understanding of the parties and revokes and supersedes all prior agreements, oral or written, between them and may not be modified or amended except in a writing signed by both parties hereto that specifically refers to this Agreement. This Agreement shall take precedence over any other documents that may be in conflict herewith. If any one or more provisions contained in this Agreement are held by any court or tribunal to be invalid, illegal, or otherwise unenforceable, each and every other provision shall remain in full force and effect.

Using the *Web Graphics For Dummies* CD-ROM

The *Web Graphics For Dummies* CD-ROM includes

- ✔ Sample files for the examples in *Web Graphics For Dummies*.
- ✔ Programs for Macintosh and PC computers.

The sample files are designed to work with many PC, Windows, and Macintosh computers. They require compatible software, such as image editing programs. The examples in the book specify appropriate software for each example. To use the sample files for a *Web Graphics For Dummies* example:

1. Insert the *Web Graphics For Dummies* CD-ROM in your Macintosh or PC CD-ROM drive.

2. Start the appropriate program, such as an image editor, on your computer.

3. Use the program to open the sample file from the CD-ROM.

4. Follow the instructions for the example.

The *Web Graphics For Dummies* CD-ROM also includes many trial programs. The appendix at the back of the book contains instructions and tips for installing these programs. Separate directories present software for Windows and Macintosh systems.

IDG BOOKS WORLDWIDE REGISTRATION CARD

ISBN Number: 0-76450-2115

Title of this book: Web Graphics For Dummies

My overall rating of this book: ❏ Very good [1] ❏ Good [2] ❏ Satisfactory [3] ❏ Fair [4] ❏ Poor [5]

How I first heard about this book:

❏ Found in bookstore; name: [6]   ❏ Book review: [7]

❏ Advertisement: [8]   ❏ Catalog: [9]

❏ Word of mouth; heard about book from friend, co-worker, etc.: [10]   ❏ Other: [11]

What I liked most about this book:

What I would change, add, delete, etc., in future editions of this book:

Other comments:

Number of computer books I purchase in a year: ❏ 1 [12] ❏ 2-5 [13] ❏ 6-10 [14] ❏ More than 10 [15]

I would characterize my computer skills as: ❏ Beginner [16] ❏ Intermediate [17] ❏ Advanced [18] ❏ Professional [19]

I use ❏ DOS [20] ❏ Windows [21] ❏ OS/2 [22] ❏ Unix [23] ❏ Macintosh [24] ❏ Other: [25]_____

(please specify)

I would be interested in new books on the following subjects:

(please check all that apply, and use the spaces provided to identify specific software)

❏ Word processing: [26]   ❏ Spreadsheets: [27]

❏ Data bases: [28]   ❏ Desktop publishing: [29]

❏ File Utilities: [30]   ❏ Money management: [31]

❏ Networking: [32]   ❏ Programming languages: [33]

❏ Other: [34]

I use a PC at (please check all that apply): ❏ home [35] ❏ work [36] ❏ school [37] ❏ other: [38] _____

The disks I prefer to use are ❏ 5.25 [39] ❏ 3.5 [40] ❏ other: [41]_____

I have a CD ROM: ❏ yes [42]   ❏ no [43]

I plan to buy or upgrade computer hardware this year: ❏ yes [44]   ❏ no [45]

I plan to buy or upgrade computer software this year: ❏ yes [46]   ❏ no [47]

Name: Business title: [48]   Type of Business: [49]

Address (❏ home [50] ❏ work [51] /Company name:)

Street/Suite#

City [52] /State [53] /Zip code [54]:   Country [55]

❏ **I liked this book!** You may quote me by name in future
IDG Books Worldwide promotional materials.

My daytime phone number is _____

IDG BOOKS WORLDWIDE

THE WORLD OF
COMPUTER
KNOWLEDGE®

☐ YES!

Please keep me informed about IDG Books Worldwide's
World of Computer Knowledge. Send me your latest catalog.